ANALOGIES *of* TRANSCENDENCE

ANALOGIES *of* TRANSCENDENCE

An Essay on Nature, Grace & Modernity

STEPHEN M. FIELDS

The Catholic University of America Press
Washington, D.C.

The paper used in this publication meets the minimum requirements of American National Standards for Information Science—Permanence of Paper for Printed Library Materials, ANSI Z39.48-1984.

∞

Library of Congress Cataloging-in-Publication Data
Names: Fields, Stephen author.
Title: Analogies of transcendence : an essay on nature, grace, and modernity / Stephen M. Fields.
Description: Washington, D.C. : The Catholic University of America Press, 2016. | Includes bibliographical references and index.
Identifiers: LCCN 2016012326 | ISBN 9780813228556 (cloth : alk. paper)
Subjects: LCSH: Nature—Religious aspects—Catholic Church. | Grace (Theology) | Thomas, Aquinas, Saint, 1225?–1274. | Catholic Church—Doctrines.
Classification: LCC BX1795.N36 F54 2016 | DDC 233/.5—dc23
LC record available at https://lccn.loc.gov/2016012326

To Greg and Matt

γρηγορἕῳ ὑπὲρ מתתיהו

Divine grace … does not by its presence supersede nature; nor is nature at once brought into simple concurrence and coalition with grace. Nature pursues its course, now coincident with that of grace, now parallel to it, now across, now divergent, now counter, in proportion to its own imperfection and to the attraction and influence which grace exerts over it.

—John Henry Cardinal Newman,
The Idea of a University, Discourse VIII, 2

Contents

Abbreviations

CC	*The Christian Commitment* (Karl Rahner)
CH	*De coelesti hierarchia* (Pseudo-Dionysius the Areopagite)
DJ	*Dominus Jesus* (Congregation for the Doctrine of the Faith)
DN	*De divinis nominibus* (Pseudo-Dionysius the Areopagite)
DS	*Enchiridion Symbolorum*, ed. Denzinger and Schönmetzer
EL	*Encyclopedia Logic* (G. W. F. Hegel)
GL	*The Glory of the Lord* (Hans Urs von Balthasar)
GSA	*Gesammelte Schriften und Aufsätze* (Johann Adam Möhler)
H	*Hominization* (Karl Rahner)
NCE	*New Catholic Encyclopedia*
PG	*Patrologiae cursus completus, Series graeca*, ed. Migne
PL	*Patrologiae cursus completus, Series latina*, ed. Migne
ST	*Summa Theologiae* (Thomas Aquinas)
TI	*Theological Investigations* (Karl Rahner)
TQ	*Theologische Quartalschrift* (Johann Adam Möhler)
UG	"Some Implications of the Scholastic Concept of Uncreated Grace" (Karl Rahner)

INTRODUCTION

Stephen Duffy observes that "no dimension of Christian life or thought can be addressed without" at least implicit recourse to the problem of nature and grace.[1] Precisely because of its fundamental importance, it embraces an exceedingly long and complex history. It has generated magisterial pronouncements, fulminated controversies that have fractured Christendom, and pitted religious orders against each other. Moreover, no commentator in whatever era can say anything meaningful about the subject without appealing to metaphysics, which finds little sympathy in today's agnosticism about universal truth claims. The question thus arises: how is it currently possible for someone to address the issue in a relatively brief work like this, or perhaps even to say anything significant about it at all?

A full-fledged defense of metaphysics is beyond the scope of this book.[2] But recent thinkers have offered compelling reassertions of some basic beliefs about Catholicism's understanding of faith and reason. Karl Rahner expresses these well when he trenchantly observes that "unphilosophical theology is bad theology."[3] Only a universal science whose object is being as such can offer a hermeneutics adequate

1. Stephen J. Duffy, *The Graced Horizon: Nature and Grace in Modern Catholic Thought* (Collegeville, Minn.: Liturgical Press, 1992), 7.

2. Together with other scholars, I have attempted such a defense in "The Metaphysics of Aquinas and Its Modern Interpreters: Theological and Philosophical Perspectives," ed. Christopher M. Cullen and Franklin T. Harkins.

3. Karl Rahner, "Philosophy and Theology," in *Theological Investigations* [hereafter "*TI*"] trans. Karl-H. and Boniface Kruger (London: Darton, Longman and Todd, 1974), 6:71–81, at 80.

for explaining a message from God, "the sustaining source of all reality, the reconciling goal of all history."[4] Avery Dulles concurs, noting that hostility to metaphysics undermines the "positive intelligibility" of the divine, reducing our transcendent knowledge to metaphor and sign.[5] For his part, Pope Benedict XVI reminds us in his Regensburg address that Christianity's importing of the Greek discoveries of mind represents no mere historical accident requiring a salutary undoing by the Enlightenment. Not to act "with *logos*"—reason's innate power of creative self-communication—"is contrary to God's nature."[6] If the God of Rahner's definition exists, then it follows that confining reason to the empirically verifiable and falsifiable not only straitjackets human nature, but also embodies a patent contradiction. In other words, if we take seriously the claim that the Holy Spirit guides the church through history "into all the truth" (Jn 16:13), then theology can hardly be the faithful servant of divine revelation by obviating what Plato terms *noesis* and Aristotle names "first philosophy." Necessity and universality belong essentially to the definition of Christianity.

"The opacity and intricacy of the issues involved" in nature and grace, together with the scholar's duty "to resist the tidal pull … to oversimplication," mean that a definitive treatment lies beyond the ken of most mortals.[7] Many specialized studies exist, both historical and systematic. As the subtitle of this book indicates, what is modestly offered here constitutes no more than an "essay." This word came into English in the late fifteenth century as a verb meaning to try or test. Montaigne made it famous a century later as a noun meaning a written composition of limited range.[8] Louis Dupré evokes both meanings in

4. Karl Rahner, "On the Relation Between Natural Science and Theology," in *TI* 19:16–23, at 19.

5. Avery Dulles, "Criteria of Catholic Theology," *Communio: International Catholic Review* 22 (Summer 1995): 303–15, at 305–6.

6. Benedict XVI, "Faith, Reason, and the University: Memories and Reflections," lecture at the University of Regensburg, September 12, 2006 (quoting the fourteenth-century Byzantine emperor Manuel II Paleologus); http://www.vatican.va.

7. Duffy, *Graced Horizon*, 11.

8. *The Compact Edition of the Oxford English Dictionary* (Oxford: Oxford University Press, 1971), 1:896.

his essay on modernity. In his work, which my own will liberally cite, he says: "Much in the argument must remain underdeveloped and a good deal of its claims less than fully supported."[9] Ladislas Orsy suggests that the essay allows insights to spark debate as disputed questions. However much insights bear the "fruits of a creative process," they still need public scrutiny. An essay should be understood, therefore, as tentative and indicative, as an effort "to reach the truth," not as the final and conclusive word.[10]

Following these leads, the present composition aims only to sound one voice entering late into a great chorus, to contribute a considered but still provisionary perspective to an extensive and weighty conversation. Accordingly, it does not treat many aspects of the problem, and treats others lightly. It does not, for instance, engage in the exegesis of the scriptures; it deals with the Church Fathers, but selectively. It does not examine some of the great controversies, such as Pelagianism, the Reformation, Jansenism, or the *de auxiliis*. It offers commentary on several statements of the magisterium, although it has striven to keep its argument consistent with the dogmatic tenor of them all.

What this study does do is focus attention on the vital role that analogy plays in developing an adequate model of nature and grace. Analogy is the keystone that coherently links God as self-manifesting transcendence, the human person as both fallen and justified, and the material cosmos that, as the apostle Paul says, "has been groaning in labor pains" while awaiting its deliverance (Rom 8:21–22). It draws broadly on the Thomist tradition, although it offers opinions about its ambiguous legacy and seeks ways to develop it. These will probably not find favor with orthodox Thomists. For reasons that it will explain, it favors the school represented in various ways by Joseph Maréchal, Henri de Lubac, Hans Urs von Balthasar, and Rahner. Nonetheless, it is critical of this school, largely because of an underdeveloped doctrine

9. Louis Dupré, *Passage to Modernity: An Essay in the Hermeneutics of Nature and Culture* (New Haven, Conn.: Yale University Press, 1993), ix.

10. Ladislas Orsy, *Receiving the Council: Theological and Canonical Insights and Debates* (Collegeville, Minn.: Liturgical Press, 2009), xii.

of analogy that weakens nature in grace's engagement with it. Redressing this weakness constitutes a major goal of the essay. In so doing, it aims to build a model that is also adapted to the intellectual struggles of our time. To achieve this purpose, it relies on Dupré's genealogy of modernity. Although it does so with modification and critique, still it accepts his argument that modernity has not been superseded. As a result, the essay's discussion of what is generally known as "postmodernism" will likely disappoint its adherents.

The book is divided into three parts of seven chapters. The first part (consisting of three chapters) is mainly historical. Probing selected understandings of nature and grace since Aquinas, it strives to find clues helpful for developing a viable model of their relation. Chapter 1 deals with the theory of "pure" nature. Encouraged by the breakdown of the Baroque, this theory worsened the problematic estrangement between nature and grace that can be traced to the thirteenth-century origins of modernity.[11] In addition to Thomas, this chapter treats the mysticism of Ignatius Loyola, justification in the Council of Trent, reason in the Augustinian tradition, and the theology of language in exegesis, both medieval and modern, and in the Second Vatican Council's *Dei Verbum*. Chapter 2 examines important nineteenth- and twentieth-century efforts to heal the estrangement between nature and grace. It draws insights from the aesthetics of Johann Adam Möhler and G. W. F. Hegel. In addition, it discusses reason in Maurice Blondel; the relation between de Lubac and Max Seckler's view of the instinct of faith in Aquinas; and Rahner's "supernatural existential." Chapter 3 studies the harmonious reciprocity between nature and grace articulated in Pope John Paul II's views on the eucharist and on faith and reason, and in Benedict XVI's views on charity and justice.

Parts 2 and 3 are primarily systematic. Part 2 takes up the task that part 1 shows to be needed. Consisting of a single chapter, it uses analogy to build what it calls a "sacramental" model of nature and grace,

11. For a study of pure nature in the work of Aquinas using a perspective different from my own, see Steven A. Long, *Natura Pura: On the Recovery of Nature in the Doctrine of Grace* (New York: Fordham University Press, 2010).

which can be defined by its own distinctive causality. This constructive effort emerges from the clues previously disclosed by the historical review. Heavily indebted to Seckler's study of Aquinas and to Rahner's metaphysics of the symbol, it also develops insights drawn from Anselm, John Courtney Murray, and Benedict XVI. These are used to explain the model's relation to modernity, to lay out the orders of creation and redemption as a continuum, and to sketch a theology of nature.

The three chapters of the third part grow out of the second part. In the spirit of an essay, they test the model by applying it to selected theological problems. On the assumption that nature never obtains without grace, chapters 5 and 6 look for philosophical insights within selected aspects of Christianity. These chapters appeal to revelation in order to incite reason to reframe the model of God's simplicity received from the Aristotelian-Thomist tradition. They reverse the "method of correlation," which uses analyses of natural experience as the warranting propaedeutic of religion. Specifically, chapter 5 treats theological aesthetics; it draws insights from Pseudo-Dionysius the Areopagite, Balthasar, and Paul Ricoeur. It also comments on the task of contemporary Christian art. Chapter 6 uses the *Spiritual Exercises* of the Jesuits' founder to study how love can ground God's relation to the spontaneously evolving cosmos. Principally indebted to Rahner's metaphysics, it considers the thought of Pseudo-Dionysius, Basil the Great, Aquinas, and Hegel. Chapter 7 endeavors to include other religions within Christianity while recognizing its definitive claim to be unique. Covering a range of patristic and Enlightenment figures, it also draws insights from Aquinas, Yves Congar, and the Second Vatican Council's *Gaudium et Spes*. Critical of Rahner's theory of the "anonymous Christian," the final chapter also offers an interpretation of *"Dominus Jesus": On the Salvific Universality of Jesus Christ and the Church*, issued by the Congregation for the Doctrine of the Faith in 2000.

The book concludes with an afterword commenting on analogy in Vatican II in light of John Henry Newman's theory of doctrinal development. It is followed by an appendix, in which Rahner's theory of the symbol, the central concept of chapter 4's constructive argument, is favorably compared and contrasted with other modern and contemporary theories, including those of Kant, Paul Tillich, Jean-Luc Marion, and David Tracy.

In addition to its other goals, this essay wishes to advance a sympathetic dialogue between Balthasar and Rahner. My experience over some years of professional conferences has made it clear that a polarity often obtains between the disciples of these two titans of contemporary theology. Dichotomizing them tends to impede the disclosure of common elements in their thought that can contribute to salutary syntheses. Finally, I would like to thank the following for permission to integrate into this expanded discussion some material previously published.[12]

12. "The Beauty of the Ugly: Balthasar, the Crucifixion, Analogy, and God," *International Journal of Systematic Theology* 9, no. 2 (2007): 172–83; *Being as Symbol: On the Origins and Development of Karl Rahner's Metaphysics* (Washington, D.C.: Georgetown University Press, 2000), 6–8, 26–29, 78–81, 101–3, www.press.georgetown.edu; "God's Labor, Novelty's Emergence: Cosmic Motion as Self-Transcending Love," in vol. 1 of *Love Alone Is Credible: Hans Urs von Balthasar as Interpreter of the Catholic Tradition*, ed. David L. Schindler (Grand Rapids, Mich.: Eerdmans, 2008), 115–40; "John Paul II and the Eucharist: Sacrifice and Sacrament of Freedom," in *John Paul II on the Body: Human-Eucharistic-Ecclesial*, ed. John M. McDermott and John Gavin (Philadelphia: St. Joseph's University Press, 2007), 203–16, from 203–8; "Mediating the Non-Christian Religions: Congar, Balthasar, Nature and Grace," in *Yves Congar: Theologian of the Church*, ed. Gabriel Flynn (Louvain: Peeters/Eerdmans, 2005), 401–26, from 403–11, 415–18; "Nature, Grace, and the Public Square," in *Catholicism in America: Proceedings from the 33rd Annual Convention of the Fellowship of Catholic Scholars, September 24–26, 2010, Baltimore, Maryland*, ed. Elizabeth C. Shaw (Notre Dame, Ind.: Fellowship of Catholic Scholars, 2012), 123–38; "Nature and Grace after the Baroque," in *Creed and Culture: Jesuit Studies of Pope John Paul II*, ed. John J. Conley and Joseph W. Koterski (Philadelphia: St. Joseph's University Press, 2004): 223–39, from 223–25, 231–36; "*Ressourcement* and the Retrieval of Thomism for the Contemporary World," in *Ressourcement: A Movement for Renewal in Twentieth-Century Catholic Theology*, ed. Gabriel Flynn and Paul D. Murray (Oxford: Oxford University Press, 2012): 355–71, from 355–66; and "The Singular as Event: Postmodernism, Rahner, and Balthasar," *American Catholic Philosophical Quarterly* 77 (2003): 93–111, from 93–97, 110.

PART 1

PROBING THE PROBLEM

Chapter 1

MODERN ESTRANGEMENT

Baroque Harmony

The contemporary philosopher of culture Louis Dupré argues that the passing of the Baroque lost for the West its last great harmony between nature and grace. The Baroque achieved this harmony through a dynamic understanding of the human person in its intrinsic relation to its transcendent source. In this understanding, human creativity is appreciated not only because it follows its own rules and standards but precisely because, in the complexity of these rules and standards, it symbolizes the divine.[1] Baroque culture is thus essentially representational.[2] In the plastic arts, for instance, Roman and Bavarian churches are filled with forms and shapes, like saints and angels, that mediate between the merely earthly and the purely heavenly. They are brightened with light and color and displayed in motion in order to radiate the transcendent glow of nature redeemed.[3] In the theatre, a recurring theme shows life alternating between truth and illusion. What is represented on stage, either in character or plot, occludes and hides reality, as well as manifesting and revealing it. The great dramatists of the age like Shakespeare and Calderón turn the theatre into a metaphor for existence: representation belongs simultaneously to both appearance and reality.[4] As a result, the theatre, like the plastic arts, depicts reality

1. Dupré, *Passage to Modernity*, 237.
2. Ibid., 240.
3. Ibid., 242–43.
4. Ibid., 240–42.

as ever expanding, as ever in the process of being created by its immanent spiritual impulse.[5]

In the realm of spirituality, Ignatius Loyola best exemplifies how nature harmoniously and dynamically represents grace. His mystical vision is the principal articulation of the explosive movement of the Baroque. Grounded in the vocation of the human person, this movement fills the mundane order with symbols that reflect the subject's own divine immanence.[6] More than any other creature, the human person, as the image of God, represents its creator, especially in the use of its freedom. Through the mystical gifts of discernment given in prayer, this freedom becomes real and authentic.[7] It is liberated from the false appearances of freedom conjured up by what Ignatius calls "the enemy of our human nature."[8] So freed, human volition can recreate the world according to its own immanent divine image by positing the highest form of symbols: acts of charity that make God apparent. According to Ignatius, grace is the *sine qua non*, the very condition without which true human freedom cannot obtain. For this reason, Dupré argues that Ignatius effects "a more radically God-centered view of reality" than had heretofore been possible.[9] In filling Renaissance humanism with mystical content, this view brings the dynamic sacramentality of the Baroque to its pinnacle: God becomes the foundation of the person, even as creator and creature each retains its appropriate autonomy. Having prayerfully met the divine in its own powers, and having been reformed in the way of Christ, the human person actively responds to the ineluctable attractiveness of grace.[10] The genius of Ignatian mysticism is embodied in the paradox that, as Dupré says, "the way down [into the person is] the way up [to God]."[11]

5. Ibid., 239.

6. Louis Dupré, "Ignatian Humanism and Its Mystical Origins," *Communio: International Catholic Review* 18 (Summer 1991): 164–82, at 181.

7. Ibid., 171.

8. Ignatius Loyola, *The Spiritual Exercises of St Ignatius*, trans. and ed. Louis J. Puhl (Chicago: Loyola University Press, 1951), 4.

9. Dupré, "Ignatian Humanism," 173.

10. Ibid., 178–79.

11. Ibid., 174.

The kataphatic vision of Ignatius nourished the Baroque world with innovations in education and contemplative life, as did the apophatic mysticism of John of the Cross and the middle ground between them charted by Teresa of Avila.[12] Although all three lived contemporaneously with the Council of Trent, it may be stretching the point to claim its teaching as the cause of their endeavors. But it is hard to see how these could have thrived without the support of its doctrine. The assertion of nature's dynamic sacramentality, which lies at the heart of Trent's project, supplied an authoritative foundation for the mysticism inherent in the Jesuit charism and the Carmelite reform. Although Trent defined transubstantiation and encouraged the veneration of sacred images as representing their prototypes, these pronouncements pale in contrast to the sixteen chapters of the *Decree on Justification* of 1545–47. In response to Luther's slogans of faith and grace alone crystallized in his challenge to "'works-righteousness,'" the decree maintained that "the gratuity of grace" does "not deprive human beings of some responsibility for their salvation."[13] God's freedom, as expressed in the merits of Christ's saving deeds, is the efficient cause of justification.[14] This state obtains only through baptism or the desire for it, justification's instrumental cause. Yet human beings are "roused and helped" by prevenient grace freely to assent to this grace and cooperate with it. They are not inactive, therefore, since they can "reject" grace or voluntarily receive it. Nonetheless, without grace, they cannot of their "own free will" turn toward righteousness (2:672).

Trent's assertion that baptism is justification's instrumental cause gives the key to its harmonious marrying of nature and grace as integrally free centers of action. According to Thomas Aquinas, an instrumental cause exercises two powers. On the one hand, the "power of

12. Barbara Mujica, "Beyond Image: The Apophatic-Kataphatic Dialectic in Teresa of Avila," *Hispania* 84 (December 2010): 741–48; Elaini Tsoukatos, "Finding God in All Things: Teresa of Ávila's Use of the Familiar" (PhD diss., Georgetown University, 2011).

13. John W. O'Malley, *Four Cultures of the West* (Cambridge, Mass.: Belknap Press of Harvard University Press, 2004), 111–12.

14. Council of Trent, *Decree on Justification*, in *Decrees of the Ecumenical Councils*, ed. Norman P. Tanner (London: Sheed and Ward, 1990), 2:671–81. Cited in the text.

the instrument" designates the innate activity that the cause effects in virtue of its defining form. On the other hand, the "instrumental power" designates the activity that the power of the instrument receives from a principal agent. The power of the instrument assumes instrumental power when the principal agent transfers to it a form that this agent possesses. When this transfer obtains, the instrumental power is incorporated into the finality of the activity intended by the agent.[15] Accordingly, Trent's teaching affirms that justification obtains by God, through Christ, as instrumentally mediated by the person's baptism. We might offer the following explanation as a further interpretation of this teaching. In baptism, the freedom of the human person constitutes the power of the instrument, because only through it can baptism's final cause be realized. Human freedom becomes an instrumental power when grace is joined to the person's voluntary acceptance of the justification effected by the sacrament. As justification's principal agent, God confers on the person sanctifying grace, God's own life, which only he can give. Prior to the reception of the sacrament, prevenient grace and human cooperation meet in an unspecified union that preserves free will intact.

Initiating a person's life of grace, this sacramental scenario respects human and divine freedom even as it weds them into a synergy. As the power of the instrument, human freedom is not compromised when it becomes an instrumental power. Nor is the freedom of God, justification's principal agent, when it effects the instrumental power. The reciprocity between human and divine freedom obtains by their common contribution to a single final cause, justification. Especially significant is Trent's incorporation of prevenient grace into the union of freedom effected by this final cause. Prevenient grace participates, however remotely, in baptism's sanctifying grace, precisely because it is oriented toward justification. As Trent says, a desire for baptism can sufficiently effect the sacrament. It is possible, then, without the water of baptism, for prevenient grace to become sanctifying grace; they can meet in the

15. James S. Albertson, "Instrumental Causality in St. Thomas," *New Scholasticism* 28 (1954): 409–35, at 412, 419, 424.

hidden continuum of human and divine freedom. Trent's teaching on justification thus refuses to affirm a theory of a pure nature totally independent of grace. Whereas justification requires the cooperation of human nature, this is always grounded in grace, both prevenient and sanctifying.

Trent's sacramental understanding of nature as grace's intrinsic medium nourishes Ignatius's development of spiritual sensibility, which lies in the heart of his mysticism. A doctrine received from Origen, Augustine, and Bonaventure, it treats the interplay among the person's faculties of sensuous intuition, intellect, and will as they strive toward knowledge of God in grace. It resolves the paradox that humanity's radical immersion in the finite world does not prevent union with the God who utterly transcends it. The crux of the resolution centers on the act of faith. It reveals the divine object to human sensibility as formal evidence.[16] This evidence is sensibly mediated, as Trent avers, by hearing, for instance (2:672). Still, as grace, this evidence is not intrinsically sensate. Because faith-inspired sensation opens the way to an experience of God, it follows that faith allows for an analogous understanding of experience. By subsuming sensation into its own form, grace allows the divine to be perceived according to humanity's sensuous forms. Religious experience in general and mysticism in particular thus become dimensions of sensory experience. While requiring sensuous mediation, they are not limited to it.

Consonant with this doctrine, Ignatius in his *Spiritual Exercises* counsels the person engaged in mental prayer to practice "applying the senses." This entails the use of memory to recall previous meditations on the scriptures, especially the events of the life of Christ. The person should most keenly attend to those aspects rich in the consoling presence of the Holy Spirit's drawing him ever more closely into divine intimacy. Placing these aspects and their associated affections clearly

16. Hans Urs von Balthasar, *The Glory of the Lord: A Theological Aesthetics* [hereafter "*GL*"], vol. 1: *Seeing the Form,* trans. Erasmo Leiva-Merikakis (San Francisco, Calif.: Ignatius Press, 1982–91), 151.

before the mind, the imagination is vicariously to evoke sensations in order to savor them with greater relish. Sights, sounds, smells, tastes, and touches are willfully to be heightened, even to the point of luxuriance. Because Ignatius believes that the creator acts "immediately with the creature, and the creature with its Creator," the exercitant's deliberate plunging into images spiritually impregnated serves to expand the ambit of grace.[17] Justified in baptism, human freedom has become grace's instrumental power. Ironically, therefore, the divine freedom is respected most when human freedom aggressively endeavors to appropriate its gifts.

In the application of the senses, Ignatius exploits his understanding of human nature as a sacramental medium of grace. The application's basic use is simple enough, even for those least initiated into the devout life. "Lovingly and contemplatively," the technique advises, "with all the feelings of your heart make everything that the Lord Jesus said and did present to yourself, just as you were hearing it with your own ears and seeing it with your own eyes."[18] But an advanced use also available could more fittingly be described as the properly mystical prayer of infused contemplation. Loyola's interpreter Juan Polanco credits the higher power of reason as its source. Yet this power is reached through a sensibility that, paradoxically, it never abandons. Thus Christ is embraced "in that pure love" that, rightly called a "sense of touch," fashions the person into his likeness.[19] The infused gifts spring from sensibility "like fire from sticks that are rubbed together."[20] Just so does Francis of Assisi embrace the divine immediacy when in the stigmata the wounds of Christ sensibly pain him.[21] Just

17. Ignatius, *Exercises*, "Fifteenth Annotation," 12.

18. *Meditationes vitae Christi*, by an anonymous fourteenth-century Franciscan, cited as Ignatius's inspiration in Hugo Rahner, *Ignatius the Theologian*, trans. Michael Barry (New York: Herder and Herder, 1968), 193.

19. Juan Polanco, *Exercitia spiritualia S. Ignatii eorumque Directoria* in *Monumenta Ignatiana, Series Secunda* (Rome: Institutum Historicum Societatis Iesu, 1955–69; rev. ed. of Madrid, 1919), 2:300–303; in Rahner, *Ignatius*, 205.

20. Balthasar, *GL*, vol. 2: *Clerical Styles*, trans. Andrew Louth et al. (San Francisco, Calif.: Ignatius Press, 1982–91), 260–362, at 323.

21. Ibid., 321.

so does Augustine claim that the love of God bathes his "inner self" in "light that is not bound by space," even while he "breathes" there a "fragrance that is not borne away on the wind."[22]

In sum, the representational culture of the Baroque embodies a vision of humanity as a divine microcosm who can fashion a macrocosm of symbolic meaning. Human freedom and sensibility retain their distinctive modes of motion even when instrumentally joined with the motion of the provident creator. From the religious experience occasioned by this fusion bursts forth a barrage of moral, social, and aesthetic creativity. In and through it, the sublunary world reflects its infinite archetype by abandoning a merely static mimesis. At the Baroque's core, human ingenuity exercises a dynamic originality akin to the creativity of its divine source. Nonetheless, however spontaneous, this dynamism sacrifices its vigor when not impelled by transcendence.

But the Baroque's synthesis of nature and grace onto which aesthetics, Trent, and mysticism open a window emerges from a homogeneously God-centered culture.[23] Its fracturing leads to a defining trait of modernity—secularization. Defined as culture's loss of the ability to interpret reality religiously, secularization results from a restricting of the mind's drive toward its transcendent term. When reason fails directly to experience the sacred mediated by the natural order but nonetheless radically different from it, the sense of the divine is not only compromised. The sense of the profane is also forfeited. Perceived only as the antithesis of the sacred, the profane constitutes the sacred's parasite. With the double loss of the sacred and the profane, the secular accordingly strews the world with impoverished and incoherent symbols. The transcendent universal that alone enriches their meaning and reconciles their diversity has, in short, evanesced.[24]

22. Augustine, *Confessions,* trans. R. S. Pine-Coffin (Harmondsworth: Penguin Books, 1961), X:211–12.

23. Dupré, "Ignatian Humanism," 180.

24. Louis Dupré, *The Other Dimension: A Search for the Meaning of Religious Attitudes* (New York: Seabury Press, 1979), 14–18.

The Clash of Thomas and Augustine

Christian theology, ironically, makes its own contribution to the advance of the secular. In ensuing centuries, as Dupré argues, it was unable to reestablish the Baroque's lost harmony.[25] It endeavored to refute the claim of the Enlightenment that any authentic philosophy either dispensed with faith altogether or forced religion to ground its beliefs in a fideism outside the "limits of pure reason alone." This last phrase, drawn from the title of Kant's last major work, signaled the Copernican revolution in religion.[26] To reassert the rationality of divine revelation over against philosophical agnosticism, several theological schools arose; but it was the Neo-Thomist revival of the mid-nineteenth century that achieved ascendancy. Centered in Rome, its greatest master, Joseph Kleutgen, a Jesuit consultor to the Congregation of the Index, sought to tread a middle ground. On the one hand, he wanted to validate the method of correlation, in which the graced truths of theology could be seen as fulfilling the insufficiency of the natural methods of philosophy. On the other hand, he wanted to assert the legitimate autonomy of these methods within their proper sphere. He therefore opposed any effort to ground human knowledge in an incipient or seminal grace.[27] Faith, deriving from an infused supernatural habit, was seen as strictly subsequent to reason, however much it served as its congenially perfecting complement.[28] The assertion of this autonomy actually caused theology to devolve into the rationalism that it sought to combat. Reason's strident prerogatives eclipsed the transcendent as its own vital source, thus estranging the wedding of nature and grace.

The Modernist controversy at the turn of the twentieth century widened the gap. A potpourri of notions drawn from the Enlighten-

25. Dupré, *Passage*, 247–48.

26. Gerald A. McCool, *Catholic Theology in the Nineteenth Century: The Quest for a Unitary Method* (New York: Seabury Press, 1977), 18.

27. Ibid., 7.

28. Ibid., 8.

ment and its Romantic aftermath selectively appeared in some Catholic thinkers. Such notions were perceived to coalesce around an evolutionary view of truth concomitant on the metaphysics of becoming. For the Neo-Thomists, this view compromised the intellect's faculty of judgment. Uniting a changeless universal concept to a datum of sensation, judgment establishes truth as the mind's correspondence to reality. The universal element grounds human knowledge in an ontology of form that gives meaning and intelligibility to the contingency of sensuously intuited data. In turn, this ontology grounds arguments from natural reason for the existence of God, the truth of faith's dogmas, and the ethical norms of the natural law. When the universal element in knowledge is undermined, the waves of contingency are undammed, causing a flood of relativism.[29] The threat of such a scenario caused Neo-Thomists and their ecclesiastical authorities to buttress the faculty of judgment. The sad upshot finds articulation in Michael Buckley's observation that theology's maturing rationalism paved the way for modern atheism. By confining religion to an intellectual defense of creed and code, theology neglected cult, thereby ignoring religion's driving energy in spiritual sensibility.[30]

But the whole blame cannot fall on the Neo-Thomists. Much of it must be accounted to Thomas's own ambiguity. In the *Summa Theologiae*, for example, he avers that humanity before the Fall existed in the state of "integral nature" untainted by sin. In this state, we could do the good of "acquired virtue." In other words, without divine grace, we could do the good proportionate to a sinless human nature (I-II, q. 109, a. 2). This good included knowing what the divine law required and being able to fulfill it (I-II, q. 109, a. 4). We could accomplish these acts of knowledge and will because we received the necessary help of God who, as the first mover, inspires us toward "any good whatsoever" (I-II, q. 109, a. 2).

29. Gerald A. McCool, "Twentieth-Century Scholasticism," *Journal of Religion* 58 (1978 Suppl.): S198–221, at S204–7.

30. Michael J. Buckley, *At the Origins of Modern Atheism* (New Haven, Conn.: Yale University Press, 1987), 362–63.

The good of integral nature, however, does not include fulfilling the law with the required spirit of charity. This good could only be realized by an "infused virtue" animated by grace, not by nature (ibid.). Thus, even in our prelapsarian state, grace was needed in addition to God's activity as first mover (I-II, q. 109, a. 4). After the Fall, humanity exists in the state of "corrupt nature." Without grace, we cannot clearly know all that the law requires, we cannot do its commands, and we cannot do them with the required charity (ibid.). Nonetheless, we continue to need the help of God as first mover to tend toward any good whatsoever (I-II, q. 109, a. 2) Thus, in both states of nature, integral and corrupt, God's activity as the redeeming giver of grace builds upon his activity as creator.

In the state of corrupt nature, under the influence of the first mover but without grace, we are capable of what might be called the good of utility. This includes "particular" goods, such as erecting buildings, planting vineyards, and other "works leading to a good which is connatural" to fallen nature (I-II, q. 109, aa. 2, 5). Because such works spring from natural virtues, especially the cardinal virtues of prudence, fortitude, justice, and temperance, the good of utility must include the whole culture of acquired virtue such as Aristotle sets out in his ethical treatises, and which Thomas incorporates into Christian moral theology. What is important, however, is that the good of utility, as such, is not meritorious before God. The person performing it is not justified by sanctifying or habitual grace (I-II, q. 109, a. 2). Nonetheless, the good of utility results from the motion of the first mover by which "everything seeks [God] under the common notion of good" (I-II, q. 109, a. 6). By common, Thomas means analogous.

The problem with this position lies in its understanding of the good. On the one hand, Aquinas says that the movement of the first cause inspires everything toward an analogous notion of the good. On the other hand, he maintains that the culture of virtue described, for instance, by Aristotle is devoid of any vestigially justifying merit. This position leads inevitably to the claim that goods resulting from the cardinal virtues, when exercised by unjustified nature, are discontinuous from the goods resulting from these same virtues when fallen nature is elevated by grace. It is hard to see how the notion of the good presupposed in this claim is analogous when it tends toward being equivocal. The equivocation can be muted by seeing the preparation for justification that occurs in a person's sincere conscience as indirectly but authentically a participation in the habitual grace to which it leads. As we saw, Trent inclines toward this view, but Thomas is far from clear on it, as Henri Bouillard's study shows.[31] The *Summa*'s incipient equivocation developed into an explicit theory of a pure nature independent of grace certainly by the sixteenth century in Sylvester of Ferrara.[32] It grew, effectively dominating Thomism until de Lubac's *Surnaturel* in 1946.

In order to uncover the reason for troubles in Thomas's relation of nature and grace, we need to plunge deeper. It lies in the ambiguity surrounding the importing of Aristotle's anthropology and metaphysics of knowledge into Christian theology. Both posit a probing critique of the Augustinian theology that had dominated Christian speculation for nearly a thousand years. The prevailing theology confronted the problem of the mind's access to truth from the Neoplatonic perspective that grounded it. If the human intellect, as created, is mutable, contingent, and temporal, then how can it make judgments about what is essentially unchanging, universal, and eternal? It is of course clear, Augustinians aver, that the mind does in fact make such judgments when it affirms the axioms of mathematics, the existence of a first cause, and the major premises of ethics. Their answer centers on the doctrine of illumination, the distinguishing hallmark of Augustinian Christianity. A metaphysical "light," as it were, radiates upon the intellect from the divine ideas, the exemplary causes of all finite realities. This light, received in reason's higher power, grounds the discursive judgments of reason's lower power in the defining qualities of metaphysics, universality and necessity. It accounts for the underived first

31. Henri Bouillard, *Conversion et grâce chez saint Thomas d'Aquin: étude historique* (Paris: Aubier, 1944), esp. 211–19.

32. Sylvester of Ferrara, *Opera* (Venice, 1535), 1:39–41; in Dupré, *Passage*, 171–72.

principles of mind, like non-contradiction, without which thinking is impossible. It explains the transcendence of finite human reason over its radical dependence on the empirical data of sensuous intuition.

Whatever problems illumination may present, it does offer a twofold genius. First, it creatively adapts Plato's anamnetic theory of knowledge to Christianity. In *Phaedo,* for instance, the problem of truth is solved by the soul's pre-existence. In a world of unchanging spirit utterly devoid of material contingency, the soul gazed on all the perfect forms that constitute the patterns of the specific objects encountered in the realm of empirical experience. For reasons Plato does not clarify, souls have fallen from their pre-existence into material bodies. Nonetheless, because the soul carries a recollection of its eternal vision, it still retains some potential to know the ideal world of pure spirit. This obtains when, in the historical world, the person learns how to know the self at its deepest level. Only an ascetical life such as Socrates pursues can effect this knowledge. The searcher of wisdom is always dying, Socrates tells his followers.[33] In other words, the philosopher is always seeking to withdraw from the sensuous stimulation that occludes inner anamnesis. When Socrates counsels his disciples "to know thyself," he is by no means presaging the merely autobiographical goals of modern psychotherapy. He is schooling them in nothing less than eternal verity. He is directing them how to render consciously explicit the knowledge that they implicitly carry.

The soul's pre-existence, on which the Platonic conception of truth depends, ran into an impasse with the teaching of the Council of Nicaea. In countering the Arian position of the Son's status as a divine creature, Nicaea ratified the doctrine of historical reality as *creatio ex nihilo*. It thus insisted on a far starker contrast between the worlds of divinity and materiality than Plato put forth. Not only heterodox is the soul's pre-existence, such as Origen had integrated into Christianity from the Academy. So also is its presupposition: that a close affinity of nature could obtain between God and the world as would ensue from locating creation within the divinity itself or within the eternal

33. Plato, *Phaedo* 67e.

sphere.[34] Therefore, because the Christian soul cannot enjoy a prehistorical vision of God, the truth of its judgments cannot find a ground in the recollection of any such vision.

With an anamnetic metaphysics ruled out, Augustine might have solved the problem of truth by recourse to the teaching of Genesis that the human being is made in the image and likeness of God. He might, for instance, have been content to ground knowledge in this image, which could have been understood in some way to mediate the eternal truth of the first cause to human judgments. In *De Trinitate*, he begins to suggest such an approach. The image of the pre-existent Word is found in the inner word of the human mind, the rational concept, that forms the acts of understanding.[35] But the apophatic Augustine is quick to remind us of the obscurity of this created image. It is an "enigma," paradoxically constituting, within its "likeness" to its infinite archetype, a great "unlikeness."[36] As a result, he saw the need for a mediating structure of nature to breach the distance between God and the enfleshed soul. Illumination, his substitute for the superannuated theory of recollection, can be discerned by the use of reason unaided by any explicit grace or act of faith.

The second genius of illumination is the intimate link it establishes between creation and divinity, especially in light of the Nicene teaching of creation from nothing. This link is well illustrated in one of the high developments of Augustinianism, the School of Chartres. Reaching its apogee in the century before the Peripatetic recovery, it comprised a group of Christian Neoplatonic love poets centered in the noted cathedral city. Chief among these is Bernardus Sylvestris, whose principal work *On the Entire World or the Macrocosmos and the Microcosmos* concerns the story of creation. Emphasizing the divine immanence in materiality, this Latin allegorical poem speaks from the point

34. Andrew Louth, *The Origins of the Christian Mystical Tradition from Plato to Denys* (Oxford: Oxford University Press, 1981), 75–77.

35. Augustine, *On the Trinity*, 15.11.20, in *A Select Library of the Nicene and Post-Nicene Fathers of the Christian Church*, ed. Philip Schaff, trans. Arthur West Haddan (Grand Rapids, Mich: Eerdmans, 1980), 3:209–10.

36. Ibid., 15.11.21 (3:210).

of view of matter that longs to receive form. The main characters include Nous, the creative mind of God, who includes the ideal patterns of creation; Urania, the heavenly spirit; Natura, the general order of the cosmos; and Physis, organic, biological nature.[37]

The poem's dramatic tension arises from the problem that the allegories must solve: how is humanity to constitute, not merely a copy of the divine ideas like the rest of creation, but something immediately joined to divinity. Physis is impotent to answer, so she calls on Urania who, as the mediatrix between Nous and Physis, possesses the potency to fashion a soul.[38] As a spirit in the world, humanity, says Nous:

> ... by his care
> Shall rule the earth, and reach the Heaven by prayer,
> ...
> He shall drag forth to light the causes hid
> In secret gloom ...[39]

Shifting its focus to erotic love, the poem continues. It seeks to restore the dignity of human sexual expression by drawing it out from under the shadow of evil. This, cast since the fifth century over sexuality even when nuptially blessed, is owing in large measure to Augustine's theory of traducianism.[40] A riposte to Pelagianism, it posits that original sin is handed down in the act of generation. Nonetheless, affirms Bernardus, "Pleasant and fitting" is the use of the body's organs, "When time and mode and measure do agree."[41] He thus charts a middle ground for eros between an immoral licentiousness on the one hand and the ascetical rigor advocated by Socrates and Augustine on the other. In turn, this mediation is possible only because of Urania's mediation between Nous and Physis. The upshot is that Natura becomes God's vicar, a synthesis of heaven and earth.

37. C. S. Lewis, *The Allegory of Love* (Oxford: Oxford University Press, 1936), 90, 93.

38. Ibid., 94–95.

39. Bernardus Sylvestris, *De mundi universitate*, in *Bibliotheca philosophorum mediae aetatis*, ed. Barach and Wrobel, 2, 9; in Lewis, *Allegory*, 96.

40. See esp. Augustine, *The Grace of Christ and Original Sin*, 2.45.

41. Bernardus, *De mundi*, 2.14.155; in Lewis, *Allegory*, 97.

Although Bernardus nowhere mentions illumination, that it forms the backdrop of his synthetic understanding of human nature can hardly be doubted. Urania confers on humanity the refracted powers of Nous. This conferral gives humanity, albeit created, its linked participation in the divine ideas. Such participation has been criticized as blurring the proper distinction between the natural and the supernatural. It is accused of rendering human beings mere "diaphanous signs, whose role is [only] to point beyond themselves to God." It supposedly deprives them of a "substantial reality of their own."[42] But the grades of created participation from Nous, through Urania, to Natura's fusion with Physis sufficiently protect the separate integrity of God and humanity without at the same time sacrificing the connection that the theory of pure nature risks sundering.

It is true that not until Bonaventure's era did the Augustinians satisfactorily synthesize the empirical data of knowledge and the divine light. And to be fair, they accomplished this task by integrating into Christian Neoplatonism a chief advance of Aristotle's: the theory of the agent intellect. But they saw, perhaps more clearly than Thomists, the problems associated with any progress. Aquinas incorporated the agent intellect into his Christian synthesis as a "created participation" in the divine intellect. It inheres intrinsically in the person, belonging naturally to it as a substance. Even as finite, it possesses the first principles of thought under whose guidance it abstracts the concept incipiently present in the intuited datum of sense. For Thomists, therefore, the intellect retains the capability, in virtue of its own immanent resources, of achieving truth. It need not be supplemented in each and every act of the mind by a higher source.[43]

Henry of Ghent, Bonaventure's Augustinian contemporary, agrees that the human intellect, without illumination, can know something of an object through sensory intuition. This knowledge obtains by

42. W. Norris Clarke, "Notes on St Thomas's Philosophy" (photocopy, course notes, Department of Philosophy, Fordham University).

43. Ibid.

"purely natural means."[44] These do not exclude the general influence of the first cause, he says following Aristotle, without which no motion whatsoever is possible. Henry asserts, however, that knowing what is true of an object and knowing its truth entail different, albeit related, mental operations. Whereas the first truth obtains by abstracting the universal from the empirical datum, the second, which posits a certain judgment, requires illumination.[45] He and Bonaventure presciently understood what Joseph Maréchal and his transcendental school of realism would claim seven hundred years later in bringing metaphysics head to head with Kant: that the universal concept in human knowledge cannot appear without an intrinsic connection to the transcendent absolute.[46] And these moderns claim to find this thesis in Thomas himself. If the agent intellect, like all human faculties, must have a final cause, then that cause cannot merely be finite. If it is not implicitly infinite, then truth can never rise above the mutable datum of its empirical ground. A pure nature connected by a vague tenuousness to God as prime mover is thus as much a metaphysical inconsistency for high Augustinianism as for some twentieth-century Thomists. In light of this similarity, it is a curious question of history as to why Bonaventure fell into an unrevived eclipse, whereas his contemporary Aquinas emerged regnant after his own eclipse.[47]

The theory of illumination, even as it differentially joined heaven, humanity, and earth, did not claim to be explicitly graced. That illumination was an uncreated light seems hard to doubt, since it claimed to ground discursive judgments in the immutable and eternal. Precisely here a crucial question of interpretation arises. If grace is the participation in God's very life, and if illumination is an uncreated participation

44. Henry of Ghent, *Summa quaestionum ordinariarum* 1.3, in *Medieval Philosophy: Essential Readings with Commentary*, ed. Gyula Klima (Malden, Mass.: Blackwell, 2007), 105.

45. Ibid., 104–5.

46. Joseph Maréchal, *Le Thomisme devant la philosophie critique*, vol. 5 of *Le point de départ de la métaphysique*, 2nd ed. (Brussels: Édition universelle, 1949). See selections in *A Maréchal Reader*, ed. and trans. Joseph Donceel (New York: Herder and Herder, 1970).

47. For some insight, see Steven P. Marrone, *The Light of Thy Countenance: Science and Knowledge of God in the Thirteenth Century* (Leiden: Brill, 2001), vol. 2, esp. chaps. 12 and 16.

in God's intelligence, then can illumination claim to be completely dissociated from grace? That illumination can be discerned by unaided reason does not therefore entail that it is purely natural. Questions along this line will be explored in subsequent chapters. What can be said at present, however, is that illumination offers a mediating structure. While belonging to nature, it at least prepares nature for the life of grace. It grounds humanity in an uncreated dimension that inhibits conceiving nature as dichotomous to its transcendent source. Moreover, if "grace perfects nature," as the commonplace observation states, then illumination allows grace to be seen less as a structure superadded on to nature than as a continuation of nature's congenial participation in the uncreated.

Language's Denouement

To the extent that the theory of pure nature contributes to the attenuation of humanity's link with its transcendent source, its influence on the devolution of language, both sacred and profane, should not be underestimated. As we shall soon see, this devolution is owing in no small measure to the incipient equivocation in Thomas previously discussed. Before turning to this issue, however, let us first discuss transcendence as the guarantor of meaning.

Just as God creates natural forms that represent his mind, observes Nicholas of Cusa, so humanity actively creates concepts, images, metaphors, and symbols that represent its own.[48] If language results from human genius even as it remotely represents the divine, then it is no mere accident that, after a hiatus of six hundred years, the allegory was revived in works such as those of the Chartrains. Allegory represents the immaterial and abstract in pictorial personifications.[49] Its origins lie in the poets of pagan antiquity, such as Virgil, Seneca, and Statius. Its high development achieved in these writers was lost after Augus-

48. Louis Dupré, "The Broken Mirror: The Fragmentation of the Symbolic World," *Stanford Literature Review* 5 (Spring–Fall 1988): 7–24, at 11–12.

49. Lewis, *Allegory*, 45, 48.

tine, although the genre continued in the relatively crude moralizings that followed.[50] C. S. Lewis, offering a gloss on Cusa, observes that for allegory "to spread its wings fully, there must be, besides the believed religion, a marvelous that knows itself as myth."[51] It is perhaps this fortuitous fusion of religion and myth that produced the unpredicted eruption of the Chartrains' creativity. In addition to Augustine's illumination that stamped their Christian Neoplatonism, they manifest a debt to tropes of his *Confessions*. In Book X, for instance, the human mind takes on decidedly allegorical contours: "Climbing up, therefore, step by step to Him that made me, I will pass beyond this faculty of my nature and come to the fields and wide pavilions of Memory."[52] Even as Augustine here echoes the metaphoric marvels of Plato's cave, so this same *Republic*, together with some of "Ovid's smirkings," are adumbrated when Bernardus Sylvestris allegorizes the sexual faculties as "Conqueror's of Death! they fill each empty place / In Nature and immortalize the race."[53]

Even before the Chartrains, allegory had already been integrated into the medieval conception of the symbol properly conceived. Developed under the aegis of divine revelation, especially for the interpretation of the scriptures, the symbol was deemed to constitute "the truest means of penetration into the mystery of reality."[54] This penetration is epitomized in the insight or intrinsic symbol as contrasted with the sign. The sign forms a *medium quo* by which an empirical object receives a signification, usually an arbitrary one, by some consensus. Like a national flag or a traffic light, its efficacy is derived from its ability to evoke or recall its assigned meaning. By contrast, the intrinsic symbol forms a *medium in quo*. Effectively representing its archetype, it contains within its own empirical substance the abstract reality that it signifies. Enunci-

50. Ibid., 49, 86.

51. Ibid., 83.

52. Augustine, *Confessions*, ed. Pius Knöll, in vol. 33 of *Corpus scriptorum ecclesiasticorum Latinorum* (Vindobonae: F. Tempsky, 1896), X.8; in Lewis, *Allegory*, 65.

53. Bernardus Sylvestris, *De mundi, Bibliotheca*, 2.14.155; in Lewis, *Allegory*, 97.

54. Helen Flanders Dunbar, *Symbolism in Medieval Thought and Its Consummation in the Divine Comedy* (New Haven, Conn.: Yale University Press, 1929), 24.

ating what it defines, it "partakes of the reality which it renders intelligible."[55] Undergirding this view is the sacramental conception of the cosmos, intrinsic to Christianity, but found as early as Heraclitus and the Stoics. They posit the "sympathy of the whole": the notion that the tensions of the visible world are ultimately reconciled in an underlying invisible harmony.[56] For the medievals, the real presence of Christ in the eucharistic bread and wine serves as the intrinsic symbol's paradigm. Thomas makes this point with succinct elegance in the sequence that he wrote in 1264 for the feast of Corpus Christi: "Here beneath symbols are hidden / Priceless things to sense forbidden; / Symbols, not things, are in view."[57] "Thing" is a translation of the Latin "res" that, in Scholastic symbol theory, means the hidden reality signified by the empirical medium. So understood, the real presence embodies Carlyle's paradox: the union of silence and speech, infinite and finite.[58]

Influenced by this view of the symbol, the fourfold exegesis of scripture, recently retrieved by Henri de Lubac's magisterial study, can be traced to Origen and Augustine.[59] They distinguish between the spirit and the letter in the interpretation of a text. Commenting on this distinction, Aquinas notes that "the first signification whereby words signify [empirical realities] belongs to … the historical or literal. That signification whereby [empirical realities] signified by words have themselves also a signification is called spiritual interpretation, which is based on the literal interpretation and pre-supposes it" (*ST* I, q. 1, a. 10).[60] Further development of this distinction trifurcated the spiritual meaning into the tropological or moral; the anagogical, which usually meant the eschatological; and the allegorical, whose rich import immediately concerns us.

55. Ibid., 16, 475. The quotation is Coleridge's, cited without source in "Symbol," from *A Handbook to Literature*, ed. William Flint Thrall et al. (New York: Odyssey Press, 1960), 478.

56. Ernst Cassirer, *An Essay on Man* (New Haven, Conn.: Yale University Press, 1944), 94–95, 222–23.

57. My adaptation of the *Roman Missal*, National Conference of Catholic Bishops, 1964.

58. Thomas Carlyle, *Sartor Resartus: The Life and Opinions of Herr Teufelsdröckh*, ed. Charles Frederick Harrod (New York: Odyssey Press, 1937), 219.

59. Henri de Lubac, *Exégèse médiévale: les quatre sens de l'Écriture* (Paris: Aubier, 1959–64).

60. Trans. in Dunbar, *Symbolism*, 498–99.

Although at root a fictional personification of an abstract value, allegory can become "a symbol when by means of it we embody an ideal content not otherwise expressible."[61] A vital premise in medieval exegesis established the union of symbol and allegory. Handed down by patristic legacy, it is well expressed by Athanasius in *On the Incarnation*: "For being the Word of the Father, and above all, [Christ] alone of natural fitness was ... able to re-create everything."[62] This premise allowed for the extension of the Chalcedonian communication of idioms, according to which what properly pertains to the savior's divine nature can legitimately be predicated of his human nature. Thus, in virtue of the unity of the incarnate person, God may be said, for instance, to have a mother, be born, suffer, and die. If the incarnate Word has recreated the cosmos, then he is to be discerned not only in the scriptures but in anything material, whether inanimate, animate, or human. In other words, what is predicated of Christ can in some vestigial sense be predicated of creation. On this basis, Bonaventure in *Mind's Road into God* affirms that all sensible objects "proclaim that in them as in a mirror can be seen the eternal generation of the Word, the Image, and the Son, eternally emanating from God the Father." This proclamation obtains because each sensible object, like the Word, is generative. In order to be known, the object must produce in the human intellect an image or species of itself.[63]

Christ therefore accounts for the fusion of allegory and symbol. All of creation is his allegory. Yet this is no fictional trope of the mere imagination. The allegory constitutes an intrinsic symbol because an authentic ontological relation obtains between creation and Christ. This relation awaits human discernment and articulation. In other words, just as scripture requires exegesis, so does nature. Language thus serves as the bridge uniting infinite and finite. But it can do so only because "in symbolism, not the word but the [object] represented by the word,

61. W. M. Urban, cited without source in *A Handbook to Literature*, ed. Thrall et al., 478.

62. Athanasius, *On the Incarnation*, trans. Archibald Robertson, in *Christology of the Later Fathers*, ed. Edward Rochie Hardy (Philadelphia: Westminster Press, 1954), 62.

63. Bonaventure, *The Mind's Road to God*, trans. George Boas (New York: Macmillan, 1986), 18.

is to be regarded as the symbol."[64] Accordingly, as Hugh of St. Victor observes, when Christ is called the Lion of Judah, "'*leo*' is said to signify Christ." It is "not the name of the animal, but the animal itself [that] signifies him."[65] Because "the [objects] signified by the words can themselves be types of other [objects]," a lion can be both Christ's allegory and symbol (*ST* I, q. 1, a. 10).[66] That language is itself an intrinsic symbol of the entities it articulates is guaranteed by the species previously mentioned. Found in Bonaventure and Thomas as from Aristotle, the species is intuited by sensibility. As subsequently synthesized by the intellect into the knowledge that is spoken, the species ensures that words both represent the empirical datum and signify the world of spirit.

This dual function of words, Dupré reminds us, is decisively sundered by the secular's loss of both the sacred and the profane. Detached from representation, language begins its devolution when it expresses merely the human subject. Symptomatically, the novel rises as modernity's premier literary form. A narrative whose development becomes more and more privatized, it is unable to offer the elevated ethical vision of tragedy or epic. In fact, its increasing idiosyncrasy approaches nihilism.[67] As the novel becomes solipsistic, language disengages itself from generally understood modes of communication.[68] It becomes the fetish of individual writers, thus entering into "war with the established reality structures" of culture.[69] Now evoking doubt and insecurity instead of signifying the true, the good, and the beautiful, speech continues to be formulated, but its meaning, ironically, descends more and more into an agnostic silence.[70]

As we have argued, the secular, which accounts for silencing language, results from the attenuation of God and reason. This in turn entails a double provenance: the demise of illumination, which inspired the Chartrains, and the eclipse of faith, which inspired symbolic ex-

64. Dunbar, *Symbolism*, 500.

65. Hugh of St. Victor, in vols. 175–76 of J.-P. Migne, ed., *Patrologiae cursus completus, Series latina* (Paris, 1844–64) [hereafter "*PL*"]; in Dunbar, *Symbolism*, 491.

66. Trans. in Dunbar, *Symbolism*, 499.

67. Dupré, "Broken Mirror," 20.

68. Ibid., 21.

69. Ibid.

70. Ibid., 22–24.

egesis. But the matter is further complicated. Tensions in the Thomist foundation of language's ability to express the transcendent also belong to this provenance. Let us now probe these by returning to the incipient equivocation lodged in Thomas's understanding of the good discussed earlier.

As previously noted, for Thomas the three spiritual senses of scripture are based on the literal level. For their part, the spiritual levels presuppose an act of faith that the literal level does not. Accordingly, the literal level provides a natural preparation for the spiritual levels. The literal level can predicate attributes of God, such as goodness, based on empirical experience. In *ST* I, q. 13, Thomas asserts that such divine attributes are, in the first instance, relative. They pertain to God's operations in the world. They are inferred from their sensible manifestations in the order of historical realities. On this basis, they can be applied analogously to God as the most perfect and real being. When they are, the attributes are no longer relative but absolute. They pertain to God as he exists in himself. Precisely because the literal level serves as a natural propaedeutic for the graced levels of the spirit, an important question arises. How can the relative attributes, which are expressed in human language conditioned by sensuous experience, be affirmed of God, when all we know of God's essence is *that* it is, not *what* it is? In *ST* I, q. 3, Thomas says that such an affirmation can be made literally. What is signified by the name goodness belongs to God and to finite objects, but the mode by which goodness signifies these beings differs. It signifies a creature in the sense of finitude, but God in the sense of infinity. Moreover, the perfection applies to God in its primary sense, asserts Thomas, because he possesses it with universal necessity. It applies to creatures only in a derived sense in virtue of their dependence and contingency.[71]

Stressing the difference in the mode of a divine attribute's significa-

71. Wilbur M. Urban, "Symbolism as a Theological Principle in St Thomas," in his *Language and Reality: The Philosophy of Language and the Principles of Symbolism* (London: Allen and Unwin, 1939), 748–50.

tion allows Thomas to affirm a predicate's literal application to all subjects without collapsing infinite and finite modes of being. The predicate is neither univocal nor equivocal. It thus avoids pantheism on the one hand and blind fideism on the other, which would deny that a divine predicate possesses some epistemic relation to human reason. But when Thomas is pressed as to the warranting ground of the differing mode of the predicate's signification, interpretive problems begin. Herbert McCabe, for instance, finds this ground in Thomas's belief that things point beyond themselves to the "no thing" that altogether transcends them. Thus, since words signify things, words can point beyond their finite mode of predication. Still, McCabe insists, it does not necessarily follow that our finite predicate should have the same literal meaning in God.[72] Thomas does deny that we can conceive any adequate notion of the divine perfections, even as he claims that their predication depends on the affirmation of God's infinite existence.[73] The ground of this affirmation lies in the mind's *excessus*, by which it negates the finite in order to affirm the infinite. The question finally focuses on seeking the ground of this *excessus*. And this focus returns us to the key question raised previously: Can the human mind affirm universal propositions, whether about finite concepts or infinite being, without an intrinsic connection to the transcendent absolute? Without a final cause that is implicitly infinite, it seems hard to warrant that the predication of the names of God can rise above the mutable datum of their empirical ground. If they are deficient in such a warrant, then they would seem to emerge, at best, only from the need of reason to

72. Herbert McCabe, "Analogy," appendix 4 in vol. 3 of Thomas Aquinas, *Summa theologiae*, trans. and ed. Fathers of the English-Speaking Dominican Provinces (New York: McGraw-Hill, 1964–66), 106–7 [hereafter "*ST*"].

73. George P. Klubertanz, "Analogy," in *New Catholic Encyclopedia* [hereafter "*NCE*"] (New York: McGraw-Hill, 1967–96), 1.465b, referring esp. to *ST* I, q. 4, a. 2. Steven A. Long, in studying the ground of predication in *ST* and *De Veritate*, highlights the intrinsic relation of the analogy of proper proportionality to the graced contents of faith. But as influenced by Jacques Maritain and Réginald Garrigou-Lagrange, OP, his approach would have less sympathy for the transcendental explanation of *excessus* that we develop next—see *Analogia Entis: On the Analogy of Being, Metaphysics, and the Act of Faith* (Notre Dame, Ind.: University of Notre Dame Press, 2011), esp. the final chapter.

satisfy the demands of its immanent operations. Thus, as Kant argues, while the predicates of God serve a useful intra-rational purpose, they spuriously evanesce as analogously divine.

We thus confront in Thomas a second incipient equivocation of the good. The first one that we discussed leads to pure nature by dichotomizing nature and grace. This one contributes to the isolation of pure nature by undermining the rational bridge of divine predication. C. S. Lewis describes the result of an independent nature closed in on itself. Hearkening to Gilson, he observes that when the danger of pantheism grows less, "the danger of mechanistic Deism [comes] a step nearer."[74] As nature becomes centripetal, the transcendent, accessed by both nature and grace, becomes centrifugal. If, for instance, the literal level of scriptural exegesis cannot assert a prerogative to the predicates that ground the levels of the spirit, then the spirit's symbolism either dries and withers, or is retained by the fideism that Thomas sought to avoid. With the crumbling of symbolism's transcendence, it is not surprising that the novel's narcissism should ascend in importance. It seems the suitable companion not only to Kant's transcendental ego but also to pure nature conceived as increasingly reclusive.

However rich and subtle the medieval relation between the scriptural letter and spirit, Thomas's framing of their distinction presents a further problem. The literal sense "would have nothing to do with faith."[75] It originates in an historical context apparently devoid of spirit, and it applies only to the correct understanding of the words of the text. Accordingly, as Thomas says, the spiritual level is added to this level, which serves as a natural base that it presupposes. Ironically, this sharp contrast between letter and spirit emerges as an ancestor of the problems that have recently come to the fore in the historical-critical interpretation of the Bible. Joseph Fitzmyer observes, for example, that whereas strictly speaking this interpretation is "neutral," it can nonetheless be used with

74. Lewis, *Allegory*, 88.

75. Joseph A. Fitzmyer, *The Interpretation of Scripture: In Defense of the Historical-Critical Method* (New York: Paulist Press, 2008), 94.

varying presuppositions.[76] The nineteenth century "rationalist, antidogmatic" assumptions of Ferdinand Baur and David Strauss and the twentieth century "demythologizing, existentialist assumptions of Bultmann" are at odds with the assumptions, for instance, of *Dei Verbum*, Vatican II's dogmatic constitution on divine revelation.[77] When integrated into the correct assumptions, the historical-critical method, Fitzmyer believes, can establish the intention of the biblical author from the words and phrases themselves, their immediate context, and the author's corpus as a whole.[78] These correct assumptions include that the text is the written word of God, and that it contains a message for the people both of old and today.[79] In addition, *Dei Verbum* would add that these assumptions include the ecclesial magisterium, the authoritative interpreter of the living tradition from which the New Testament emerges.

One might dispute Fitzmyer's claim that any method can be neutral, but much to his credit he shows a sensitivity to the problem inherent in the medieval distinction between the letter and the spirit. He rightly affirms a reciprocity between them. Not only does the literal sense ground the spiritual sense, but it presupposes the spiritual sense. In other words, if the historical-critical method aims at disclosing the original intention of the author, then it cannot obviate the author's faith that necessarily informs the words. To do otherwise would reduce the method to historical positivism.

Yet historical criticism entails problems deeper than Fitzmyer indicates. He tends to underestimate its limits, together with the consequences when these are not respected. In one of his last books, for example, the German exegete Rudolf Schnackenburg observes that this method can only "inadequately" achieve a "reliable view of the historical" Jesus.[80] Commenting on this, Pope Benedict XVI finds that, with

76. Ibid., 69.

77. Ibid., 66–68.

78. Ibid., 68–69.

79. Ibid., 84.

80. Rudolf Schnackenburg, *Jesus in the Gospels: A Biblical Christology*, trans. O. C. Dean, Jr. (Louisville, Ky.: Westminster John Knox Press, 1995), 316; originally *Jesus Christus im Spiegel der vier Evangelien* (Freiburg-im-Breisgau: Herder, 1998); in Benedict XVI, *Jesus of Nazareth: From the Baptism in the Jordan to the Transfiguration*, trans. Adrian J. Walker (New York: Doubleday, 2007), xiii.

the advance of historical-critical interpretation, the layers of scriptural tradition become excessively fine. The first result, he ironically observes, entails the loss of the historical Jesus altogether. When critical reconstructions of him clash, so many contradictions emerge that the only salvageable remains would seem to be Jesus as the moral prophet of Jeffersonian Deism. The second result entails the obscuring of Jesus as the object of faith. His divinity comes to be seen merely as the subsequently developed theory needed to resolve the historical contradictions.[81] Thus, spirit once again becomes split from letter. Schnackenburg himself evinces a tendency in this direction. In the New Testament, he claims, "the historical ground is presupposed but is superseded [*überschritten*] in the faith-view of the evangelists."[82] By this he means that the immediate demands of those who believed in Jesus assumed paramount importance over his historical foundation.[83] Although the distinguished scholar does not eliminate this foundation, his use of "supersede" implies that it can be forced out of use as inferior or replaced with something preferable. If it is thus superseded, history crumbles as a bulwark guarding the Jesus of the scriptures from the Gnosticism, for instance, that is inimical to orthodox Christianity.

When its methods are narrowly pursued, critical interpretation runs the risk of ending in an untenable bifurcation. The Jesus of historical positivism and the Jesus of supersessionist fideism repel dissonantly. Only when history and faith are held together in harmony can the Jesus of the scriptures accord with the doctrine of nature and grace proclaimed by Chalcedon. According to the council, the human and divine natures of Christ obtain "without confusion," "division," or "separation." Even so, they combine in "one person," himself "not divided or separated."[84] Jesus consequently admonishes Thomas when in the fourth Gospel he asks to be shown the Father. The reply is un-

81. Benedict XVI, *Jesus*, xii.

82. Schnackenburg, *Jesus in the Gospels*, 321 (*Jesus Christus*, 353); in Benedict XVI, *Jesus*, xiii.

83. Schnackenburg, *Jesus in the Gospels*, 321.

84. "The Chalcedonian Decree," trans. Edward Rochie Hardy, in *Christology of the Later Fathers*, 371–74, at 373.

equivocal: whoever sees Jesus sees the Father (Jn 14:9). As an icon, the flesh is charged with divinity, however much it retains human integrity. Although Christ, as incarnately active in time and space, can to some "inadequate" extent be grasped by historical criticism, still this criticism must perforce be grasping something of his divinity. Just so, this divinity is transmitted in the text perforce by the faith of the author who perceives it. Yet since Christ's divinity utterly transcends the history in which it is immanent, historical interpretation will only "inadequately" ascertain the text's spiritual sense immanent in its letter.

Consistent with his understanding of historical criticism, Fitzmyer argues that "spiritual exegesis" is nothing more than the "actualized literal sense of Scripture."[85] This sense means that what the message authentically says, as discerned by the method's proper orientation, can homogeneously address contemporary circumstances.[86] He cautions against interpretations like elaborate medieval allegories that foist a meaning on the text.[87] Hence when Pope John Paul II in *Redemptoris Mater* applies a text of Colossians to Mary, Fitzmyer diagnoses "the accommodated sense of Scripture." However useful this sense may be as a biblical meditation, it does not correspond to the meaning that Colossians' principal author (God) or its human author "ever intended."[88]

Although Fitzmyer's view of the actualized literal sense does not in itself presuppose a theory of pure nature, it suffers from an inadequate understanding of the reciprocity between nature and grace. De Lubac expresses this reciprocity well when he observes that the data of the Bible possess an inner significance "by virtue of their finality; they are already, in time, charged with eternity." Because of the incarnation, "the spiritual meaning is everywhere, not only or especially in a book, but *first and foremost in reality itself*."[89] Thus, he hearkens to the me-

85. Fitzmyer, *Interpretation*, 99.

86. Ibid., 84.

87. Ibid., 93, 98.

88. Ibid., 98.

89. Henri de Lubac, *Catholicisme: les aspects sociaux du dogme* (Paris: Cerf, 1947), 136, citing Maximus the Confessor, *Quaestiones ad Thalassium*, 9.17 (in J.-P. Migne, ed., *Patrologia cursus completus, Series graeca* [Paris, 1857–66], 90:304; [hereafter "*PG*"]); in Peter Casarella, "Introduction to the 2000 Edition," in Henri de Lubac, *Scripture in the Tradition*, trans. Luke O'Neill (New York: Crossroad, 2008), xiv.

dieval ground of allegory's union with the symbol: the entities signified by words can be types of other entities. If, as Balthasar observes, "profound *interconnections* [exist] within the history of salvation," then it seems a legitimate application of the spiritual sense for John Paul to speak of Mary's life in Nazareth as "hidden with Christ in God," even though the human author of Colossians would not have intended this meaning directly.[90] The spiritual finality pervading both the scriptures and reality as a whole warrants such a use. John Paul's meditation is not, therefore, a gratuitous foist on God's written word, but a deeper explication of this word's divine symbolism. As a result, the spiritual sense cannot be conveniently reduced to the actualized literal sense. The spiritual sense embraces the literal sense. Moreover, because it speaks through the literal sense, it requires the literal sense as its necessary condition, even while transcending it.

We thus see that historical-critical interpretation, when its limits are not respected, contributes to the denouement of language. Insofar as it tends to quarantine the letter, keeping at bay the spirit that harnesses it as a medium, language's ability to sustain a symbolic world of meaning is jeopardized. Language's decline, however, meets a strong countervailing force in *Dei Verbum*. Locating language within an interlocking system of intrinsic symbols, the dogmatic constitution teaches that God's revelation is not first and foremost communicated in words. The "mediator and the fulness of all revelation" is nothing less than the person of Jesus Christ, the Father's image in history.[91] As the incarnate Word, Christ reveals the Father not only "by his words," but by "works, symbolic acts and miracles" (par. 4). What Christ says and does, therefore, are secondary symbols immediately ensuing from, and reflective of, his theandric identity, the fundamental symbol.

For their part, the apostles faithfully "handed on, by their own

90. Hans Urs von Balthasar, *Le Cardinal de Lubac: l'homme et son oeuvre* (Paris: Lethielleux, 1983), 100, cited in Susan Wood, *Spiritual Exegesis and the Church in the Theology of Henri de Lubac* (Grand Rapids, Mich.: Eerdmans, 1998), 141; in Casarella, "Introduction," xiv.

91. Vatican Council II, *Dei Verbum*, in *Decrees*, ed. Tanner, 2:971–81. Cited in the text.

preaching and examples and by their dispositions, whatever they had received," whether from Christ's words and example, or under "the prompting of the Holy Spirit" (par. 7). Hence, the apostles' words and deeds constitute a third emanation of symbols in history. Ensuing from, and reflective of, Christ's words and deeds, their endeavors initiate Christian tradition. Developing in the church under the Spirit, tradition causes "growth in understanding of what is handed on, both the words and the realities they signify" (par. 8). From this understanding emerges the New Testament, which tradition causes to be more effectively realized in the church (par. 8). Accordingly, the scriptures are the fourth historical emanation of symbol. As inspired, the words of their authors present a divine meaning (par. 12), but the scriptures reciprocally communicate with tradition (par. 9) As Congar observes, tradition, in relation to the scriptures, is both *regula regulans et regulata.*[92] In other words, tradition interprets that which, having developed from it, nonetheless binds it.

Dei Verbum thus understands scriptural interpretation decidedly as a theological enterprise, however much scientific hermeneutics must attend to the historical media that serve the divine revelation. Indebted to de Lubac's retrieval of the medieval symbol that inspires it, the document advises historical criticism to perceive the divine realities signified by the words. "Indeed, God's words," it says, "expressed through human language, have taken on the likeness of human speech, just as the Word of the eternal Father, when he assumed the flesh of human weakness, took on the likeness of human beings" (par. 13). When the full import of this teaching is appropriated, religious culture will have taken a long stride toward recreating the harmony of nature and grace. *Dei Verbum* embodies the message of Nicholas of Cusa lying in this harmony's heart: human creativity is sustained when its freedom is dynamically joined to its transcendent source. Accordingly, God's free revelation in Christ in no sense compromises the genius of individual authors, whose words can be studied by historical criticism. On

92. Yves Congar, *Tradition and Traditions: A Historical and a Theological Essay*, trans. Michael Naseby et al. (New York: Macmillan, 1967), 205.

the contrary, it instrumentally seizes this genius, endowing it with a divine significance dynamically mediated through the words of Christ, the apostles, and the ecclesial tradition. A continuous system of symbols, grounded in the theandric Christ, heals the incipient equivocation in the Scholastic understanding of the spirit and the letter. Even as interpretation is called to its transcendent task in and through the verbal media, nature is nowhere conceived as independently pure and free-standing. For these reasons, it is no surprise that Benedict XVI should view *Dei Verbum* as one of the least assimilated pronouncements of Vatican II and yet one of the three keys to its meaning, along with *Lumen Gentium* and *Sacrosanctum Concilium*.[93] His own *Jesus of Nazareth*, aware of the multivalence that faith gives language, seeks to unfold the "inner potentialities" of scriptural words and so discover afresh "'the face of the Lord'" in the mirror of the inspired text.[94]

Conclusions

This chapter has probed selective developments in the modern estrangement of nature and grace. It has argued that modernity begins with the West's recovery of Aristotle and its clash with the reigning Augustinian synthesis. The tentacles of a theory of pure nature independent of the grace that is added on to it as a free-standing foundation extend widely through the seven hundred years of our purview. They underlie two important, albeit incipient, equivocations in Thomas's understanding of the good. They contribute to the theological rationalism that in part brought down the Baroque synthesis. Although this collapse receives a compensating thrust in *Dei Verbum*, pure nature is not moribund. It is alive and well in some contemporary applications of historical criticism which obscure the Jesus of faith. As contributing therefore to positivism, fideism, secularism, and atheism, it offers

93. Claudio Burgaleta, "Benedict XVI: Theology of the Word of God," paper presented at 11th Jesuit Colloquium on Papal Thought, Georgetown University, June 7–10, 2009.

94. Benedict XVI, *Jesus*, xix, xxiii, citing Ps 27:8.

little, if any, discernible hope for Christianity's continuing dialogue with modernity.

Our probings have not only exposed the problem of pure nature. They have also pinpointed clues for formulating a viable model of nature's relation to grace. The Baroque, for instance, offers two. First, nature should be dynamically conceived in its intrinsic relation to the transcendent source that grounds it. This dynamism should respect the conjunction of human and divine freedom. The clash between Augustine and Thomas shows that nature should be conceived as providing a bridge to the divine. While not compromising grace as utterly free, human reason should find its implicit ground in the infinite. Grace would then appear less as nature's superadded structure than as a continuation of nature's congenial participation in the divine. Instrumental causality provides a second clue; it is helpful in explaining this congenial participation. *Dei Verbum* offers a final clue. Like the relation between the letter and the spirit, nature and grace should be conceived as reciprocal, however much their difference needs respecting. In other words, nature should be represented as grace's intrinsic symbol.

The next chapter will continue our probings. It will take us into those nineteenth- and twentieth-century thinkers who, aware of some of the problems that we have outlined, propose a range of solutions. We will begin with a thinker of seminal importance, Johann Adam Möhler, the recognized chief of the Catholic School of Tübingen. According to Joseph Ratzinger, the ferment of this movement is responsible for bringing forth *Dei Verbum*'s innovative achievement.[95] We will continue with Henri de Lubac and Max Seckler and conclude with Karl Rahner's supernatural existential. In passing, Hegel's philosophy of art and Maurice Blondel's understanding of the supernatural will also occupy us. Throughout, we will look to augment the clues that we have already gleaned for fostering a viable union of our estranged partners.

95. Joseph Ratzinger, "Dogmatic Constitution on Divine Revelation, Origin and Background," in *Commentary on the Documents of Vatican II*, ed. Herbert Vorgrimler (New York: Herder and Herder, 1967–69), 3:155–66, at 155–56.

Chapter 2

ATTEMPTED REUNIONS

Aesthetics

We have seen that *Dei Verbum* expansively recapitulates medieval exegesis. Building on the letter as the intrinsic symbol of the spirit, it understands divine revelation as a system of continuous symbols that join together Christ, his words and works, the apostolic tradition of the church, and the written scriptures and their interpretation. Whenever a synthesis is grounded in symbolism, its aesthetic dimension cannot help but be invoked. Heidegger reminds us, for instance, that symbolism constitutes the essence of art.[1] In the creative fashioning of an artifact, truth itself is preserved as beauty. Accordingly, if the Son is the Father's image, then the incarnation manifests God's consummate artisanship. In fact, Pseudo-Dionysius the Areopagite goes so far as to claim that God's being, which Aquinas posits as irreducible, emerges as a function of God's beauty.[2] This divine quality, even more fundamental than being, is coterminous with God's eros.[3] If love entails freedom, then in creating and redeeming, God spontaneously shows forth his beauty as "the cause of initiation" of all beings.[4] It therefore follows that

1. Martin Heidegger, "The Origin of the Work of Art," in *Poetry, Language, and Thought*, ed. and trans. Albert Hofstadter (New York: Harper and Row, 1971), 17–87, at 20, 71.

2. Hans Urs von Balthasar, "Denys," in *GL* 2:144–210, at 189, referring to *De divinis nominibus* [hereafter "*DN*"], chap. 5.

3. Ibid., referring to *DN*, chap. 4.

4. Pseudo-Dionysius the Areopagite, *De ecclesiastica hierarchia* III.1 (164D); in Balthasar, *GL* 2:196.

the interlocking symbols of *Dei Verbum,* which ensue from the incarnation, are charged with the primal beauty of God's self-communication.

The concept of beauty, so vital in the Baroque and recently brought into theological renown by Balthasar, suggests a means of integrating nature and grace. We will examine Balthasar's handling of this topic in a later chapter. Here we will study its proximate origins in Johann Adam Möhler's masterwork, *Symbolism.* Möhler defines the title of his book as both a method and a set of sources. Symbolism means "the scientific exposition of the doctrinal differences among the various religious parties opposed to each other, in consequence of the ecclesiastical revolution of the sixteenth century, as these doctrinal differences are evidenced by the public confessions or symbolical books of those parties."[5] The method had already enjoyed an extensive history prior to Möhler.[6] The sources refer, for instance, to the decrees of Trent and the Articles of Smalcald. Unlike Balthasar, Möhler does not directly work out a theological aesthetics. But he does put forth a system of interlocking symbols that, like *Dei Verbum,* implicitly calls forth the beautiful. It is the structure of this implicit aesthetics that will especially interest us in seeking clues to reunite nature and grace.[7]

Möhler grounds the symbolism of religious confessions or doctrines in a metaphysics of ecclesial history, which is itself implicitly symbolic. In positing this metaphysics, Möhler wishes to navigate between two erroneous and opposing views. On the one hand, he wishes to avoid the pagan view of antiquity that, knowing nothing of divine provi-

5. Johann Adam Möhler, *Symbolism or Exposition of the Doctrinal Differences Between Catholics and Protestants as Evidenced by Their Symbolical Writings,* trans. James Burton Robertson, 5th ed. (London: Thomas Baker, 1906), 1. Unless noted otherwise, citations to *Symbolism* are taken from this source.

6. For this history, see Josef R. Geiselmann, "Zur Einführung," in vol. 1 of Johann Adam Möhler, *Symbolik oder Darstellung der dogmatischen Gegensätze der Katholischen und Protestanten nach ihren öffenlichen Bekenntnisschriften,* 5th ed. (Mainz: Kupferberg, 1838), ed. Josef Rupert Geiselmann (Darmstadt: Wissenschaftliche Buchgesellschaft, 1958), 44–54.

7. Michael J. Himes, *Ongoing Incarnation: Johann Adam Möhler and the Beginnings of Modern Ecclesiology* (New York: Crossroad, 1997), 285–86, notes that, although aesthetics was not a new category of Catholic theology, Möhler gave it new meaning, especially in *Symbolism,* where Christ is both the artist of the church and its artifact.

dence, reduces history to an irrational fatalism. On the other hand, he wishes to avoid those idealists who reduce history to strict rational necessity and thereby undermine the graciousness of God and the freedom of humanity.[8] His theory seeks, therefore, to synthesize two realities: the spontaneous contingency of human action in history and the divine teleology that, guiding and shepherding history, provides its ultimate meaning.

Accordingly, Möhler's synthesis centers on the notion of organic evolution. Existing within time, the church constitutes a living consciousness that develops by dialectically resolving the challenges presented to it by historical contingencies. Although the church is a unified organism that retains its substantial identity through the successive resolutions of crises, its doctrines and institutions, which constitute its empirical manifestations, must necessarily be changed and modified. Sometimes, for instance, under pressure from hostile forces one of the church's constitutive elements may assume a disproportionate importance and thereby require a future curtailment.[9] Crucial for Möhler, the organic evolution of the church's visible manifestations is derived from an "internal force" that must actively respond to external exigencies.[10] If, for example, a particular institution dies because it fails to respond to current needs after having served well for a period of time, the historian may conclude, says Möhler, that the institution was not essential to the church's identity.[11]

The internal force that drives organic evolution is not reducible to a form of human self-consciousness, although human rationality is an important factor in Möhler's notion of organic evolution. Rather, the internal force is derived ultimately from the Trinity, from Christ's incarnation, a mission received from the Father that the power of the

8. Edmond Vermeil, *Jean-Adam Möhler et l'école catholique de Tubingue (1815–1840)* (Paris: Librarie Armand Colin, 1913), 155–56.

9. Johann Adam Möhler, *Gesammelte Schriften und Aufsätze* [hereafter "*GSA*"], ed. Johann J. I. von Döllinger (Regensburg, 1839–40), 2:273–77; in ibid., 156.

10. Johann Adam Möhler, *Theologische Quartalschrift* [hereafter "*TQ*"] (1826), 434; *TQ* (1827), 487–88; *GSA* 1, 68; in ibid., 157.

11. Möhler, *TQ* (1826), 430–32; *TQ* (1827), 73; in ibid., 157.

Holy Spirit continues in time.[12] According to Möhler, "the Church is Christ acting and manifesting himself through the ages."[13] In history, the Son of God continues "to appear in human form" because the church represents "his permanent incarnation."[14] Just as humanity is "won again to God" by the merits of the sufferings, works, doctrines, conduct, and death of Christ that remain undivided from the God-man, so the church derives its inner life undivided from the Son and communicates this life undivided to the doctrines and institutions that historically emanate from it.[15] Möhler's metaphysics of ecclesial history thus reconciles the transcendent and the immanent, divine teleology and historical contingency, by a twin ontological participation. The organic life of the church's internal force is derived from Christ's organic unity with God, whereas the church's doctrines and institutions that empirically appear through the ages are derived from, and reciprocally act upon, the life of the church's internal force.

Möhler's model of human reason follows from his theory of this twin ontological participation. The analytic and synthetic powers of the mind, *Verstand* and *Vernunft*, function in tandem. Whereas *Verstand* examines the empirical data in order to establish a sequence of historical events, *Vernunft* must penetrate into the sequence in order to discern the intelligibility immanent in it. This penetration must first diagnose patterns in the sequence that partially explain the events. But beyond this diagnosis, *Vernunft*, enlightened by faith that believes in the immanence of providence in history, must further discern in the

12. See Johann Adam Möhler, *Die Einheit in der Kirche oder das Prinzip des Katholizismus dargestellt in Geiste der Kirchenväter der drei ersten Jahrhunderte* (Tübingen, 1825), ed. E. J. Vierneisel (Mainz: Matthias Grünewald, 1925), 24; in Gustav Voss, "Johann Adam Möhler and the Development of Dogma," *Theological Studies* 4 (1943): 420–44, at 428. See also Joseph Fitzer, *Moehler and Baur in Controversy, 1832–38: Romantic-Idealist Assessment of the Reformation and Counter-Reformation* (Tallahassee, Fla.: American Academy of Religion, 1974), 19.

13. Johann Adam Möhler, *Symbolik*, 4th ed., 2 vols. (Mainz: Kupferberg, 1835), 1:301; in Hervé Savon, *Johann Adam Möhler: The Father of Modern Theology*, trans. Charles McGrath (Glen Rock, N.J.: Paulist Press, 1966), 95.

14. *Symbolik* (4th ed.), 1:335; in ibid., 95.

15. *Symbolism*, trans. Robertson, 3rd ed. (New York: Catholic Publication House, n.d.), 178; in Fitzer, *Moehler and Baur*, 41.

sequence something of the divine causality that sustains history and leads it to its perfection in Christ.[16] This second task does not imply, however, that Möhler's notion of *Vernunft* aims fully to encompass history by reason.[17] On the contrary, *Vernunft* for Möhler endeavors more modestly to grasp the phases of the church's organic evolution in their interdependent unity and to measure their relative importance and particular contributions.[18]

The ecclesial historian who embraces this model of reason knows that, because history is partially conditioned by human freedom, it will inevitably escape the full comprehension of human intelligence. Furthermore, this historian knows that, because God is history's ultimate ground, human reason must submit to the inscrutability of the divine mind. Nonetheless, because history does not fully explain itself but leaves open many questions including its final destiny, the historian can affirm that the laws of reason demand "something eternal that will stand over the temporal; they demand that the divine be grasped in the human."[19] If history is implicitly religious, it follows that the principles of divine revelation, far from being externally imposed upon history, are a necessary complement to the use of *Vernunft* in historical investigation.[20]

Möhler's metaphysics of the internal force that drives the church's organic evolution implicitly constitutes ecclesial history as an intrinsic symbol. Because history makes present in time and space the saving work of the incarnation, it is the empirical medium in which the Holy Spirit maintains the living presence of the God-man. If history is thus essential to the divine economy of salvation, the church's internal force

16. Fitzer, *Moehler and Baur*, 17.

17. See Möhler, *GSA* 2:269–71, in Vermeil, *L'école*, 156.

18. Möhler, *TQ* (1826), 324–25; *GSA* 2:281–85; in Vermeil, *L'école*, 160.

19. Johann Adam Möhler, "Die Idee der Geschichte und Kirchengeschichte," in *Geist des Christentums und das Katholizismus: Ausgewählte Schriften katholischer Theologie im Zeitalter des deutschen Idealismus und der Romantik*, ed. J. R. Geiselmann (Mainz: Matthias-Grünewald, 1940), 391–96, at 392; in Fitzer, *Moehler and Baur*, 17.

20. Fitzer, *Moehler and Baur*, 17, 19.

that animates history mediates the activity of the Spirit to ecclesial doctrines and institutions. As a result, these empirical manifestations, however much they are historically conditioned, are implicitly consecrated as intrinsic symbols of the internal force. Doctrines thus embody a paradoxical synthesis: they are eternally true, yet they are expressed in changing forms. Möhler explains this paradox by distinguishing between the objective and the subjective senses of doctrinal language.

The objective sense of doctrine means that the church at its inception received the immutable divine revelation in its full truth.[21] This truth, the source of all subsequently formed doctrines, necessarily must evolve because, as Möhler says, the Word of God lives perpetually "in the hearts of believers."[22] Accordingly, the subjective sense of doctrine means that the church is able to unfold the objective revelation. As its self-consciousness matures, the church gains clearer and more distinct insights into the truth that it received.[23] The continuing immutability of these evolving insights is guaranteed by the Holy Spirit who, present throughout ecclesial history, cannot admit of contradiction.[24] As new insights emerge through the church's internal force, the church, using its authoritative organs, incorporates as doctrines what it discerns to be authentic.[25]

Möhler's notion of doctrine's subjective sense makes it clear that human self-consciousness plays an important role in his metaphysics of organic evolution. The form of doctrine is necessarily expressed in concepts and images. Although this form is temporal, perishable, and exchangeable, Möhler takes care to observe that, when subjective doctrines articulate objective revelation, the inner truth of the revelation perdures.[26] The difference between, for instance, the language of the

21. *Einheit* (Grünewald), 24, 325; in Voss, "Development," 428, 430.

22. *Symbolik*, 9th ed. (Mainz: Kupferberg, 1884), 357; *Symbolism*, 279; in Voss, "Development," 428.

23. Voss, "Development," 429.

24. *Einheit* (Grünewald), 24; in Voss, "Development," 428.

25. *Einheit* (Grünewald), 33; in Voss, "Development," 429.

26. *Einheit* (Grünewald), 22; *Symbolik* (9th ed.), 369–71; *Symbolism*, 289–90; in Voss, "Development," 430–31.

Gospels about God and the Nicene dogma of the Trinity is formal, not substantial. The difference applies only to the conceptual formulation of the revelation.[27]

Möhler does not seem to comment directly on the extent to which doctrines that have been defined by the church in one age may be revised by it in another. On the one hand, the logic of the internal force, together with Möhler's statements about the exchangeability of subjective formulations, suggests that the church is free to modify, even to retract, what it has defined. On the other hand, his avowal that the Holy Spirit who cannot err is the animator of the church's definitions suggests otherwise. Given that Möhler's comments on the development of doctrine intend to restate the canon of Vincent of Lérins, which affirms the abiding consistency of the church's doctrines, the second position seems more likely to be Möhler's.[28]

If Möhler's metaphysics of ecclesial history can be considered intrinsically symbolic, so can his theory of doctrine that follows from it. Doctrine is intrinsically symbolic because its subjective sense, its historically conditioned form, expresses its objective sense, the immutable revelation received by the church at its beginning. Doctrine develops as the Christian consciousness matures in its understanding of revelation. The objective revelation, which is the reality symbolized, therefore needs the subjectively expressed doctrine, which is its symbol, in order more to become itself. Although divine revelation does not require the church's doctrines in order to be true, it does need them in order for the Christian consciousness to recognize and appropriate the depth of its truth. This recognition, conditioned by the need for an organic consciousness to evolve, is nonetheless animated by the internal force that, under the guidance of the Spirit, leads the church to its *telos*, the fullness of Christ.[29] In sum, Möhler's understanding of doctrine as intrinsically symbolic, however implicit, explains why hu-

27. *Symbolik* (9th ed.), 368; *Symbolism*, 288; in Voss, "Development," 434.

28. Voss, "Development," 434–44.

29. *Einheit* (Grünewald), 33; in Voss, "Development," 429.

man concepts and images can represent a divine surplus of meaning that transcends their finite symbolic form.[30]

Möhler strongly affirms the importance of the forms of rational self-consciousness as factors in the organic evolution of doctrine. Accordingly, not only is his view of doctrine's intrinsic symbolism derived from his metaphysics of ecclesial history; it also corresponds to his model of human reason. In this model, the categories of *Verstand* function in the service of a metaphysically constituted *Vernunft*. As an ontological propaedeutic, these categories organize empirical data into an intelligible form. *Vernunft* is the penetration of intelligence into the intelligible; it discloses pattern and meaning in this form. This disclosure is a result, not only of the metaphysical power of *Vernunft*, but of *Vernunft* enlightened by faith, which is thereby graced with some insight into the divine teleology that sustains the temporal order. Nonetheless, Vernunft does not fully comprehend time by unfolding it according to a strictly immanent necessity. *Vernunft* for Möhler preserves something of the apophaticism strong in the Catholic view of God's relation with the world. According to this view, all positive or kataphatic manifestations of the divine discernible in creation must be followed by negations. These deny that God's identity is co-equal with any or all of the predicates affirmable of him.[31] As a result, *Vernunft*, although efficaciously endowed with metaphysical insight and graced with faith, fails exhaustively to disclose the divine intelligibility.

Corresponding to this model, doctrines, as intrinsic symbols, are both metaphysical and non-reducible. As metaphysical, they import real knowledge of God that *Vernunft* can apprehend and articulate. Although their form consists of historically conditioned concepts and images, the finitude of this form implicitly carries the immanence of

30. See Karl Rahner, "Theology of the Symbol," in *TI* 4:221–52, at 225, citing Friedrich Theodor von Visher, "Das Symbol," *Altes und Neues* (Stuttgart: A. Bonz, 1889); see also Dupré, *Other Dimension*, 108.

31. For a study of the principles of apophatic predication according to Pseudo-Dionysius, see Bernard McGinn, *The Presence of God: A History of Western Christian Mysticism* (New York: Crossroad, 1994), 1:157–82, at 173.

the Spirit's activity. As non-reducible, doctrines cannot be rendered by *Vernunft* into a more univocal form that would allow the objective revelation they express to become more transparent to *Vernunft*. Although *Vernunft* acting in the church under the Spirit's direction can gain further insight into previously expressed doctrines, that insight remains necessarily symbolic. Conditioned by time and space, doctrines cannot articulate with full intelligibility the reality that they nonetheless ontologically represent.

In sum, the heart of Möhler's synthesis lies in the graced consecration that the church confers on history, even as the natural order dynamically mediates the grace that it signifies. Itself lodged in history, the church is nonetheless animated by the Holy Spirit. The divine life endows the church with an internal force that harmoniously fuses a twin ontological participation. Just as the internal force is derived from the salvific mission of the triune God, so the church's doctrines and institutions, precisely as they appear in history, are charged with the grace of this force. As the empirical medium in which the Holy Spirit maintains the living presence of the God-man, history dynamically communicates the divine life to ecclesial doctrines and institutions. This means that history retains its own exigency when wedded to grace. It also means that language, although sensuously conditioned, can incarnate a divine surplus of meaning. Furthermore, Möhler's notion of human reason shows that the natural order does not explain itself. Only when *Vernunft* is enlightened by faith can the deeper intelligibility in history be discerned. Möhler thus affirms that grace sustains the natural order, which is neither free-standing nor independent of it. Revelation is reason's necessary complement if reason is to avoid ultimate frustration.[32]

The aesthetic dimension of Möhler's synthesis is best exposed by discussing its relation to Romanticism. Disagreement exists about the extent of this influence on Möhler. Hegel, Schelling, and Schleier-

32. For more on nature and grace in *Symbolik*, see Himes, *Ongoing Incarnation*, chaps. 6–7.

macher have all been cited as his sources.[33] It is more plausible that Möhler's debt to Romanticism is derived less from individual thinkers as such and more from the reaction to the rational ahistoricism of the Enlightenment that he shares with them.[34] The father of this reaction, Goethe, opines that "through art and act" the one, everlasting idea is manifested and apprehended.[35] But Romanticism reaches its apogee in Hegel. As a result, he perhaps best represents the tradition that nourished Möhler. It is ironic that we should advert to Hegel. After all, though a profoundly Christian philosopher, he can hardly be considered theologically orthodox. His view of human reason as infinite leads to the collapsing of the distinction between God's transcendence and immanence preserved by metaphysical realism. As a result, there is a Gnostic dimension to Hegel's thought that confers on human reason a divine transparency. As we have indicated, Möhler is careful to avoid this dimension. Nonetheless, we find in Hegel, as in Möhler, a system of ontologically continuous, interlocking symbols. Hegel's view that these constitute aesthetic media of divine activity can tease out Möhler's implicit evocation of beauty.

It might be said at the outset that Hegel's entire system is symbolic, if we mean that all finite forms manifest, in appropriate degrees, the

33. For Hegel's influence, see Karl Eschweiler, *Johann Adam Möhlers Kirchenbegriff* (Freiburg-im-Breisgau: Herder, 1930); for rebuttals, see Yves M.-J. Congar, "Sur l'évolution et l'interprétation de la pensée de Moehler," *Revue des sciences philosophiques et théologiques* 27 (1938): 205–12; and Martin Preis, review of Eschweiler's *Johann Adam Möhlers Kirchenbegriff*, in *Zeitschrift für katholische Theologie* 56 (1932): 101–3. For Schelling's and Schleiermacher's influence, see Henry Nienaltowski, "Johann Adam Möhler's Theory of Doctrinal Development: Its Genesis and Formulation" (PhD diss., The Catholic University of America, 1959), 6–8; and Fitzer, *Moehler and Baur*, 15–16.

34. See A. Minon, "L'attitude de J. A. Moehler dans la question du développement du dogme," *Ephemerides Theologicae Lovanienses* 16 (1939): 328–82, at 362–67; and Vermeil, *L'école*, 1–8.

35. Johann W. von Goethe, *Maximen und Reflexionen*, in *Sämtliche Werke, Jubiläumsausgabe*, ed. Edward J. von der Hellen (Berlin: Cotta, 1902–7), 35:305, cited in Elizabeth M. Wilkinson, "The Poet as Thinker," in *Goethe: Poet and Thinker*, ed. Elizabeth M. Wilkinson and Leonard A. Willoughby (New York: Barnes and Noble, 1962), 133–52, at 134; also *Maximen und Reflexionen*, § 313, in *Goethes Aufsätze zur Kultur-, Theatre-, und Literaturgeschichte*, vols. 12–13 of *Sämtliche Werke*, ed. Max Hecker and Fritz Bergemann (Leipzig: Inselverlag, 1913–14).

unique spirit that struggles, in and through history, to express itself through them. Spirit is the infinite act that includes, transforms, and surpasses all oppositions in the finite order of experience.[36] In this sense, it may be called God. Since for Hegel, "beauty is God's appearance," his entire system might be considered aesthetic.[37] Like Thomas, Hegel posits the convertibility of the beautiful with the true and the good. In the realm of aesthetics proper, however, as distinct from philosophy's other branches, spirit has begun its final self-explication. It will continue this work in religion and philosophical science. Art represents spirit as implicitly infinite, although it does this in sensuous forms.[38] These are intended to point away from themselves and so signify the spirit that, through perception, they bring before the mind's eye (30). Through sensuousness, therefore, the aesthetic mind enables spirit to see the eternal vision of itself.[39]

If on the one hand the entire manifold of finite experience manifests spirit, it is only through the mediation of the human mind that spirit properly effects its aesthetic revelation. Art arises necessarily from the nature of humanity as a rational spirit. In other words, spirit requires humanity to draw forth its rationality from within itself, to render it explicit, and thus to duplicate itself externally (57). Art exults the inner world through this self-emanation of spirit. Just so, the outer world of sense is consciously drawn into the eternal when its forms, imbued with spirit, become artifacts (59). Although spirit's aesthetic self-replication is mediated through the imagination, art loosens the hold of particular forms on perception. "While remaining within the sensuous sphere," Hegel claims, art delivers mind "at the same time from the power of sensuousness" (79). It is the universal truth in the

36. James Collins, *The Emergence of Philosophy of Religion* (New Haven, Conn.: Yale University Press, 1967), 308.

37. Robert Wicks, "Hegel's Aesthetics: An Overview," *Cambridge Companion to Hegel*, ed. Frederick C. Beiser (Cambridge: Cambridge University Press, 1993), 348–77, at 349.

38. Georg W. F. Hegel, "On Art," trans. Bernard Bosanquet from *Vorlesungen über die Aesthetik, Erster Band*, in *On Art, Religion, and Philosophy*, ed. J. Glenn Gray (New York: Harper and Row, 1970), 23–127, at 29. Cited in the text.

39. Georg W. F. Hegel, *Hegel's Logic* [hereafter "*EL*"] trans. William Wallace (Oxford: Clarendon Press, 1975), 278.

particular image of beauty that the aesthetic mind expresses and that captivates a person's appreciation of the artifact.

The special challenge of Hegel's aesthetics is to find in the various historical types of art the "true unity ... of the sensuous and the rational" (93). Art is only true when its sensuous form attains an immediate and adequate unity with the idea that it seeks to represent (108). Qualitatively, therefore, art can be judged as more or less perfect depending on the degree of spiritual interiority possessed by its medium. The more the medium is invested with mind, the more appropriately will art signify the idea. The more appropriate this signification, the more beautiful the artifact. Hegel of course takes it for granted that the idea can only articulate spirit in and through the agency of human intelligence. But because this articulation occurs in time and space, art as spirit's expression will evolve in history (106).

Art's highest form is reached in the Christian era. This offers the breeding ground for what Hegel calls romantic art. In the incarnation, art posits "the unity of the human and divine nature." Consequently, finite mind, now properly understood as infinite, can become the adequate form of aesthetic representation (115). Language, especially poetry, emerges as mind's most fitting aesthetic medium. It is least conditioned by time and space and, conversely, the most spiritually interior. In the word, mind produces "out of itself the infinite space of its ideas" and unites these "with the temporal character of sound" (125). In language, both the medium and its idea emerge from spirit (126). As a result, for Hegel, as later for Heidegger, poetry is the highest art form, and therefore the most beautiful. It lies at the heart of all artistic forms (127). Aesthetics entails composition, and poetry is composition's consummate mode.[40] It follows, therefore, that because language constitutes the spiritual summit and center of art, in it art transcends itself, even while retaining a foothold in the sensuous (116).

However much the beauty of art discloses spirit, for Hegel it does not shine forth spirit's greatest radiance. Art possesses a permanent defect: even as it takes as its object mind's infinite universality, it posits

40. Heidegger, "Origin," 72.

this in contingent entities (114). To realize its full freedom, art's object must sacrifice poetry to the prose of philosophical science. This alone is capable of explicating spirit's immanent necessity. Hegel's friend Hölderlin sings an elegy on the death of the Greek gods:

> But where are the thrones? Where are the temples,
>   the songs,
> The vases full of nectar for the pleasure of the gods?
> Where are the oracles that shine for miles and miles?
> Delphi sleeps, and where does great Fate resound?[41]

It is a sad irony that Hegel's aesthetics, in providing philosophical support for his friend's lament, may seem to signal the death of art itself.[42]

In sum, beauty, defined as the appearance of truth perceived in history's sensuous forms, can for Hegel be broadly predicated. It establishes a link among reality's animate and inanimate forms, history, human intelligence, and the divine. Because material forms manifest spirit in varying degree of adequacy, they constitute a hierarchical range of ontologically continuous and interlocking symbols. Hegel thus posits an analogy of beauty, although all distinctions entailed in it are ultimately subsumed into the one eternal spirit. At once analogous and univocal, beauty constitutes, like infinite and finite modes of reality, a cosmically irreducible unity-in-difference. Given the historical exigency of spirit's self-manifestation, the chief issue of aesthetics proper is discovering that sensuous form most adequate to its idea. Hegel finds it in the poetic language of Christianity, which might consequently be called art's paradigm.

If beauty is the appearance of God in the sensuous forms of history, then Möhler's synthesis of nature and grace is aesthetic. Nature is beautiful because, as a sensuous form, it dynamically mediates the radiance of grace. But grace is the source of nature's beauty, even as nature signi-

41. Friedrich Hölderlin, "Bread and Wine," in *Poems of Friedrich Hölderlin*, trans. James Mitchell (San Francisco, Calif.: Ithuriel's Spear, 2004), 10.

42. For more on this issue, see Wicks, "Aesthetics," 369.

fies grace. As the fundamental artifact, the incarnation preserves the beauty of divine truth in the church, through whose internal force this truth is communicated to the language of Christian doctrines. Because of the incarnation, all of nature can be considered analogously related to grace. If all of nature, as Irenaeus of Lyons observes, is recapitulated in Christ, then all sensuous forms are incorporated into a new synthesis.[43] This is especially true of humanity, in whom and for whom the incarnation most properly obtains. Only human beings are capable of the vision of faith that confers on intelligence the insight into the radiant beauty of history's provident purpose and destiny. The more history's sensuous forms submit to this vision, the more their adequacy to grace becomes patent.

Moreover, of material realities, only human beings can, like God, utter the word that brings forth inner truth. The Father posits his truth in the Word, who becomes beautiful in signifying him. Just so, under the church's graced aegis, human beings utter the truth of the Word incarnate in written scriptures and dogmatic pronouncements. Language thus lies, irreducibly, in Christianity's heart. Because God is intrinsically word, human language, for its part, can embody a surplus of beauty. But *pace* Hegel, Christian language, even when spoken in the prose of the scriptures and ecclesial doctrines, can never essentially be prose. The Father's Word is necessarily his image. Rahner defines this last title well when he calls the Son the Father's "*Realsymbol*."[44]

This means that, however much the Son is other than the Father because of their relational opposition, the Father nonetheless perfectly expresses himself in the Son who shares the Father's essence. If images are the essence of poetry, and poetry is the word of the Trinity, then it follows that poetry is the prime analogate of all expression. Consequently, all human language, especially when it communicates graced realities, is derived from the divine image whose beauty it signifies. In

43. Irenaeus, *Against the Heresies*, in vol. 1 of *Ante-Nicene Fathers*, trans. and ed. Alexander Roberts and W. H. Rimbaud (Peabody, Mass.: Hendrickson, 1996), 315–567, at 548, citing Eph 1:10.

44. Rahner, "Symbol," 235–36.

Christianity, therefore, because the poetic constitutes the core of the prosaic, art will always provide a living synthesis of nature and grace. We will develop this topic in greater detail in a subsequent chapter.

Dynamic Desire for God

If the school of Tübingen brought about a Romantic ferment in the early nineteenth century, it was Leo XIII's 1879 encyclical *Aeterni Patris* and the subsequent *ressourcement* movement that galvanized a Thomist revival in the twentieth. For his part, Leo wished to "bring the old to completion by the new."[45] His vision included nurturing the fledgling Thomism of Kleutgen and the prolific Matteo Liberatore, who in 1850 became an early editor of *La Civiltà Cattolica*, which served as an organ of the revival. Even more ambitiously, Leo hoped that an expansive strengthening of Catholic intellectual life would in turn leaven the secular order.[46] Although Modernism slowed innovations in Thomism, by no means did it bring them to a halt. The *ressourcement* gave them new momentum. Its initiators did not, however, envisage their movement as primarily oriented toward Thomas. They proposed a creative return to the church's theological past that focused mainly on the patristic legacy as "the very headwaters of the Christian tradition."[47] In these, they believed, lay the hermeneutical keys to coping with modern problems. Nonetheless, given his pervasive and growing importance, Thomas came under their purview and generated a controversy that bore rich fruit for the relation between nature and grace.

45. Bernard Lonergan, *Insight: A Study of Human Understanding* (San Francisco, Calif.: Harper and Row, 1978), 747, citing Leo XIII, *Aeterni Patris*.

46. James Hennesey, "Leo XIII's Thomistic Revival: A Political and Philosophical Event," *Journal of Religion* 58 (1978 Suppl.), S185–97, at S195–96, citing Yves Congar, *L'église de saint Augustin à l'époque moderne* (Paris: Cerf, 1970), 451, and Friedrich Heer, *The Intellectual History of Europe*, 2 vols. (Garden City, N.Y.: Doubleday, 1968), 2:313.

47. Marcellino D'Ambrosio, "*Ressourcement* Theology, *Aggiornamento*, and the Hermeneutics of Tradition," *Communio: International Catholic Review* 18 (1991): 530–55, at 532, citing Henri de Lubac, *Mémoire sur l'occasion de mes écrits* (Namur: Culture et vérité, 1989), 94. D'Ambrosio is cited in the text.

On the one hand, from the perspective of the ressourcement's leaders, no tension existed between their aspirations and Thomas himself.[48] For the Dominicans of Saulchoir and the Jesuits of Fourvière, the real enemy of theology was Neo-Scholasticism. Lacking an historical sense, its "excessive preoccupation with clarity and systematization" made it "oblivious to human subjectivity," even as it caused a "'rupture between theology and life'" (534–36).[49] These deficiencies led to the irony that the antagonists of Thomas were his interpreters. Chief among these, according to de Lubac, was Cajetan, who altered the whole meaning of Thomas's understanding of the relation between nature and grace.[50] Others also fell under censure, such as John of St. Thomas, Suárez, and Bañez, for example. These thinkers long enjoyed a hegemony in the post-Tridentine church that prevented an authentic retrieval of the Angelic Doctor (543).[51] Aquinas's own genius, the *ressourcement* opined, constituted a kindred spirit. Like the Fathers, Thomas "held theology, spirituality, and pastoral practice in a dynamic and vital unity," even as he maintained a dialogue with the currents of his time (546–47). As such, he served as a paradigm of the movement's aims (545).[52] The criticism leveled against the *ressourcement,* therefore, by the Dominicans Labourdette and Garrigou-Lagrange that it rejected Thomism would appear to be self-serving (551). In failing to distinguish between Aquinas himself and outmoded Thomist accretions, they exculpated themselves from a fresh retrieval of the thirteenth century's inspiration.

Yet the controversy runs deeper, certainly from the perspective of the movement's Neo-Thomist critics. Maritain, for instance, even while

48. This sentence begins a section previously published within Stephen M. Fields, "*Ressourcement* and the Retrieval of Thomism for the Contemporary World," in *Ressourcement,* ed. Flynn and Murray, 355–71, from 355–57, 360–64.

49. Citing M.-D. Chenu, "Position de la théologie," *Revue des sciences philosophiques et théologiques* 24 (1935): 232–57, at 244, and Jean Daniélou, "Les orientations présentes de la pensée religieuse," *Études* 249 (1946): 1–21, at 6, 14.

50. Henri de Lubac, *The Mystery of the Supernatural,* trans. Rosemary Sheed (New York: Herder and Herder, 1967), 10–11.

51. Citing Étienne Gilson, *Letters of Étienne Gilson to Henri de Lubac,* trans. Mary Emily Hamilton (San Francisco, Calif.: Ignatius Press, 1988), 23–4 (July 8, 1956), 33n6.

52. Citing Yves Congar, *Vrai et fausse réforme dans l'église* (Paris: Cerf, 1950), 337.

endeavoring to remain faithful to the spirit of Thomas, contended that the *ressourcement* was introducing a new anti-intellectualism into theology.[53] Others feared that the rejection of the Scholastic method portended a return to Modernism (2). A wave of "historical and doctrinal relativism" could be undammed if the correspondence of the mind to the object known were replaced as the criterion of truth with the correspondence of the mind to life (10–11).[54] Labourdette argued not only that Thomism contains the resources for a theology of event and history, but that its metaphysics is "quite simply, true" (12–13).[55] It followed for him that the job of Thomas's interpreters was not merely to retrieve his spirit, but to integrate issues of contemporary import into his universal verity (13–14).

From within this polemic emerged the seminal genius of de Lubac's approach to nature and grace. At the heart of this lay a fresh study of the natural desire for God in Thomas and a wide range of other sources. Cajetan had denied the supernatural end of this desire as authentically Thomist.[56] According to de Lubac, however, this end appears throughout Thomas's corpus, including in this important instance: "the rational creature, which can attain the perfect good of happiness, but needs the Divine assistance for the purpose, is more perfect than the irrational creature, which is not capable of attaining this good, but attains some imperfect good by its natural powers."[57] While endeavoring to see the meaning of texts such as this clearly, de Lubac also lent his ear to the dynamic metaphysics sounded by Maurice Blondel and echoed in Rousselot and Maréchal. He thus revolutionized post-Tridentine theology by directly challenging the incoherence lodged in the core of the theory of

53. Aidan Nichols, "Thomism and the Nouvelle Théologie," *The Thomist* 64 (2000): 1–19, at 7. Cited in the text.

54. Referring to Garrigou-Lagrange, "La nouvelle théologie, où va-t-elle?," *Angelicum* (1946): 126–45.

55. Citing letter of Reginald Garrigou-Lagrange (July 17, 1946), in Étienne Fouilloux, "Dialogue théologique? (1946–1948)," in *Saint Thomas au XXe siècle: actes du colloque centenaire de la 'Revue Thomiste.' Toulouse, 25–28 mars 1993*, ed. Serge-Thomas Bonino (Paris: Éditions Saint-Paul, 1994), 170.

56. De Lubac, *Mystery*, 11–12.

57. Aquinas, *ST* I-II, q. 5, a. 2, ad 2, in de Lubac, *Mystery*, 198.

pure nature. On the assumption that "a nature is an essence which *rests content* with the good that is proportionate to it," the pure nature theory posited that grace alters the natural end of human beings.[58] Suarez, for instance, supposed that as punishment for original sin God withdraws humanity's supernatural finality.[59] As a riposte, de Lubac pointed out that because a being's end necessarily dictates its structure, an end cannot be changed without modifying the entire species.[60] In consequence, the supernatural order is not properly inferred from the natural. On the contrary, "it is not nature ... which requires grace; it is rather grace which ... calls into being spiritual creatures to receive it."[61] In other words, it is not possible to envisage "a concrete nature in existence prior to or without its supernatural finalization."[62] Congenially intrinsic to nature, grace is no extrinsic conferral, which could make it seem an alien imposition, however much the adage "*gratia perfecit naturam*" be insisted upon.

Although the natural desire is central for de Lubac, in none of his works on nature and grace does he undertake a rigorously systematic exposition of it in Thomas.[63] For this we will have recourse to Edward Schillebeeckx's study of the work of Max Seckler on the relation in the Angelic Doctor between the natural desire and the instinct of faith.[64] Schillebeeckx contends that this work "surpasses everything [on the subject] that we have hitherto been offered."[65] From a distinctly Thomist per-

58. Charles Boyer, "Nature pure et surnaturel dans le *Surnaturel* du Père de Lubac," *Gregorianum* 28 (1947): 279–95, at 291; in de Lubac, *Mystery*, 196–97.

59. Francisco Suárez, *De gratia*, prolog. 4, c. 1, n. 5, in *Opera omnia*, vol. 7 (1857), 18; in de Lubac, *Mystery*, 89.

60. Henri de Lubac, "Le mystère du surnaturel," *Recherches de science religieuse* 36 (1949): 80–121, at 94–95; in Duffy, *Graced Horizon*, 76.

61. Anton C. Pegis, "Nature and Spirit: Some Reflections on the Problem of the End of Man," *Proceedings of the American Catholic Philosophical Association* 23 (1949): 62–79, at 79; in Duffy, *Horizon*, 70n9, as summarizing de Lubac.

62. Duffy, *Horizon*, 70.

63. The closest he comes is *Surnaturel: études historiques* (Paris: Aubier, 1946), 231–60. This, however, was "written in haste" (De Lubac, *Mystery*, 65).

64. Max Seckler (1927–) is professor emeritus in the faculty of Catholic theology in the University of Tübingen.

65. Max Seckler, *Instinkt und Glaubenswille nach Thomas von Aquin* (Mainz: Matthias-

spective, therefore, Schillebeeckx's account of Seckler gives the advantage of further developing the chief elements of de Lubac's position. Moreover, whereas de Lubac's work has received wide attention, Schillebeeckx on Seckler brings a less known but incisive perspective to greater light.

In analyzing the instinct of faith in Thomas, Seckler, according to Schillebeeckx, emphasizes the creativity of the human subject. The instinct constitutes a moment within the differentiated unity of God's free will. As "the divine impulse which prompts ... us to believe," it is "suited to bring about activity" in life (30, 33). For Thomas, the instinct lodges within the structure of the divine "creative act" (33). This one act is, at the same time, the means by "which all creatures are flowing out from God" and "the principle of their return to God" (34).[66] Within this act, "one and the same grace," says Thomas, "both calls [nature to faith] and justifies [nature in faith]" (52).[67] According to Seckler, this call, even as associated with grace, is seen by Thomas as belonging to nature. If these claims can be warranted, it follows that the subject's creativity, precisely as freely human, is linked intrinsically to the free revelation of God in Jesus Christ.

Seckler grounds his demonstration by linking revelation and value. The instinct represents the subjective action of grace moving the human heart (mind and will) to apprehend the objective value of revelation as it comes externally to the person (37). The intrinsic goodness of this object attracts the subject precisely because the subject possesses a potential to be attracted. A congeniality thus obtains between divine and human actions—between, in other words, divine and human goodness, grace and nature. The potential to be attracted to revelation is not, in the first instance, an explicitly articulated experience. It obtains as a formal, *a priori* predisposition. Nonetheless, once activated, it is ca-

---

Grünewald-Verlag, 1961), as discussed by Edward Schillebeeckx in vol. 2 of his *Revelation and Theology*, trans. N. D. Smith, 2 vols. (New York: Sheed and Ward, 1967–68), 2:30–75, at 32. Seckler and Schillebeeckx are cited in the text; all citations are from vol. 2.

66. Citing a similar reading in Bouillard, *Conversion*.

67. Citing Aquinas, *ST* I-II, q. 113, a. 8, ad 2.

pable of reflexive explication as conscious experience (38). As a natural predisposition, the instinct grounds the subject's ability to respond to any objective value. As an inner motive or prompt to faith as value, the instinct admits of an analogical potential capable of embracing the divine revelation freely offered in history (40).[68] This analogy embraces all of the following qualities of the instinct: "a tendency of the human spirit itself"; "the beginning of the entire act of faith" (40, referring to Seckler, 110); and "the grace that invites us to believe" (33). In sum, Seckler, in accord with de Lubac's inspiration, sees Thomas endowing the act of creation as such with a supernatural potential. This is fully realized only in the beatific vision, the human person's one and only end (41, referring to Seckler, 128–29). Given human freedom, however, this end is by no means necessarily realized by any human being.

The key issue raised by Seckler's analysis concerns the precise relation in the instinct between nature and grace. In order to explain this, a question needs to be addressed. It expresses the nub of the criticism also leveled against de Lubac.[69] Does Seckler's position exact grace and so undermine its gratuity? Does it, in other words, fall into semi-Pelagianism by holding that "the natural desire of salvation is already the seed of salvation"?[70] On the one hand, his exposé makes it clear that nature is perfected by grace when the Gospel, apprehended as a value, is accepted as the supreme good. It could appear that revelation would not be exacted, therefore, because its advent in history is utterly gratuitous (47). Were it not to appear, other values would have to fill its gap, and humanity would be left ultimately unfulfilled (44–45). It might be argued, on the other hand, that if this were the case, then God would have fashioned a creature whose end he would have withheld fulfilling. If so, God's goodness would be compromised. It would seem, in consequence, that if Seckler's position is to avoid this conclusion, it would have to concede that nature does seem to exact a supernatural

68. Referring to Seckler, 110, citing Aquinas, *ST* II-II, q. 2, a. 9.

69. See Duffy, *Horizon*, 77, and de Lubac, *Mystery*, 68.

70. Duffy, *Horizon*, 34. See also Karl Rahner, "Concerning the Relationship Between Nature and Grace," in *TI* 1:297–317, at 310n1.

end. In other words, if God's goodness is to be upheld, Seckler would seem to confer on humanity a natural claim to the beatific vision.[71]

In answer to this objection, Seckler would reply that redemption should be seen as a continuation of creation (47). Conversely, creation should be seen as a function of God's free, primordial plan of redemption. Schillebeeckx does not further explain these claims of Seckler, but they can be defended by the following argument.[72] Because God is infinitely self-present, it cannot be said that God decides first to create and then, once the Fall occurs, second to redeem. On the contrary, God's eternally free intention to create must be understood as foreseeing the Fall and hence as including within it the intention to redeem. The free intention to create in light of its consequences embraces, therefore, the gratuity to redeem (and vice versa). Redemption and creation are reciprocally entailed. If it seems from human nature's having one supernatural end that grace is exacted, this is an appearance, not the reality. God's infinite goodness is vindicated by his primordially free decision to create. In other words, it may seem that God owes us revelation, because without it our end would remain unfulfilled. But the truth is that God owes us nothing but what he has intended freely and primordially. This is the fulfillment of creation in the redemption, and conversely, the beginning of the redemption in creation. These claims cannot be made *a priori*, but only *a posteriori*. They are evident only in light of the revelation that, in fact, has been freely posited in history.

A second question raised in Seckler concerns whether the instinct belongs to the order of nature or grace. On the one hand, he affirms that Thomas identifies the instinct of faith with the natural desire for the absolute that is ontologically prior to conscious intellection and volition (42). On the other hand, in keeping with the continuity of creation and redemption, he argues that the instinct cannot be characterized as belonging distinctly to either, nor as a medium between

71. Ibid., 33.

72. Based on Karl Rahner, "Salvation," in *Sacramentum Mundi: An Encyclopedia of Theology*, ed. Karl Rahner et al. (New York: Herder and Herder, 1970), 5:430b.

them. It is "*of grace, without actually being grace*" (50, citing Seckler, 213). By this, Seckler seems to mean that the human person as created receives, in and through the instinct, not sanctifying grace, but prevenient grace. This predisposes the person to accept the revelation that, in an explicit act of faith, justifies and sanctifies. In other words, the "spiritual core" of the person constitutes "a *promise of* [sanctifying] *grace*" (48, citing Seckler, 178). This promise is the divine movement that "sets up in man the inner dimension of return" in grace to the God of creation (49, citing Seckler, 178).[73] To hold otherwise would replace reflection on the concrete reality of humanity with moot speculation about a natural end that never obtains in history. And this, claims Seckler on the heels of de Lubac, is alien to Thomas (49–50, citing Seckler, 207).[74]

We will continue our analysis of Seckler in a subsequent chapter. For the moment, this treatment will serve to lay out the basic tenets of the position that he develops under de Lubac's aegis. Its advantages will become more apparent when shortly we view it against the backdrop of the supernatural existential, the model of nature and grace that has tended to dominate recent discussion. Before doing so, however, we need to consider Seckler and de Lubac's vitally important debt to Blondel. In his great work *Action* of 1893, he develops a metaphysics that cuts away the fundamental premise of the pure nature theory: namely, that a nature is an essence which rests content with the good that is proportionate to it.

On the one hand, *Action* wishes to respect the autonomy of reason and the transcendent freedom of God. On the other hand, it wishes to demonstrate the need for a divine revelation without making it necessary.[75] In reconciling this paradox, Blondel analyzes the sequence of

73. See also Schillebeeckx, *Revelation and Theology*, 2:51, citing Seckler, 214–15; and 2:64, citing *In I Sent.*, dd. 14, 15.

74. Duffy, *Horizon*, 74.

75. Henri Bouillard, "Philosophy and Christianity in the Thought of Maurice Blondel," in *The Logic of the Faith* (New York: Sheed and Ward, 1967), 161–85, at 161–62. Cited in the text.

human strivings that constitute endeavors like art, language, education, family, and country. He desires principally to grasp action's conditions of possibility and, through these, to understand humanity's ultimate fulfillment (167).[76] First he establishes the insufficiency of action to satisfy the aspirations of the person. The demands of these transcend action even when action is considered as the aggregate of all its expressions in their consummate totality. Given action's impotence to realize its goal, the supernatural does not emerge as an ontological imposition on humanity from an external absolute alien to nature. On the contrary, it arises immanently from within the person, whose action nonetheless strives to realize a transcendence naturally inaccessible to it. Since the supernatural is thus necessary for ultimate human fulfillment, Blondel concludes that the person remains open to some possible action of the supernatural. Such an action would satisfy humanity's deepest yearning that none of its strivings can fulfill. This supernatural action could be the divine revelation embodied in Christianity, although its truth is not presumed and its gratuity is not compromised (179–80).

The core of Blondel's argument, laid out in the third of *Action*'s five parts, centers on the dialectical relation between the "willed will" and the "willing will." The willed will refers to any specific choice of action. It represents those limited and defined expressions of volition that seek to satisfy the incessant demands of human desires. The willing will refers to the ontological dynamism that drives the specific choices of the willed will. The willed will is known directly by consciousness. The willing will is known only reflexively through an analysis of the conditions of possibility of the willed will. In an analysis reminiscent of the breadth of Hegel's *Phenomenology of Spirit*, Blondel demonstrates that the dialectic between the willing will and the willed will manifests itself in the creation of successively more complex orders of

76. Citing Maurice Blondel, *Action (1893)*, trans. Oliva Blanchette (South Bend, Ind.: University of Notre Dame Press, 1984), 473, 475; originally *L'Action (1893)* (Paris: Presses Universitaires de France, 1950). Blanchette's translation gives the pagination of the original in the margins; this and all subsequent pages of this work refer to the original.

action. By surveying the spheres of human endeavor from sensation through individuality, society, thought, and religion, Blondel exposes the ontological delusion that action evokes in human consciousness. This delusion causes the human person to devolve into "superstition": the collapsing of the two ultimate orders of action, thought and religion, into each other. In mistakenly believing that the successive orders generated by the willed will are capable of bringing about ultimate fulfillment, human consciousness objectifies the absolute. By making the absolute a specific product of the willed will, consciousness tries to capture the ultimate. It thus commits superstition, the error of limiting and defining the unlimitable and indefinable.

As the crisis to which action's dialectic inevitably leads, superstition shows that none of the orders generated by the willed will, not even the products of human thought, can offer action an adequate surcease. Even humanity's highest aspiration, the desire for the absolute, fails to be equaled in any and all of action's practices. Because the willed will does not sufficiently account for the source of humanity's highest aspiration, this source must lie in the willing will, the willed will's necessary condition of possibility, the origin of the willed will's strivings. If the absolute is the cause of human action, then no limited expression of the willed will can ever adequately match it. Consequently, action must remain dynamic, always seeking its consummation by expressing itself in successively higher orders. Only the possession of the absolute can confer on action the final peace that gives ultimate fulfillment to the person. Such fulfillment therefore becomes for Blondel a function of the absolute transcendence that his metaphysics of action reveals to be necessary for the achievement of humanity's potential (168–72).[77]

Developing this argument, *Action*'s fourth part shows that the idea of the supernatural represents the necessary solution to the crisis of superstition. The supernatural becomes the "one thing necessary," the "inaccessible necessity," the goal of action. Although the supernatural

77. Summarizing *Action*, 43–322.

remains absolutely transcendent to humanity, the knowledge of its existence arises immanently from the recognition of action's impotence to consummate humanity's destiny (173–75).[78] The supernatural cannot be conceived as an alien action added on to human nature. On the contrary, it is a congenial action arising from within human nature. As both transcendent to humanity and immanent in it, the idea of the supernatural generates in consciousness an awareness of the idea of God (180).[79] Thus showing the metaphysics of action to be the precursor of religion, *Action* concludes by correlating reason's idea of God to the Christian idea of the supernatural.

Blondel counterpoises his dialectic of action to both critical and absolute idealism. On the one hand, *Action*'s analysis of the crisis of superstition offers a critique of Hegel, for whom the absolute exhaustively communicates itself within human consciousness. On the other hand, its demonstration of the necessary immanence of the absolute in human action offers a critique of Kant, whose transcendental ego is metaphysically agnostic about the absolute's existence. For its part, *Action* has been criticized as failing satisfactorily to ground the absolute's metaphysical necessity. Unlike Kant and Maréchal, for instance, it offers no transcendental deduction. As a result, its phenomenology proves only, critics claim, that action generates the absolute as reason's subjective or psychological necessity. In Blondel's defense, it should be noted that he agrees with Hegel for whom intelligence is compenetrated by being. While rejecting Hegel's infinite reason, Blondel understands action as intrinsically metaphysical. On this basis, his affirmation of the absolute as action's inaccessible necessity claims universal objectivity.[80]

78. Citing *Action*, 339, 388.

79. Citing Maurice Blondel, "Lettre sur les exigences de la pensée contemporaine en matière d'apologétique et sur la méthode de la philosophie dans l'étude du problème religieux," in his *Les premiers écrits de Maurice Blondel* (Paris: Presses Universitaires de France, 1956), 5–95, at 86–87.

80. Maurice Blondel, *Pages religieuses*, ed. Yves de Montcheuil (Paris: Aubier, 1942), 28, 42, 56–57; in Albert Milet, "Les 'Cahier' du P. Maréchal. Sources doctrinales et influences subie," *Revue néoscholastique de philosophie* 43 (1940–45): 225–51, at 246.

In sum, the deepest significance of Blondel's thought for nature and grace lies in its understanding of humanity as implicitly baptized by divine desire. If the supernatural is both "absolutely impossible and absolutely necessary," then human nature is constituted by a "felt expectation of an unknown messiah" to which it cannot give birth.[81] As created, humanity is, in itself, a religious vocation: an obediential potential, from the Christian perspective, for union with God in grace. Dynamically open, nature struggles in "a perpetual dissatisfaction," whose solution is more practical than speculative.[82] Knowledge cannot be taken "as the complete substitute for actual existence."[83] It is the will that yearns for surcease in a "gift" of supernatural value.[84] This, as Seckler explains from Thomas, comes freely as a fulfilling revelation that dovetails with humanity's deepest longing. If nature, as created, is thus oriented to grace, then it can be concomitantly affirmed that grace is already at work in nature, at least implicitly. As de Lubac avers echoing a principle as old as Plato, no being can possess an end that does not affect its entire constitution. In other words, if action is a function of being; and if a being's end gives the key to what a being signifies; then the end is implicit in the action. Let us for the moment leave this line of thought, albeit temporarily, and continue our probing into recent reunions of nature and grace.

Supernatural Existential

Particularly associated with Karl Rahner, the supernatural existential has sometimes been seen as a response to the criticism that Pius XII's 1950 encyclical *Humani Generis* purportedly leveled at de Lubac.[85] It

81. Blondel, *Action*, 388, cited in James Le Grys, "The Christianization of Modern Philosophy According to Maurice Blondel," *Theological Studies* 54 (1993): 455–84, at 481.

82. Le Grys, "Christianization," 480–81.

83. Maurice Blondel, *The Letter on Apologetics and History and Dogma*, trans. Alexander Dru and Illtyd Trethowan (New York: Holt, Rinehart, and Winston, 1964), 176; in Le Grys, "Christianization," 480.

84. *Action*, 388, in Le Grys, "Christianization," 481.

85. Joseph A. Komonchak, "Fifty Years After *Humani Generis*," paper presented at annual

claimed that the gratuity of the supernatural is destroyed by those who contend that God "cannot create intellectual beings without ordering and calling them to the beatific vision."[86] The document, however, did not name de Lubac explicitly, and this quotation constitutes its unique mention of the supernatural's gratuity. Moreover, de Lubac's position does not advance the censured position, nor does Seckler's. De Lubac in fact wanted to maintain God's double gratuity: in offering the beatific finality on the one hand and in creating a nature capable of enjoying it on the other.[87] The supernatural existential actually emerges more from the influence of the response to the encyclical by the Jesuit Superior General, John Baptist Janssens. Apparently having in mind de Lubac's Blondel-inspired critique of Cajetan, the Belgian took upon himself the prerogative of further specifying the meaning of *Humani Generis*. In an official letter to his order, he declared: "Henceforth, [Jesuit theologians] will not say that the thesis that a spiritual creature could have been not destined to supernatural beatitude is simply an interpretation of dogma by means of a defective philosophy."[88] In an effort to comply with this instruction, Rahner put forth one of the most influential and ingeniously conceived notions in contemporary theology. By contrast with de Lubac and Seckler, he "never suggested that humans, simply by reason of their *nature*, are possessed of an exigency for personal union with the Trinitarian God."[89]

On the one hand, according to Rahner, humanity, by nature, is necessarily ordered to affirm the existence of the absolute being. This affirmation is grounded in a philosophical analysis of the conditions of the possibility of human thinking. It makes no appeal to divine rev-

---

meeting of Catholic Theological Society of America, Milwaukee, Wis. (June 8, 2001), 19 (photocopy, privately circulated). Pope Pius XII, *Humani Generis*, Encyclical Letter, August 12, 1950; all English translations are drawn from www.vatican.va.

86. *Humani Generis*, par. 26, in Komonchak, "Fifty Years," 19.

87. For a criticism of this double gratuity, although one that, in light of Seckler, seems lacking in force, see Duffy, *Horizon*, 79–80.

88. John Baptist Janssens, "A Letter of Very Rev. Father General on the Encyclical 'Humani Generis' (11 February 1951)," *Woodstock Letters* 80 (1951): 291–316, at 299–300; in Komonchak, "Fifty Years," 19.

89. Duffy, *Horizon*, 103.

elation or the grace of faith. It appeals only to the finality of the agent intellect. In Thomist metaphysics of knowledge, this faculty knows the universal or conceptual element in sensuously intuited data. In order to know it, however, the intellect must be able to transcend the limits of all the particular concepts that it knows.[90] To affirm a limit is necessarily to surpass it. Given the necessary dynamism of human reason, absolute being is therefore pre-apprehended, according to Rahner. In other words, it is not objectified like finite realities. On the contrary, it is the infinite horizon against which all finite objects can be known.[91] Although the absolute is humanity's goal, end, and purpose, it must nevertheless be immanent in the intellect.[92] Rahner is merely applying the previously mentioned principle that de Lubac takes from Plato: all causes are present in their effects. This immanence gives the intellect and will their dynamism. God thus becomes a constitutive *a priori* of human rationality known, however, only reflexively: only as the explanation of the finite judgments that, in the first instance, are consciously present to the mind.[93] Affirmed in this way, knowledge of God's existence, but not his essence, falls appropriately within nature's ambit as what Rahner calls general revelation.

On the other hand, faith shows us that God has revealed himself, not just generally, but categorically: concretely and historically in Jesus Christ. This utterly gratuitous event cannot, in any sense, be inferred from nature. But it has perpetually altered nature. It therefore follows that the pre-apprehended horizon of infinite being actually exists within the order of grace, which is the only concretely existing historical order. The horizon represents a disposition for grace, even an implicit offer of grace. In no sense does it compel human beings to accept grace. This implicit offer of grace is the supernatural existential. Were there no grace, general revelation would continue to obtain. In this sense,

90. Karl Rahner, *Spirit in the World,* trans. William V. Dych (New York: Herder and Herder, 1968), 209.

91. Ibid., 145, 209.

92. Karl Rahner, *Foundations of Christian Faith: An Introduction to the Idea of Christianity,* trans. William V. Dych (New York: Seabury Press, 1978), 21.

93. Ibid., 21–22.

the pre-apprehended horizon can be considered a natural desire for God and an instinct of faith. The theoretical possibility of its existence without grace safeguards grace's gratuity. This possibility entails that humanity could be fulfilled in a natural end as unaided reason might infer it.[94] It also renders pure nature into what Rahner calls a remainder concept. In other words, pure nature would be left over were we able to subtract grace from the concrete historical order that we know. We cannot, of course, do this, nor has humanity ever been bereft of grace.[95]

Just as in Seckler so also in Rahner, an important question concerns the relation between the natural desire for God and prevenient grace, the gift that calls or disposes humanity to justification. Seckler identifies the natural desire with the instinct of faith, Rahner with general revelation. By contrast with Seckler's instinct, Rahner's pre-apprehended absolute retains the possibility of its own natural end. Formally, general revelation for Rahner is distinct from prevenient grace, which is divinely gratuitous and oriented toward sanctification. Materially, however, the pre-apprehended horizon and prevenient grace are united in the one concrete historical order. Because nature and grace are joined materially but not formally, general revelation represents grace's implicit offer. But their material union is not so congruent as to obviate nature as the locus of concupiscence and sin.[96] Although freedom can resist the offer, the offer can become explicit when, as Trent teaches, an awakening obtains leading a person to desire baptism. In other words, the general revelation that yearns for the absolute can become a call to justification when prevenient grace and human freedom meet in the instrumentally causative synthesis discussed in the previous chapter. In this synthesis, grace, as materially united with nature, becomes formally united with nature in the consciousness that the absolute ineluctably desired as an unknown messiah is, in fact, the God revealed in Christ.

94. See ibid., 55–57, and chap. 4, esp. 126–33.

95. Rahner, "Relationship Between Nature and Grace," 312–13.

96. Gerald A. McCool, introduction to Karl Rahner, "Nature and Grace," in *A Rahner Reader*, ed. McCool (New York: Seabury Press, 1975), 175; see also Rahner, "Nature and Grace," in *TI* 4:165–88, at 180.

In the case of those justified by baptism of desire without explicit faith in Christ, where precisely the natural desire becomes prevenient grace, and where this in turn becomes sanctifying grace would be difficult to specify. Such progress, however, must implicitly obtain since, as we have seen, Trent teaches that it does, and it cannot be doubted that Rahner wishes to be consistent with its doctrine.

Like de Lubac, both Seckler and Rahner are indebted to Blondel. In all three thinkers, nature's dynamism cannot rest content with a good that is proportionate to it. This point is clear enough in de Lubac and Seckler. According to them, the end of nature's primal desire is nothing less than the beatific vision. By contrast, Rahner's approach is more complex. Through a reflexive analysis of the yearning intellect, the pre-apprehended absolute emerges as both the source and the end of nature. Because this end can be discerned by unaided reason, it is rightly called natural. But because, unlike finite objects, it constitutes a horizon incapable of objectivation, it is also rightly defined as infinite, as transcending the human faculties, and hence as supernatural. This meaning of supernatural does not, for Rahner, entail grace.

Rahner thus clearly maintains the natural knowledge of God that Vatican I declares as orthodox.[97] But de Lubac and Seckler also maintain it. They affirm that reason can discern a natural desire for God, however much revelation shows this also to be an instinct of faith. They would probably not deny that the supernatural end of this desire could be called the unobjectified absolute. But they would most likely be wary of this epithet. They might first point out that Rahner's consideration of general revelation, at best, only establishes the absolute's necessity as humanity's rational ground. It does not establish that, beyond its pre-apprehension, the absolute is actually achievable as the existential end of the human person.

Second, they might emphasize that nature stands before the super-

97. Vatican Council I, *Dei Filius*, in *Decrees*, ed. Tanner, 2:804–11, here 806. In his study of Vatican I's use of the concept of nature, Balthasar observes that nothing that the council says "prevents the theologian from maintaining ... that all natural knowledge of God occurs *de facto* within ... the supernatural order." *Theology of Karl Barth: Exposition and Interpretation*, trans. Edward T. Oakes (San Francisco, Calif.: Ignatius Press, 1992), 307.

natural as utter mystery. Although this is also Rahner's claim throughout his writings, de Lubac and Seckler might well understand the supernatural existential as effectively mitigating it.[98] Interposing itself between the beatific vision and nature, the supernatural existential gives nature a purported entitlement that falls desperately short of actually satisfying nature's exigency. Accordingly, it could be seriously misleading. For them, the crux of Blondel's contribution lies in the necessity that only some action of the supernatural, precisely in history, can fulfill nature's immanent demands. A nature oriented to the unobjectified absolute says nothing about history's consummation. Developing this point, Balthasar opines that the distinction between a general and a categorical revelation sounds equivocal.[99] "Our natural capacity for knowing God," he claims, "is incorporated as an inserted moment in the ultimate" knowledge given by grace.[100] Accordingly, since grace envelops nature, any overlap between an apparently natural knowledge of God and that knowledge given in faith must be analogical.[101] Fundamentally, therefore, Balthasar underscores that a natural right to the infinite, however theoretical, still posits for nature the two ends that de Lubac has shown to be incoherent.

Let us explore another problem in the supernatural existential. It centers on an ambiguity in its definition as an intrinsic, permanent, ontological "modification (*Modifikation*)" of the human spirit.[102] This definition means that, whereas human nature possesses, theoretically in the order of thought, a purely natural end, this end, concretely in the order of history, has never existed. It has always been subsumed into the order of grace. Quite rightly, Rahner claims that "God's self-communication is given not only as gift, but also as the necessary

98. For insight into Rahner's understanding of the supernatural as mystery, see "The Doctrine of the Spiritual Senses in the Middle Ages," in *TI* 16:104–34.

99. Balthasar, *Theology of Karl Barth*, 314.

100. Ibid., 318.

101. Ibid., 311.

102. Rahner, *Grundkurs des Glaubens: Einführung in den Begriff des Christentums* (Freiburg-im-Breisgau: Herder, 1976), 135; *Foundations*, 129; see also McCool, introduction to Karl Rahner, "Relationship Between Nature and Grace: Supernatural Existential," in *Reader*, 185.

condition which makes possible an acceptance of the gift which can allow the gift really to be God."[103] But this claim leads us to ask how prevenient grace, as justification's necessary condition, could modify the transcendence of the human faculties. In the first instance, to call it a modification implies that humanity existed, or could have existed, without it. Rahner's rejection of pure nature obviates the first possibility. If prevenient grace is not a modification obtaining in history, then it must have been given with the act of creation. This, of course, is de Lubac and Seckler's point. Perhaps, therefore, it is a modification obtaining only in the theoretical order of possibility. Perhaps, in other words, God, from all eternity, conceived humanity with two ends in mind. Nonetheless, from all eternity, he intended, when actually creating us, graciously to modify our natural end by subsuming it within our graced end. Why, we might wonder, would God do this? To protect his own gratuity? This is not necessary if, as we have previously argued, creation and redemption constitute a continuum that, in itself, is gratuitous. God has no need to ensure the double gratuity of what is gratuitous from the beginning.

A further problem concerns the view of nature to which the supernatural existential leads. On the one hand, Rahner appears to posit a robust notion of nature, because nature retains its own theoretically possible end. Yet on the other hand, his defining nature as a remainder concept that exists only theoretically in the one concrete order of grace serves to blur the distinction between the orders. Nature can be lost in grace like a thimble of water in a glass of wine. A problem thus obtains opposite to that of the pure nature theory. Nature does not stand freely and independently of grace but rather becomes dissipated in it. The supernatural existential thus poses a danger to nature's theological significance. In so doing, it shares a problem found in the reformed tradition. Barth, for instance, asserts that grace, as the "'wholly other,'" breaks in upon nature as a tangent "'perpendicularly from above.'"[104]

103. Rahner, *Foundations*, 128.

104. Karl Barth, *The Humanity of God*, trans. John Newton Thomas et al. (Atlanta: John Knox Press, 1960), 41.

But his view of nature is so deeply corrupted by the Fall that it retains little, if any, integrity for grace to support and perfect.[105] Thus, while purporting to offer a theory of pure nature in strong dialectical opposition to grace, Barth effectively crushes nature, leaving only the graced order.[106] It is hard to see how, despite its Thomist provenance, the supernatural existential retains, any more than Barth, a robust notion of nature. To avoid this problem, we need to find a conceptual framework that protects nature's dignity in its cooperation with grace.

In sum, Rahner's supernatural existential does not shine with bright theological promise. Nonetheless, other aspects of his thought remain trenchant. In subsequent chapters, we will have recourse to them.

Conclusions

Our probings into recent efforts to reunite nature and grace reveal that, for the congeniality between nature and grace to obtain, the seeds of grace need to be planted in nature without in any way violating the integrity of either order. Möhler develops a solution that centers on the implicit aesthetics of nature as grace's intrinsic symbol. The incarnation charges the natural order, especially history and language, with its beauty. In turn, they signify the beauty that they embody. To the extent that grace is immanent in nature, nature is itself a poetic artifact: it expresses the Father's unique image through whom it was created and redeemed. The divine aesthetics thus lies in the heart of nature and grace and offers us potential for fruitfully developing their synthesis.

For their part, Blondel, de Lubac, Seckler, and Rahner all develop a solution centered on nature's dynamism. This is driven by, and oriented to, a supernatural end that, in the concrete historical order, can only come as gratuitous. Blondel has aroused deep skepticism about the tenability of any pure nature. Philosophy shows that nature is not free-standing but is constituted by a transcendent exigency that makes a divine revelation reasonable and even likely. Developing the theo-

105. Ibid., 44.

106. See Balthasar, *Theology of Karl Barth*, 272.

logical implications of this thesis, de Lubac and Seckler see that grace is required precisely for nature to obtain. Accordingly, if an end is implicit in its effects, then prevenient grace can be seen as rendering the natural desire for God into a religious vocation. To answer the charge that this rendering undermines the divine gratuity, an understanding of creation and redemption as a continuum needs developing. We began to meet this need in our consideration of Seckler, but we must enhance our efforts. His approach offers greater potential for preserving grace as gift than Rahner's supernatural existential; its ambiguity jeopardizes nature's theological significance.

In short, we can glean from this chapter a rich recovery of the reciprocity between nature and grace. In the next chapter, we shall turn to recent papal thought in order to continue exploring this reciprocity. Underscoring nature as the sacrament of grace, John Paul II and Benedict XVI plunge us deeply into three relations: faith and reason, freedom and the eucharist, and love and justice.

Chapter 3

RECENT WEDDING

Influenced by recent efforts to reunite nature and grace, the thought of Popes John Paul II and Benedict XVI seizes on the harmonious interpenetration of both orders. Exploiting the creative tension between these orders, the pontiffs expound a paradox: nature realizes its own autonomy only when it mediates a higher synthesis. A theme thus uniting their work concerns nature as grace's sacrament. In John Paul, this theme undergirds the reciprocity between faith and reason and guides his reflections on the eucharist. In Benedict, nature understood as grace's sacrament structures the relation between justice and charity. In developing this relation, the German scholar lays a foundation for a theology of nature that complements his Polish predecessor.

Faith and Reason

In *Fides et Ratio,* John Paul contends that for nature's sacramentality to be understood rightly, reason in the first instance must rightly understand itself. He implicitly hearkens to reason's dynamism as seminally developed by Blondel, thus distancing himself from those post-Baroque thinkers who depict nature as statically independent of grace.[1] Modeling reason as incomplete and restlessly eager for its own fulfillment, he ar-

1. For more on Blondel's relation to John Paul II, see Peter Henrici, "The One Who Went Unnamed: Blondel in the Encyclical *Fides et ratio,*" *Communio: International Catholic Review* 26 (Fall 1999): 609–21.

gues that, despite humanity's poignant sense of finitude, reason "yearns for the infinite riches" beyond it.[2] The source of this yearning is a nostalgia for God that, constituting reason, defines the human person's essence as a seeker of truth (24, 28). Reason's infinite goal thus occupies at least a virtually immanent presence in the human person.

The encyclical does not explain how this presence obtains, declining to canonize specific philosophical concepts, such as Rahner's preapprehension of the absolute. But the pope does affirm that finite realities can mediate reason to itself by bringing this virtual presence more fully to consciousness (22). This mediation is possible because, although the fullness of truth transcends all finite realities, it is immanent in them even as it is in reason (20). Through them, reason seems, ironically, "almost to surpass [its] natural limitations" (22). By synthesizing the knowledge that it acquires from the sensory faculties, reason gains an intuition of its own self-transcending capacity. It grasps the majesty and divinity of the ultimate cause (22–23). If reason fails to acknowledge this cause as the fullness of truth, it is not because reason is incapable but because the will impedes it (17). Thus opposed to the reduction of reason to the utilitarian ends of mere power and pleasure, John Paul links reason's search for ultimate meaning with "the religious impulse innate in every person" (47, 81). This link echoes Blondel's understanding of human action as implicitly baptized by desire.

Creating in reason the nostalgia for God, the religious impulse is anterior to all of reason's yearnings. Because it is the cause that drives these, they become the impulse's sacrament. Humanity's pluriform searchings for meaning are the outward sign of the restlessness for the divine that initiates them in an effort to obtain satisfaction. This sacramentality makes it clear for John Paul, as for the Tübingen thinkers, de Lubac, Seckler, and Rahner that the divine is ingredient in nature, which it originates, stimulates, and completes. In a telling footnote, *Fides et Ratio* exemplifies this divine ingredience. Reiterating the teaching of Vatican I on the unity of truth in the orders of nature and grace,

2. John Paul II, *Fides et Ratio*, Encyclical Letter, September 14, 1998, par. 17; all English translations are drawn from www.vatican.va. Cited in the text by paragraph.

John Paul alludes to Galileo, who sensed in his scientific research the creator's presence stimulating his ingenuity and assisting his inquiry (9, 34, 53).[3] This allusion underscores the need of God's dynamic immanence to bring the created order to full integrity. It shows that the divine, which is the source of reason's searching, is also discovered by reason in the objects of its search. On the one hand, God inspired the questions that Galileo asked of nature. On the other hand, Galileo found God in the answers that nature supplied. According to John Paul, therefore, objective reality mediates a fuller consciousness of God to human intelligence. When it does, the order of nature attains the fullness of its own truth. Nature is thus sacramental, not only because it is an outward sign of its creating cause, but more especially because it is an efficacious sign that causes what it signifies. Nature brings knowledge of God to light in reason.

If the pope posits that reason's engagement with empirical reality is epistemically fruitful because it is religiously grounded, he further argues that Christian revelation is the lens that uniquely opens for reason its potential to see the full sacramentality of creation. In order for reason to make use of this lens, however, it must critically assess both its limit and its capability. In defining reason's limit, the encyclical, without explicitly mentioning Blondel, seems nonetheless to caution against the superstition that he diagnoses. This obtains, we will recall, when reason mistakenly believes that any finite object or idea will satisfy its innate yearning. According to John Paul, reason must admit its own contingency, question its own sufficiency, and move beyond the natural conclusion that an ultimate cause exists (79). "At the summit of its searching," he says, "reason acknowledges that it cannot do without what faith presents"—"the person of the Word made flesh" (41–42). Only this reveals the "fullness of the seminal plan of love which began with creation" (15). Only this gives a foretaste of the "definitive vision

3. See Vatican I, *Dei Filius*, in *Enchiridion Symbolorum: Definitionum et Declarationum de Rebus Fidei et Morum*, ed. Heinrich Denzinger and Adolf Schönmetzer (Barcinone: Herder, 1973), 3008 [hereafter "*DS*"]. See also John Paul II, "Address to the Pontifical Academy of Sciences" (November 10, 1979), in *Insegnamenti* 2, no. 2 (1979): 111–12.

of God"—the unique surcease of reason's yearning, the single cure for its nostalgia (15).

If the encyclical shows that reason's limit leads ineluctably to revelation, it also contends that revelation strengthens and enhances reason's capability. Consisting of the "boldness" of human intelligence to perceive and articulate "universally true propositions," this capability is grounded in the knowledge of being that conforms to, and is evinced from, objective reality (48, 59). Demonstrated by the history of human cultures, this boldness, when exercised, generates wisdom, the contemplation of goodness, truth, and beauty (70, 81). Because revelation embodies a divinely inspired source of wisdom, it augments reason's potential (56). "Without the stimulus of the word of God," asserts John Paul, "a good part of modern and contemporary philosophy would not exist" (76). Such ideas as creation and original sin have been appropriated from revelation by philosophy, which has then developed them according to its own object and methods (76). So fecund a union, the marriage between revelation and reason "cannot be separated without diminishing" humanity's capacity to know itself and its world (16).

In short, for John Paul revelation is the sacrament of reason's integrity. Graciously incarnating the divine in history, revelation is an outward sign that manifests to reason its limit and its boldness, which reason can nonetheless discern through a critical self-examination. Moreover, revelation is an efficacious sign because it answers the question of ultimate meaning that reason's limit generates even as it expands reason's bold capacity to know universally true propositions about wisdom. Because of this sacramentality, revelation enjoys a circular relation to reason. Sensing its limit as a result of the divine nostalgia that constitutes it, reason appropriates revelation, which then stimulates reason's universal power "to explore paths which of itself it would not have suspected it could take" (73). New syntheses in the empirical disciplines and in philosophy and theology thus ensue for the benefit of human culture.

In sum, *Fides et Ratio* advances the post-Baroque understanding of the relation of nature and grace by evolving within the church's magisterium various strains of thought developed in philosophy and theology since the early nineteenth century. Indebted to the Tübingen school, it posits the transcendent as ingredient in reality. On this basis, it positions reason's integrity and autonomy squarely within the sacramentality of nature. It defines this integrity as reason's capacity for self-transcendence grounded in a restless nostalgia for God. Thus, it is indebted to Blondel, who envisages the divine ingredience in nature as reason's dynamic striving toward a transcendent destiny that nature cannot supply. In addition, the encyclical owes a debt to Seckler and Rahner. For John Paul, when reason acknowledges the insufficiency of its own methods, it can assent in faith to the revelation that complements reason. This circularity in the relation between faith and reason hearkens to Seckler's instinct of faith that, in responding to revelation as value, brings human freedom to perfection. Similarly, it implicitly adverts to Rahner's categorical revelation that incarnates the meaning of the general revelation given in the pre-apprehended absolute. Moreover, *Fides et Ratio* evokes de Lubac. Just as for him grace calls into being spiritual creatures to receive it, so for John Paul the order of creation is the outward and efficacious sign of grace, which nature incarnates in every person.

However boldly *Fides et Ratio* makes its case, it does not take into account the modern plight of the religious believer who must dwell in a secular world. This world, as Dupré reminds us, is marked by an attenuated sense of representation in which the symbols of art and religion, if not yet moribund, have at least lost much of their lustre as beacons of meaning guiding us on our journey through time. Although agreeing with John Paul that reason is sufficiently capacious to reach a transcendent term, Dupré nonetheless observes that, when reason is restricted, language becomes silent. In such a context, public religious symbols like verbal revelation and ecclesiastical doctrines fail decisively to convey a sacred experience—an existential sense of nature's graced dimension.[4] It is becoming increasingly difficult for the modern person

4. Louis Dupré, *Transcendent Selfhood: The Loss and Rediscovery of the Inner Self* (New York: Seabury Press, 1976), 29.

to point to anything in direct experience that is sacred, or even for this person meaningfully to conceive the term. Although contemporary society has witnessed religious revivals, many of these, Dupré opines, are only marginally religious. All too often they merely evoke romantic remembrances and sentimental imitations of the past.[5]

An assessment of modernity such as Dupré's offers a tempering balance to *Fides et Ratio*. Stamped by the secular, nature is now uniquely experienced in western culture.[6] As a result, he believes that anyone who wishes to cultivate the life of grace must make a commitment to become separated from the public sphere and deliberately to turn inward. There, more or less alone, the subject can experience a mediated sense of the sacred that cannot be known directly in the patent symbols of the world. Thus isolated from secular society, the contemporary religious subject lives in a painful state of tension. Caught between culture's impoverishment of the human capacity for transcendence and the interior will to believe, the subject must reconcile the orders of nature and grace in the personal cultivation of religious experience. Only as a result of an enriched inner life can the believer subsequently impose a sense of the sacred on the objects of experience. Although inner conviction has become the genesis of the sacred, the total integration of reality that religion promises is still possible.[7] But in secular modernity, "the center of human piety has moved" from a religiously accessible cosmos to an individual choice.[8] However much this shift might cause us to grieve over what culture has lost, still, exhorts Dupré, it should spur institutional religion on to develop structures that mediate the sacred for its adherents. These structures should especially encourage the mystical life.[9] Above all, it is the direct experience of grace, personally appropriated deep within the human faculties, that reconnects the order of faith to that of nature.

In the complementary guidance they offer to the modern believer,

5. Ibid., 26.

6. Ibid., 25. This position aligns Dupré more with Blumenberg and puts him at odds with Robert Bellah.

7. Ibid., 27, 29.

8. Ibid., 29.

9. Ibid., 30.

both John Paul and Dupré creatively retrieve the Augustinian tradition. On the one hand, John Paul's view of reason hearkens to the first book of the *Confessions*, where the human heart is restless until it rests in God.[10] The pope develops this metaphor into a model of reason boldly extroverted in its searching for meaning. The world of empirical reality, to which reason is directed, represents the rich intelligibility of nature ready to answer many of humanity's driving questions. On the other hand, Dupré evokes the ninth book of the *Confessions*. In Augustine and Monica's vision at Ostia, we see that the rivulet of divine immanence in the heart can, in prayer, be followed to its source: the fountain of love, the divine subject itself, that overflows its abundance into humanity, this subject's image and likeness.[11] In contrast with John Paul, Dupré reminds us that nature now represents a world of impoverished meaning. He is thus less sanguine than the Pontiff that reason's extroversion will lead it to its transcendent term. Reaffirming humanity's power to articulate the graced symbolism of the natural order, however necessary, is not sufficient to heal the post-Baroque breach between nature and grace. Also needed is reason's inner reappropriation of its own transcendence, where the power to generate religious experience is lodged. Prayer creates an inner culture revealing the sacramentality of nature to a public culture ignorant of it. Dupré thus rightly underscores the urgency of individual acts of pious recollection as means of grasping the divine.

Nonetheless, Dupré exaggerates private experience as the bridge between nature and grace. We might wonder, for instance, how the individual can find the divine life within when the intellect's quest for its transcendent term is so restricted. It is here that *Fides et Ratio* offers Dupré a tempering balance. The encyclical guides us to behold the culture of institutional religion as an oasis of meaning for the human heart parched by secularity. If public symbols are sacramentally opaque, the Christian church remains to radiate its beacon. In its tra-

10. Augustine, *Confessions*, trans. R. S. Pine-Coffin (Harmondsworth: Penguin, 1961), I.1 (21).

11. Ibid., IX.10 (196–99).

ditions of worship and prayer and its systems of creed and code, the church mediates reason's transcendence to itself. Moreover, without the church to guard and regulate religious experience, personal piety easily devolves into delusion and fantasy, as the great doctors of the spiritual and mystical life have reiterated. Such a devolution, far from reconnecting faith to nature, distorts them both into another form of the fetish that Dupré deplores in the modern novel.

In sum, the role of ecclesial religion should not be underestimated as offering hope for refashioning a cultural synthesis between nature and grace analogous to the Baroque. This community of meaning is efficacious both for the modern believer and secular culture. For the believer, it stimulates and protects the religious experience that fulfills reason. For culture, it prophesies against the diminishment of public symbols. It thus gives witness that empirical reality is properly appreciated only when grasped as a moment within its transcendent constitution.

Eucharist and Freedom

John Paul's eucharistic reflections also provide insights into the relation between nature and grace. They not only retrieve from the church's tradition the twin aspects of sacrament and sacrifice, consecrated act and sacred meal. They harmonize them with striking originality and contemporary appeal. Interpreting these themes against the backdrop of his own personalist metaphysics, John Paul shows the eucharist to be the "source and summit," not only of the Christian life, as *Lumen Gentium* asserts, but also of freedom—both individual and social, both human and divine.[12] Because his understanding of freedom is "perhaps the most profound in modern philosophy," the pope presents us with an innovative approach to expanding the old by com-

12. John Paul II, *Dominicae Cenae,* Encyclical Letter, February 24, 1980, in Edward J. Kilmartin, *Church, Eucharist, and Priesthood: A Theological Commentary on "The Mystery and Worship of the Most Holy Eucharist"* (New York: Paulist Press, 1981), 69–100, at 74, citing *Acta Apostolicae Sedis* 57 (1965): 15. The encyclical is cited in the text by page number in Kilmartin.

plementing it with the new.[13] John Paul thus challenges his critics who accuse his reflections of arresting their development at Trent.[14]

Standing in the ecclesial tradition, the pope holds that, as a sacrament, the eucharist is an efficacious sign: it causes what it signifies. "Just as the Church 'makes the Eucharist,'" he writes, "so 'the Eucharist builds up' the Church" (73). By this he means that Christ's eucharistic body signifies Christ's mystical body, even as it molds the church ever more into that body. Moreover, the "Eucharist," he says, "is above all else a sacrifice," a "consecrated offering" representing Christ's own sacrifice of propitiation that irrevocably reconciles God and humanity (81–82). The eucharist is a sacrifice, not principally because we make an offering to God, however perfectly. It is a sacrifice because Christ, as Son and Logos, has first condescended to us by initiating the new covenant on our behalf (79). Thus John Paul intrinsically links the eucharist as sacrament and sacrifice. What establishes the *sacrament* is the self-*sacrifice* of God for humanity. The church is able to make its offering to God only because the divine Son and Logos has made his kenotic offering in the incarnation. Similarly, the eucharist is able to build up the church only because it "makes available always" to us the newness of the incarnate Word's paschal offering (81). For the Pontiff, therefore, the heart of the efficacious causality of the eucharist is the theandric sacrifice that redeems all humanity even as it incorporates the church.

As we delve more deeply into John Paul's understanding of the eucharist as an efficacious sign, we discover how creatively he appropriates and interprets what he has received. Although theories explaining sacramental causation can be traced at least to Augustine, they tend to be formalistic rather than existential. In other words, they emphasize defining the causal mechanics that obtain between the sacrament's signs and its grace. Insufficient attention is given to the origins of these

13. John M. McDermott, "The Theology of John Paul II: A Response," in *The Thought of Pope John Paul II: A Collection of Essays and Studies*, ed. McDermott (Rome: Editrice Pontificia Gregoriana, 1993), 55–68, at 58.

14. Kilmartin, *Commentary*, 14.

mechanics in the divine freedom that offers the grace and in the human freedom that integrates the effects of the grace into the dynamics of personal consciousness. For instance, Augustine and Isidore of Seville posit that, although the signs of the sacraments resemble the spiritual reality that they signify, they are efficacious only because God externally infuses grace into the recipient each and every time a sacrament is received.[15] Thus, the sacramental signs, such as water in baptism and oil in confirmation and orders, become, not the intrinsic media of grace, but merely part of the ritual occasion concomitant upon God's conferring the grace. This approach affirmed that the sacraments are efficacious because first and foremost they convey knowledge. They remind the recipient of the grace that they are simultaneously receiving, not in and through the sign, but through God's free choice to confer it directly and particularly whenever the ritual is performed.[16]

The concomitance theory had to be adapted to the eucharist, especially after the heresy of Berengar of Tours denied the real presence. In order to buttress this doctrine and coherently to interrelate the sacrament's rite, its signs, and its conferral of grace, theologians found inspiration in Augustine to develop the *res et sacramentum* or "symbolic reality."[17] This new category reinforced what was previously believed but not so clearly expressed: that the action of the Mass objectively and permanently consecrates the bread and wine which, in turn, become the means conferring grace.[18] The theorists of concomitance, although affirming the symbolic reality of the eucharistic species, nonetheless continued to claim that God acted separately in consecrating them on the one hand and in conferring grace along with them on the

15. David Bourke, introduction to vol. 56 of Aquinas, *ST*, xiii–xxiii, at xvi; also Peter B. Garland, *The Definition of Sacrament According to St. Thomas* (Ottawa: University of Ottawa Press, 1959), 46, 85, 88.

16. Henry of Ghent, Bonaventure, Ockham, and Biel, among others, held versions of the concomitance theory. See Bernard Leeming, *Principles of Sacramental Theology* (Westminster, Md.: Newman Press, 1960), 287, 290–94.

17. See Augustine, *In Johannis evangelium tractatus* 26, n. 17, in *PL* 35, col. 1612; cited in Leeming, *Principles*, 252. Augustine borrows his doctrine of signification from Origen and the Alexandrians (see Bourke, introduction to *ST*, xv).

18. See Leeming, *Principles*, 251.

other. Some thinkers differed, however, holding the symbolic reality to be the instrumental cause of the grace. According to Thomas, for instance, God acts in and through the objectively consecrated signs; these then intrinsically mediate the grace to those receiving the sacrament.[19]

Chapter 1 explored Trent's integration of Aquinas's understanding of instrumental causality into its doctrine of justification. Thomas's own integration of this causality into the symbolic reality brought about an important advance in understanding efficaciousness. It shifted the sacraments from merely concomitant occasions of grace to grace's intrinsic media. The gist of Thomas's account runs as follows. As God's incarnate Word, Christ is the exemplary cause of the divine life of grace made available in the sacraments. Christ is also the principal agent of the sacraments, because he instituted them and is encountered in them through the Holy Sprit. As principal agent, he confers on the natural signs a graced power that operates in and through the innate power of the signs. Thus, when in the eucharist bread and wine physically nourish, the signs, having been consecrated by the words of an appropriate minister, accomplish immediately their spiritual effects: they nourish spiritually. According to this view, therefore, the signs are constituted as the sacraments' instrumental cause. Christ, as exemplary cause and agent of divine life, communicates grace to the recipient in and through their innate power.[20] The signs manifest the hidden power of sanctifying, Thomas affirms, "because [they are] not only a cause but in some sense an effect, inasmuch as [they are] moved by the principal agent" (*ST* III, q. 62, a. 1).

John Paul presupposes this understanding of efficacious causality, even as he creatively relates it to freedom. For the pope, first and foremost, the eucharist really manifests and immediately makes present an infinite love freely sacrificed. God's freedom thus lies at the core of

19. *ST* III, q. 62, a. 4; see also Leeming, *Principles*, 264, 288, 324–30; and E. Neveut, "La pensée de saint Thomas sur la causalité des sacrements de la Nouvelle Loi," *Divus Thomas (Piacenza)* 40 (1937): 267–70, at 269.

20. I have interpreted Thomas in light of Albertson, "Instrumental Causality," 409–35.

the sacrament. Above all, this freedom is exposed in Christ's voluntary annihilation that, in crucifying the world with himself, transforms all that is human (71, 78). When we ritually celebrate this freedom, in no sense do we add to it. Rather, because what we enact flows from Christ alone, we "reopen" in time and space "the central moment in the work of redemption."[21] As both priest and victim, Christ is the unique offerer of the eucharist and the one uniquely offered (79). Therefore, as the consecrator and the one consecrated, he continues God's loving intervention among us. In so doing, he dynamically makes possible *theosis,* our divinizing union in him (79).[22] Just as God's freedom lies at the core of the sacramental sign, so our divinizing union lies at the core of Christian worship. God's sacrificial love evokes in the faithful a reciprocal love: an act of our own freedom that responds to the divine initiative and, in Christ, adequately compensates for it (71–72). All authentic praise of God thus has its origins in this "profound thanksgiving," as does the church, which continues to build itself into what it is, Christ's body, by a cicumincession of love freely posited and freely requited (78).[23]

We begin to see the outlines of John Paul's innovative interpretation of the eucharist as an efficacious sign. On the one hand, it signifies the divine freedom at the heart of the sacrifice that establishes the sacrament. On the other hand, it causes human freedom to be perfected: it elicits our loving response to the God who first loves us. John Paul developed this last theme when, as archbishop of Crakow, he delivered a homily at the 1976 Eucharistic Congress in Philadelphia. Placing the eucharist within the context of Jesus's ministry of proclaiming "release for all who are deprived of freedom" (Lk 4:18–19), he asserts that its food intends to satisfy the deepest hunger of the human person—the

21. "General Audience of May 12, 1993," in John Paul II, *The Church: Mystery, Sacrament, Community* (Boston, Mass.: Pauline Books and Media, 1998), 316; vol. 4 of *A Catechesis on the Creed.*

22. See also ibid., 320–21.

23. See also "General Audience of September 11, 1991," in *Church,* 61.

yearning for freedom.[24] As "the principal trait of humanity and the source of human dignity," freedom is a gift, because it endows humanity with the power of self-determination. But the gift entails a task: self-determination involves doing good and avoiding evil. Freedom achieves its purpose only when it mounts the summit of goodness—the love of God and neighbor (111–12). Yet John Paul is clear that this summit must be negotiated spontaneously if the human person is authentically to *self*-determine his destiny (111). Compulsion and coercion have no role in this effort, even when, through good intentions, they direct the person to what is, after all, his proper end and goal in God.

Positing his central point, the pope affirms the eucharistic Christ as the guarantee, protection, and fulfillment of authentic human spontaneity. Liberating the power of love latent in the human heart, Christ loosens the bonds that would shackle our freedom. He redeems us from the slavery of sin and concupiscence, while serving as the counterfoil to self-indulgence, the allure of the flesh, and monetary gain (113–14). The eucharistic Christ teaches us to give ourselves utterly, in loving service of God and neighbor, even as he himself has done. But the hunger for freedom is not confined to the existential realm of the person. It is cosmic, for John Paul, and cultural and historical. The struggles of peoples and nations for the unhindered exercise of conscience and religion and for deliverance from all forms of social and political injustice give additional witness to its driving exigency (115–16). Absorbing this struggle into his own sacrifice, the eucharistic Christ enters into solidarity with freedom-starved humanity, offering them continually, along with himself, to the Father. Thus the tragedies of our own age become co-actors with the chief protagonist on the stage of the altar in the paschal drama that is forever old and forever new (117).

The message that John Paul develops in this homily draws deeply from the well of his own philosophy in order to pour forth a refresh-

24. Karol Wojtyła, "The Eucharist and Man's Hunger for Freedom," in Ludvik Nemec, *Pope John Paul II: A Festive Profile* (New York: Catholic Publishing, 1979), 110–17, at 110. Cited in the text.

ing synthesis of personalist and sacramental metaphysics. The creative tension between freedom as a gift and as a task lies at the center of his homily. But it also lies at the center of his anthropology, which is focused on, and derived from, human moral activity.[25] This activity is constituted by those deeds for which we are responsible and through which we intend the true and the good.[26] As a gift, "freedom is expressed by efficacy," he writes in *The Acting Person*, "and efficacy leads to responsibility."[27] By efficacy he means, not only that our moral acts *affect* other persons and things, but more importantly that they *effect* us. Bringing about self-determination through morality is the root of human responsibility.[28] It cannot be escaped. Self-determination results from every moral choice, because every choice implies a prior knowledge of self. As an immediate intuition, self-knowledge accompanies choosing.[29] Through choosing, the person brings into harmony with his conscious agency his own bodiliness on the one hand, which is the means by which choices are enacted, and the external world on the other hand, where the objects of choice reside.[30] In sum, freedom for the pope is a gift, because moral action establishes the unity of the person, even as it reflects this unity.[31]

Freedom is also a task. Self-determination is not mere autonomy divorced from the order of objective reality.[32] *Pace* Kant, the moral law for John Paul does not emerge from the necessary structure of reason alone. To be sure, it requires the exercise of conscience, but this is reason's capacity to enter into dialogue with "the values and disvalues

25. McDermott, "Response," 58, citing Karol Wojtyła, *The Acting Person*, trans. Andrzej Potocki, *Analecta Husserliana* 10 (Dordrecht: D. Reidel, 1979), 107, 121, 135, 266.

26. George Huntston Williams, *The Mind of John Paul II: Origins of His Thought and Action* (New York: Seabury Press, 1981), 192.

27. *Acting Person*, 180, cited in Kenneth L. Schmitz, *At the Center of the Human Drama: The Philosophical Anthropology of Karol Wojtyła/Pope John Paul II* (Washington, D.C.: The Catholic University of America Press, 1993), 83.

28. Schmitz, *Center*, 83.

29. McDermott, "Response," 58, citing *Acting Person*, 16, 37, 42, 181, 261.

30. McDermott, "Response," 62.

31. Robert F. Harvanek, "The Philosophical Foundations of the Thought of John Paul II," in *Collection of Essays*, 1–21, at 12.

32. McDermott, "Response," 59.

among the range of possible actions" that confront us heteronomously.[33] Precisely put, the task of freedom requires us creatively to integrate the world of objective value into the complex dynamism of our own consciousness. It requires us to synthesize self-determination and natural value, but not by statically assimilating what we accept as true and good.[34] On the contrary, self-determination realizes both autonomy and truth, not merely by surrendering to the objective order, but by fashioning it into "an internal principle" of action.[35] When this task is negotiated, a "horizontal transcendence" results. We come into harmony with the world around us. More importantly, we give ourselves over to the selves whom we are able to become.[36] Ultimately, horizontal transcendence, since it is oriented to truth, drives beyond itself to vertical transcendence: the living source of truth that is God enfleshed in Christ, the truth made a human person.[37] This drive is not so much a necessity of nature for the pope as an encounter of divinity and humanity in the mutually free exchange of grace and loving response.[38]

We are now in a position to appreciate the originality of John Paul's integration of freedom into the eucharist. On the one hand, freedom is itself *the* sacrament of the human person. It causes what it signifies: moral choices reflect the inner orientation and existential unity of the person, even as they strengthen and cause them. John Paul thus harnesses Thomas's understanding of a sacrament as an instrumental cause in order to exploit its implications for philosophical anthropology. Freedom is the power by which the person innately determines himself. Like any instrumental cause, freedom, as a gift, remains open to an indeterminate range of applications until, as a task, it is intentionally directed toward the accomplishing of specifically chosen ends.

33. *Acting Person*, 158–65, 173, in Schmitz, *Center*, 84.

34. McDermott, "Response," 59, citing *Acting Person*, 111, 191, 195, 199, 202, 212, 255.

35. McDermott, "Response," 62, citing *Acting Person*; and Wojtyła, *Amore e Responsabilità*, 2nd ed., trans. A. Milanoli (Torino: Marietti, 1978), 110, 179–82; and Wojtyła, "The Person: Subject and Community," *The Review of Metaphysics* 33 (1979): 273–308, at 282–87, 296.

36. Schmitz, *Center*, 86.

37. McDermott, "Response," 63, citing John Paul II, *The Whole Truth About Man*, ed. James V. Schall (Boston, Mass.: St. Paul, 1981), 273.

38. McDermott, "Response," 63–64.

The fulfilling of these brings about a far more important finality, the person's existential integrity. This is the hidden reality that specifically chosen ends cause and whose effects they are. John Paul's pinpointing of freedom as the person's core accentuates humanity's responsibility and develops its existential energy. Nonetheless, it seems to shortchange the intellection that, at least in Thomism, precedes volition even while impregnating it (see *ST* I, q. 82, a. 4).

There is a final aspect of the pope's originality. If on the one hand freedom is *the* sacrament of the person, still on the other hand the eucharist is *the* sacrament of the church that perfects freedom. In liberating the love latent in the human heart, the eucharist frees us from sin and concupiscence. Meanwhile it empowers us to offer ourselves sacrificially for others just as the divine freedom offers itself in the eucharist for us. John Paul thus exposes the eucharist as the catalyst for synthesizing the dialectic of human freedom. It integrates our autonomous drive for self-determination with the heteronomous demands not only of avoiding the sin opposed to objective value but also of loving others even to the end. When we receive the divine freedom that the eucharist signifies, and when we assimilate it as an internal principle of action, we attain freedom's twin goals: horizontal and vertical transcendence. We bring into harmony with our conscious intentionality our corporeal actions and the external world in which our actions have effects. Moreover, we intimately imbibe the living truth itself, making its divine freedom our own. For John Paul, let us recall, every choice results in self-determination, because every choice implies self-knowledge. It therefore follows that our choice freely to surrender to the loving power of the eucharist builds up the self from its deepest and most fundamental ontological roots: the union of knowledge and freedom, truth and goodness, bound together in love.

In sum, John Paul's eucharistic thought, like *Fides et Ratio*, posits nature as grace's sacrament. Whereas his synthesis of faith and reason owes a heavy debt to Blondel, his view of the church's principal act of worship presupposes Thomas's dynamics of efficacious symbolism. Nonetheless, the pope takes us a long way from the instrumental causality of the Angelic Doctor, just as Thomas shed new light on Augustine's view of signs. The heart of both nature and grace for John Paul is freedom. As the instrumental cause of the person, freedom attains its perfection when incorporated as a living moment in the free kenosis of Christ. As such, human freedom is congenially assumed by the instrumental causality of grace. In the eucharist, the commingling of love between God and the person empowers human freedom to reconcile the dialectic of autonomy and heteronomy. Aiming by nature at self-determination, freedom reaches in grace the highest good, loving self-sacrifice. In thus effecting what it signifies, the eucharist dynamically draws the person forth to become what Irenaeus calls *homo vivens, gloria Dei.*[39] Preserving and establishing human autonomy, this summit of faith molds us ever more into what our nature requires: harmony with the ordered goodness of a freely created world charged with divine vestiges.

Love and Justice

Like his predecessor, Benedict XVI understands nature as grace's sacrament. His first encyclical, *Deus Caritas Est,* focuses on the relations between eros and charity and charity and justice. Striking is the German Pontiff's sensitivity to the nuanced reciprocity that structures both relations. Disputing, for instance, the well-known thesis of the Lutheran bishop Anders Nygren, he argues that eros and charity are analogical, not equivocal.[40] God's redeeming activity is the prime analogate of both loves. In the incarnate Word, eros and charity are perfectly conjoined. They flow forth from God's universal self-sacrifice on the one hand and from his passionate yearning to save sinful humanity on the other.[41] For its part, the eros between husband and wife mirrors the divine charity, especially when it comes to completion in conceiv-

39. Irenaeus, *Against the Heresies* 4.20.7 (in the numeration of Massuet), in *PG* 7.

40. Anders Nygren, *Agape and Eros,* trans. Philip S. Watson (London: SPCK, 1953).

41. Pope Benedict XVI, *Deus Caritas Est,* Encyclical Letter, December 25, 2005, pars. 10, 13; all English translations are drawn from www.vatican.va. Cited in the text by paragraph.

ing children, nurturing a family, and spreading further to embrace the needs of neighbors and friends (18).

In relating charity and justice, the Pontiff contends that charity for the church "is not a kind of welfare activity which could equally well be left to others. Charity is part of her nature, an indispensable expression of her very being" (25). The work of charity is, in fact, sacramental in a broad sense. It is both a sign and an instrument of the church's essence. The church's "*service of charity*" is the overflowing of the life of the Spirit, whose energy "transforms the heart of the ecclesial community, so that it becomes a witness before the world of the love of the Father" (19). This emanation of love must necessarily extend "beyond the frontiers of the Church." In so doing, it causes what it signifies. Acting to "purify" humanity, it clarifies rational judgment and aids the state in better ordering the norms of political life (25, 28).

In developing this thesis, Benedict explicitly addresses Marxism, perhaps Christianity's leading recent nemesis. Its central critique, he argues, rests on the notion that those who stand on the social and political margins demand justice, not charity. Charity merely assuages the consciences of the privileged by treating the symptoms of the disease. It makes no attempt to diagnose and heal the underlying causes of injustice. These are structural; they cannot be eradicated by the purveyors of voluntary goodwill (26). In agreement with Marxism, the pope defines justice as giving people their rightful share of the community's goods. Justice, he says, is the "aim and criterion of politics" (28). It falls properly under the aegis of the state. In parting company with Marxism, however, he reasserts a fundamental imperative of Catholic social teaching. The state bears the moral burden of acting according to the principle of subsidiarity (26). As Benedict claims in his 2009 encyclical *Caritas in Veritate*, this principle is designed to guard against the paternalist encroachments of "an all encompassing welfare state" by protecting the legitimate autonomy of intermediate social organizations.[42] Far from imposing on the commonwealth a dictatorship of

42. Pope Benedict XVI, *Caritas in Veritate*, Encyclical Letter, June 29, 2009, par. 57; all English translations are drawn from www.vatican.va.

the proletariat, subsidiarity requires the higher orders of society to encourage the lower ones to assume their proper share of responsibility. Without this assumption, neither human freedom nor social participation can flourish.[43] The higher should not perform what the lower can do best for itself.[44]

Moreover, the principle of subsidiarity entails that, however pervasively justice reckons social structures, it never obviates love (28). Without solidarity, subsidiarity can create social privatism.[45] "One does not make the world more human," the pope asserts, "by refusing to act [lovingly] here and now" (31). From deep within their spontaneous initiative, people are "always capable of freely giving something to others" (28).[46] Suffering and loneliness never cease to need compassion and care. Because these qualities often fall outside the state's aegis, solidarity respects the reciprocity between persons that lies at the core of humanity's constitution. The state must not only respect this reciprocity but also promote it. For this reason, the church casts a wary eye on all ideologies that would compromise the legitimate sphere of responsible human endeavor. These include partisan strategies and programs, including proselytism, that envisage charity tendentiously: merely as a means of promoting an agenda, not as an end in itself. Because love constitutes the essential bond between God and man, its free exchange is "the best defense" of both (31).

Benedict further develops his notion of justice by locating its promotion squarely within the realm of practical reason (28). Wisely, he understands that achieving justice within the complex organization of modern society presents ethical problems whose solutions are often translucent or even opaque to the best minds of the best persons. Moreover, the political order is often blinded by power and special interests (28). To help lift these shadows, the church has developed a "set of fundamental guidelines" to enlighten the deliberations of prac-

43. Ibid.

44. See Pope Pius XI, *Quadragesimo Anno*, Encyclical Letter, May 15, 1931, par. 79; all English translations are drawn from www.vatican.va.

45. Benedict XVI, *Caritas in Veritate*, par. 58.

46. Ibid., par. 57.

tical reason (27). Called Catholic social thought, these guidelines are grounded in "the natural law" (28). As such, they are "valid even beyond the confines of the Church" (27). Although the church offers its teaching to purify the political order's understanding of justice, "the political task … cannot be the Church's immediate responsibility" (28). Not itself a political organ, the church has no interest in building a theocracy. Consistent with *Gaudium et Spes* (par. 36), its interest lies in respecting the appropriate autonomy of the state (28).[47]

To further enhance the church's respect for this autonomy, Benedict makes a vitally important distinction. On the one hand, the church's role concerning justice is indirect. Its mandate serves to awaken "those moral forces without which … just [social] structures are neither established nor prove effective in the long run" (28). Its mandate is hortatory and prophetic. It serves to inform the consciences of the faithful, and more generally all people of goodwill (29). They in turn are mandated to form society according to the virtuous use of their own practical reason. On the other hand, the church's role concerning charity is direct (29). As a theological virtue, love is the essence of grace that is the very life of God. The church's work of charity elevates the state's notion of justice (29). The pope is careful not to say that charity is the state's direct concern. He does argue, however, that the church's witness of love leavens the humanitarian efforts of secular agencies, whether public or private (30). These efforts share with religion a common motivation. "Love of neighbor," the pope reminds us, "is inscribed by the Creator in man's very nature" (31). Consequently, state-sponsored programs like subsidies and relief for heavily indebted countries promote human solidarity. They concretely embody charity. In so doing, they congenially join with the culture of life preached by the church. This preaching serves to deepen all motivations, whether secular or religious, that are grounded in self-sacrifice (30).

The pope concludes his reflection by squarely incorporating the Christian notion of justice within love. No doubt intending to reorder

47. Vatican Council II, *Gaudium et Spes,* in *Decrees,* ed. Tanner, 2:1069–1135.

the recently popular slogan "the faith that does justice," he says, referring to Galatians 5:6, that Christians should "be guided by the faith which works through love" (33). Reminding us of 1 Corinthians 13, he further asserts that "practical activity will always be insufficient, unless it visibly expresses a love for man" (34). For Benedict, justice is not an absolute in itself, but a sign of love and a means to love. Its sustaining furnace is a loving "encounter with Christ" (34, 36, 37). Without this, justice becomes dissipated. It devolves into the delusion that its promotion could fully resolve every social problem (36). Justice cheap in love, even when luxuriant in faith, offers us only the ideologies against which the pope prophesies. Even worse, when justice stiffens into ideology, then fanaticism, terrorism, and despair often result. Love acts justly by being patient and humble in the face of sustained poverty and suffering (37). Persevering when its own actions seem powerless, justice grounded in the faith that works through love cleaves to the crucified Christ, the paradigmatic victim of injustice, whose wounds never ceased to pour forth life (38–39).

Mounting a critique of Benedict's vision in *Deus Caritas Est,* Tissa Balasuriya would have the Pontiff broaden his reading of the signs of the times to include stern challenges to "neo-liberal capitalism."[48] Regrettably, he contends, Catholic social teaching from *Rerum Novarum* through *Centesimus Annus* remains the hostage of this and other ideologies, such as European colonialism and white racism (245).[49] As a first riposte to Balasuriya, it should be noted that this tradition, which *Deus Caritas Est* intends to develop, deplores the corrosive effects of unbridled capitalism, as does *Caritas in Veritate.*[50] Undergirding Bala-

48. Tissa Balasuriya, "A Companion to the Encyclical of Pope Benedict XVI on 'God is Love,'" *Cross Currents* 56, no. 2 (Summer 2006): 229–60, at 247. Cited in the text.

49. Pope Leo XIII, *Rerum Novarum,* Encyclical Letter, May 15, 1891; Pope John Paul II, *Centesimus Annus,* Encyclical Letter, May 1, 1991. All English translations are drawn from www.vatican.va.

50. See, e.g., *Quadragesimo Anno* (pars. 58, 61); Pope John XXIII, *Mater et Magistra,* Encyclical Letter, May 15, 1961, pars. 14, 73, 74, 96, 112. For a recapitulation of these themes, especially in Pope Paul VI, *Populorum Progressio,* Encyclical Letter, March 26, 1967, see Benedict XVI, *Caritas in Veritate.* All English translations are drawn from www.vatican.va.

suriya's entire critique, however, is his opposition to a central tenet of Benedict's anthropology: its "mythical presupposition of original sin" (257). By this Balasuriya means the notion that "the whole of humanity is placed in sin as offenders against God" (257). His critique of original sin as myth is not further developed. But from what he says even so briefly, we can infer that he and Marxism share a common ideological source in Pelagianism. It is precisely Benedict's awareness of this source that leads him to single out Marxism for special censure. Let us probe this awareness more deeply.

The Judeo-Christian doctrine of original sin stands as a bulwark against all ideologies based on the naive notion that the human person is innately perfectible. As John Henry Newman writes in his intellectual autobiography *Apologia Pro Vita Sua*, original sin is striking because of its empirical verifiability. No profound insight into the signs of the times, or into human history as we know it, is needed to perceive that, if an all-good God exists, then the human species stands in a consistently radical opposition to him.[51] For his part, Augustine in *Confessions* traces this opposition to a disease located deep in the human heart over which the person is powerless. Observing its symptoms even in reputedly innocent children, he wonders why a toddler would aggressively force his infant brother away from his mother's breast. Milk aplenty flows for both to share, even as the infant depends on it for his very life. Augustine concludes that the concupiscent drive of self-love is natural. By this he means that human nature acts spontaneously and pre-reflectively from a primeval disorder from which only the power of divinity can redeem it.[52]

Augustine's battle against Pelagius brought the main contours of the Christian doctrine of original sin into relief. The British monk, desiring to spare Christians from the charge of ethical laxity leveled at them by the pagan aristocracy of Rome, contended, in effect, that sinful behavior is learned by sociocultural conditioning. On this basis

51. John Henry Cardinal Newman, *Apologia Pro Vita Sua* (New York: Doubleday, 1989), 319–20.

52. Augustine, *Confessions*, I.7 (27–28).

he could then argue that Christianity believed in vigorous moral action—strength of will—in order to overcome the influence of a corrupt and errant environment. The incarnate Word shines amidst this milieu as a luminous example of perfection. To be saved, we need to emulate him by a freedom firmly and consistently steeped in virtue.[53]

Augustine saw the error lightly hidden in this position. If original sin is learned by bad example, if it is merely external to the human person, and if Christ's role is principally exemplary, then it is logically possible for human volition to save itself. For Augustine, therefore, the deepest problem in Pelagianism is not anthropological but soteriological. He answers Pelagius with the traducianism mentioned in chapter 1. Original sin, inbred in humanity, is handed down in the person's very generation in sexual intercourse. This is a compellingly reasonable position once it is granted that original sin must condition human nature. And so it must, if Christ is to be humanity's necessary perfecter, not merely an aid in humanity's task of self-perfection.

For his part, Benedict locates the modern rehearsal of the error of human perfectibility in the thought of Joachim of Fiore.[54] For Joachim, history is a divine progression in which the Holy Spirit will ultimately render both church and state redundant.[55] Joachim is subtler than Pelagius in that he attributes humanity's perfectibility in time and space to a divine agency. Nonetheless, to the extent that his immanent soteriology loses its fulfillment in a supernatural future that is divine, it is Pelagian at root. Joachim's thesis became secularized with the exploitation of the inductive method of empirical science. According to Bacon, this method, as the pope argues in his 2007 encyclical *Spe Salvi*, would produce "'the triumph of art over nature.'"[56] According to Kant,

53. See Henry Chadwick, *The Early Church* (Harmondsworth: Penguin, 1983), 227; and Professor Rowan Greer of Yale University (personal communication).

54. Ratzinger deals with Joachim and his relation to Bonaventure in his *Habilitationschrift: The Theology of History in St. Bonaventure,* trans. Zachary Hayes (Chicago: Franciscan Herald Press, 1971).

55. D. Vincent Toomey, "The Mind of Benedict XVI," in *Claremont Review of Books* 4 (Fall 2005): 66–71, at 66.

56. Francis Bacon, *Novum organum* I.117; in Pope Benedict XVI, *Spe Salvi,* Encyclical Letter, November 30, 2007, par. 16; all English translations are drawn from www.vatican.va.

this triumph would fulfill the kingdom of God by the kingdom of humanity: reason would regain its dominion over the world lost by the Fall.[57] This putative overcoming of original sin, which positive religion affirms lies as deep in the person as it does in "the structure of society," surely jeopardized the credibility of faith.[58] It created another reason for religion to evanesce from public culture and to seek confinement in the privacy of individual devotion.[59]

For his part, Marx, in contrast to the Enlightenment, did not devolve progress from inductive reason. After all, this had produced the miseries of the industrial revolution. He placed hope in political action. It would secure redemption by precipitating the socialization of the means of production.[60] This, in turn, once finalized in the dictatorship of the proletariat, would fulfill the same promise of Bacon and Kant—a new messiahship for the human race.

Ultimate hope in secular progress, whatever its form, recapitulates errors that Christianity has long countered. Progress, says Benedict quoting Adorno, simply means moving "from the sling to the atom bomb." Whatever its possibilities for good, they are offset by those for evil.[61] Infected by an immanent soteriology that rejects traducianism, progress as secular redemption proffers a dangerously delusional hope for humanity. A more mature Kant, for instance, would observe that the kingdom of humanity would likely end in perversion. Should Christianity cease to be loved, he says, reason itself would usher in the reign of the Antichrist.[62] Instinctively aware of Pelagianism's power, Kant's wisdom seems to have escaped Balasuriya's critique of Benedict. To the extent that Balasuriya's reading of the signs of the times is thus grounded in a bias, it might fairly be deemed as deluded as the

57. See Immanuel Kant, *Religion Within the Limits of Reason Alone*, chap. 3, in *Werke* IV, ed. W. Weischedel (1956), 777; in Benedict XVI, *Spe Salvi*, par. 17.

58. Benedict XVI, *Caritas in Veritate*, par. 34.

59. Benedict XVI, *Spe Salvi*, par. 17.

60. Ibid., par. 20.

61. Ibid., par. 22.

62. Immanuel Kant, *Das Ende aller Dinge*, in *Werke* VI, ed. W. Weischedel (1964), 190; in Benedict XVI, *Spe Salvi*, par. 19.

ideologies that it assimilates. Correcting such a bias, the Pontiff trenchantly observes that the crux of the human struggle in this world constantly entails winning freedom "over for the cause of good."[63] This victory can obtain only when the divine "gift" of "unconditional love," which is the heart of redemption, is freely accepted by individual human beings.[64]

Balasuriya's critique also takes issue with the paradigm that Benedict develops for the relation between love and justice. According to Balasuriya, justice, as entailed in charity, should occupy the church's direct work, especially the clergy's. He would have bishops and priests develop their own social analyses, plan their own strategies based on them, and then serve as the executors of these strategies in the political arena (245–47). Compromising the autonomy of the temporal order that *Gaudium et Spes* calls upon the church to respect, this proposal is seriously flawed. It misunderstands the necessary relation, not first and foremost between love and justice, but between justice and prudence.

Although Thomas defines justice as what is "properly and in itself right," he nonetheless understands justice to be the subject of prudence as it discerns the natural law.[65] In determining what is right, justice mediates between humanity's need for self-defense and its vindictive instincts on the one hand and its fundamental tendency toward social communion on the other hand.[66] Prudence consists in the skilled ability to choose and execute appropriate means to bring about objectively good ends. Prudence governs justice, therefore, when the question of how a complex social organization prone to conflicts among rights can best promote the mediation required by justice. In the first instance,

63. Benedict XVI, *Spe Salvi*, par. 24.

64. Ibid., pars. 26, 31.

65. Josef Pieper, *The Four Cardinal Virtues: Prudence, Justice, Fortitude Temperance*, trans. Donald Coogan et al. (New York: Harcourt, Brace, and World, 1954), 164.

66. Gerard Gilleman, *The Primacy of Charity in Moral Theology*, trans. William F. Ryan and André Vachon (Westminster, Md.: Newman Press, 1959), 332; cited in John P. Langan, "What Jerusalem Says to Athens," in *The Faith That Does Justice: Examining the Christian Sources for Social Change*, ed. John C. Haughey (Ramsey, N.J.: Paulist Press, 1977), 152–80, at 163.

this question is not religious but fittingly secular. It is, in other words, a matter for rational refection apart from any consideration offered by the church, based as it is on natural virtue.[67] Consequently, as Benedict rightly adumbrates, people of sound prudence, whether Christian or not, will differ about what constitute apt means to achieve just ends. Because love mandates justice through the agency of prudence, it follows that, if the church closely allies itself with a particular social and political agenda, its credibility risks serious compromise. The Gospel's eternal truths entail ends that ought not to be sacrificed on the public arena's altar of reasonably disputable means. Doing otherwise exposes the church's kerygmatic mission as prey to partisan ideology.

Balasuriya's naivete in urging the clergy to direct political action is further underscored when we consider that promoting justice within the complex organization of modern society will involve conflicts among rights. When a person's *prima facie* rights collide with those of others, the result is often aggressive tension and angry impasse. These can be transcended only by the voluntary "resignation of rights [and] normally justified claims."[68] If, as Balasuriya argues, love demands justice, it is equally necessary that justice defer to self-sacrificing love if social communion is to obtain.[69] Long aware that justice needs to be enfolded in love, the church realizes that a justice unyielding to love can never bring about secular order, much less the fullness of the kingdom of heaven.[70] To love, says Benedict, means not merely to give another his due; it means "to offer what is 'mine.'"[71] For this reason, the humane development of peoples can only obtain by faith-inspired love.[72] In proposing these themes, the Pontiff echoes Paul VI, who in *Progressio Populorum* observes that only true charity motivates people to uncover the sources of misery and to find effective means to combat it.[73] The deep sickness

67. Langan, "Jerusalem," 153, 163.
68. Ibid., 168–69.
69. Ibid., 175, citing Augustine, *On the Morals of the Catholic Church*, esp. chap. 15.
70. Langan, "Jerusalem," 172.
71. Benedict XVI, *Caritas in Veritate*, par. 6.
72. Ibid., par. 9.
73. Paul VI, *Populorum Progressio*, par. 75.

of the world, Paul opines, ensues more from a lack of brotherly solidarity than from problems in the means of production.[74] In Benedict's own Johannine vision, the struggle for justice lodges, therefore, within the pierced side of Christ, the living font of wounded love that serves as the "starting-point" and focus of *Deus Caritas Est* (12).

If for Benedict justice finds its fulfillment and inspiration in faith-infused love, it is because the natural order embodies intractable contradictions. That the ends of justice rarely emerge clearly and univocally offers a sign of nature's opaqueness without grace. In fact, he asserts, again quoting Adorno, that true justice can result "'where not only present suffering would be wiped out, but also that which is irrevocably past would be undone.'"[75] Nature's impotence to resolve this conflict proves a chronic frustration to both reason and will. Other contradictions also confront us. For instance, although we naturally desire happiness as the meaning of life, we find ourselves unable to specify its content. "When we think we can reach out and touch it, it eludes us," Benedict astutely observes.[76] In these quandaries, we share the plight of the Gentiles living during Christianity's origins. The purposes that the learned and cultured sought to give life ultimate meaning were increasingly moribund. Roman religion had degenerated into politics and fossilized into magic. Astrology struggled vainly to penetrate into the providence that governs the cosmos.[77] Death, the final frontier, hung a closed curtain of despair around existence that even the renowned wisdom-seekers of the age lacked the conviction to lift.[78] To them as well as to us, the light of the Gospel's grace opens nature's "dark door of time."[79]

Thus, in a phenomenology reminiscent of Blondel, the Pontiff denies to nature any permanently meaningful ends. Ironically, in the very experience of attaining what he can attain, the human person attains

74. Ibid., pars. 66–67.

75. Theodor W. Adorno, *Negative Dialektik*, third part, III, 11, in *Gesammelte Schriften* VI (Frankfurt-am-Main: Suhrkamp Verlag, 1973), 395; in Benedict XVI, *Spe Salvi*, par. 42.

76. Benedict XVI, *Spe Salvi*, par. 11.

77. Ibid., par. 5.

78. Ibid., par. 6.

79. Ibid., par. 2.

his inadequacy. Justice, happiness, and meaning illusively defy satisfactory incarnation. Benedict's conclusion similarly evokes Blondel. "Only something infinite will suffice for [humanity]," he posits, "something that will always be more than [humanity] can" grasp.[80] Expanding Blondel with Augustine, he adds that our natural plight is so impoverished that, unless in the first instance God stretches our desire, we cannot even yearn for what God alone can satisfy.[81] This seems tantamount to affirming Seckler's interpretation of Thomas: that nature rests in grace's cradle. In the next chapter, we will further develop these implications when we consider Benedict's theology of nature in greater detail.

Conclusions

Our probings into recent papal thought show that John Paul II and Benedict XVI continue to develop the reciprocity of nature and grace laid out in the thinkers discussed in the previous chapter. From different perspectives and topics of concern, both posit nature as grace's sacrament. In other words, they affirm that nature attains its integrity by mediating a graced transcendence. In John Paul, this sacramentality obtains between reason and faith and between human and divine freedom. In Benedict, it obtains between eros and charity and between justice and charity. In presenting their syntheses, both pontiffs manifest similarities with Blondel: John Paul in reason's nostalgic yearning for God; Benedict in nature's darkness about disclosing a proportionately immanent end. In addition, John Paul creatively draws on instrumental causality and personalist metaphysics, whereas Benedict, hearkening to Augustine, enters into dialogue with a range of modern and contemporary sources. It would be stretching the point to claim that either pope decisively rejects the theory of pure nature. Nonetheless, the thought of both shows sufficient congruence with themes running through recent efforts to reunite nature and grace that, combined with

80. Ibid., par. 30.

81. Augustine, *In 1 Joannis* 4.6 (*PL* 35, col. 2008); in Benedict XVI, *Spe Salvi*, par. 33.

their debt to Blondel, they seem to signal a turn away from it. Neither pope, however, can be said to favor de Lubac and Seckler's position over Rahner's.

Furthermore, John Paul emphasizes nature's capabilities, especially reason and freedom. By contrast, Benedict, more in line with Dupré's awareness of the secular's corrosive effects, reminds us of nature's chronic flaw. Original sin vitiates all hope for progress and perfectibility not rooted in Christ. Nonetheless, although important nuances differentiate the pontiffs' views of nature, it seems fair to say that no fundamental disagreement divides them. Together they present a complementary understanding of nature as an ambiguous reality. Ultimately opaque without the grace that sustains and purifies it, nature is yet capable, without explicitly adverting to grace, of finding some meaning and bearing some accountability.

PART 2

DEVELOPING A MODEL

Chapter 4

SACRAMENTAL CAUSALITY

The previous three chapters have selectively probed into the last seven hundred years of nature and grace's relation. Let us take stock of our findings. In the first place, we have seen what blind alleys to avoid. On the one hand, we have concluded that the theory of pure nature, at least as putatively grounded in Thomas, contains two equivocations of the concept of the good. These continue problematically to influence some modern theology, in addition to having contributed to the breakdown of the Baroque synthesis. Perhaps sensitive to this contribution, recent papal thought tends to signal a turn away from pure nature. On the other hand, we have concluded that the supernatural existential as advanced by Rahner is not needed to preserve grace's gratuity. It also runs the risk of positing a misleading end for nature and of undermining nature's theological significance. We are thus led to Seckler's position, inspired by de Lubac and Blondel, as offering us a beginning for healing the troubled marriage of nature and grace.

We have also gleaned other insights that any healing needs to incorporate. An especially important theme runs from Trent, through the Baroque, and into the twentieth century. It concerns nature and grace's reciprocity. The Baroque highlights nature's dynamic relation to the transcendent source that grounds it. Driven by, and oriented to, a supernatural end, nature attains its integrity in, and by mediating, grace. Blondel provides a philosophical foundation for this mediation. John

Paul II uses instrumental causality to explain it. Thus hearkening to both Aquinas and Trent's decree on justification, he posits the unity-in-difference of divine and human freedom. A person's spontaneity fuses with the divine action to cause a common finality, salvation, even while each order retains its distinctiveness. All of these insights drawn from our historical review coalesce, we have argued, around nature and grace's sacramental relation. This relation affirms nature as grace's intrinsic symbol.

Our probings have also brought to light several other aspects of our problem that need developing. Let us state these serially. If the pure nature theory holds little hope for advancing Christianity's dialogue with modernity, then we need to put forth a model that does. If Thomas's position contains equivocations, then we need to work out an analogy between nature and grace. If the gratuity of grace is to be firmly grounded, then a deeper consideration of creation and redemption as a continuum is needed. If nature is to retain its significance, then a broader elaboration of its theology, such as recent papal thought adumbrates, is required.

Based on these findings, our book's first part, "Probing the Problem," leads us to conclude that the way forward entails three immediate tasks: assessing how Seckler's position addresses modernity; discussing how his position advances a sacramental model of nature and grace; and expanding this model by incorporating into it the remaining aspects of the problem. As just mentioned, these include the analogy of nature and grace, the continuum of creation and redemption, and the theology of nature. Once this chapter completes these tasks, subsequent chapters will be able to use the results to explore other theological issues.

Let us begin by examining modernity more carefully. This topic has been previously broached: first in chapter 1, when we sought the origins of the pure nature theory; and then in chapter 3, when we studied *Fides et Ratio* in light of the secularization that confronts the modern religious believer. Now we will more systematically isolate modernity's defining characteristics.

Modernity

In seeking a working definition of this problem, two main strains of analysis present themselves.[1] The first finds clear expression in Nietzsche, who views the modern project as homogeneously developing from the Socratic origins of mind in the West. Also found in Heidegger, Derrida, and Rorty, it avers that any solution to modern problems must entail a radical reworking of the roots of thought and culture.[2] By contrast, the second strain, found in Hans Blumenberg, Eric Voegelin, Alasdair MacIntyre, and Charles Taylor, sees modernity as resulting from the disintegration of a homogeneity that can be resynthesized.[3] Following this strain, Dupré's nuanced account focuses on a careful diagnosis of modernity's complex causes. It is laudably reticent of offering a critique of a project that it considers unfinished.[4]

Dupré argues that modernity is caused by a realignment of three components that constitute the origins of the West's ontotheological synthesis: the noetic human subject as the interpreter of reality, the extra-subjective cosmos, and the transcendent source of both. A crucial shift occurred when fourteenth-century humanists like Dante and Petrarch articulated what has come to be validated as modernity's defining principle: "Mind stands in a creative relation to that physical reality on which it in other respects depends."[5] Until this time, the intelligibility of the objective world, crystallized in the notion of form, had assumed priority over the human knower.[6] Transcendence, whether understood as the infinite good, the prime mover, or a personal God obtained either in an immediate or a causally necessary relation to the objective forms of the world received by the subject. Aesthetics well reflects the influence of this shift. Mere mimesis gives way to a view expressed by Lessing. It may well be, he says, that ours represents the

1. This sentence begins a section previously published within Stephen M. Fields, "*Ressourcement* and the Retrieval of Thomism for the Contemporary World," in *Ressourcement*, ed. Flynn and Murray, 355–71, at 358–60.

2. Dupré, *Passage to Modernity*, 5.

3. Ibid.

4. Ibid., 5–6.

5. Ibid., 249–50, 252.

6. Ibid., 18.

best of all possible worlds, as Leibniz claims, but this is hardly apparent. The world's ultimate opaqueness, Lessing continues, establishes a distinctive role for art. Its products can create small worlds more perfect than the incoherent fragments of the universe that we experience. Human creativity thus adds a surplus to the broken reality that otherwise confronts our minds.[7]

Flowering from the branch of fourteenth-century humanism, the Baroque emerges as modernity's paradigm. As we have seen, it posits humanity as a microcosm who can fashion a macrocosm of symbolic meaning. Human freedom lodges in the core of this fashioning. Functioning in tandem with a God-enlightened reason and imagination, the creative spontaneity of the human person becomes more than a mere metaphor of the divine artisan. It establishes an ontological analogy. Integral in its own right, human freedom bursts forth into a myriad of moral, social, and aesthetic productivity. This obtains, however, precisely because it is derived from the transcendence that it represents.

Yet an irony ensues from the aggressive assertion of the prerogatives of subjective ingenuity over mind's more passive assimilation of the objective cosmos. As we argued in chapter 1, mind's growing detachment from representation leads to the progressive silencing of language. Allegory, severed from religion, descends into mere myth, even as metaphor and imagery are rendered into fetishes. Concomitantly, a new view of skepticism is introduced. It becomes, as Newman regrettably opines, not an aberration, but lauded as the healthy development of human reason.[8] Thus d'Holbach, placing God in the eighteenth-century dock, could utter a belief echoed with little emendation by today's popular pundits: "To discover the true principles of morality, men have no need of theology, of revelation, or of gods.... They have only to commune with themselves, to reflect upon their own natures."[9]

7. Maurice Marache, *Le symbole dans la pensée et l'oeuvre de Goethe* (Paris: A. G. Nizet Editeur, 1960), 26.

8. Newman, *Apologia*, 336.

9. Paul, Baron d'Holbach, *Common Sense: or Natural Ideas Opposed to Supernatural* (New York: n.p., 1795), 8–9; originally *Le bon sens: ou idées naturelles opposées aux idées surnaturelles* (Amsterdam: n.p., 1772). See Sam Harris, *The End of Faith: Religion, Terror, and the*

Skepticism has been broadened and reinforced, moreover, by modern developments in empirical science that highlight nature's spontaneous capacity for emergent novelty. These have further strained the credibility of form as the stable link between transcendence and the knowing subject.[10]

For its part, secularization, a more recent trait of post-Baroque modernity, rolls forth in skepticism's momentum. It entails not merely doubt about the mind's religious attitude but the loss of it. Stunted, the mind's innate drive now restricts the raising of those questions that could impel it toward its transcendent term. Accordingly, the profane is sacrificed along with the sacred. Secularization thus emerges only in a world that subordinates form to individual genius. As we have seen, as the human subject withdraws centripetally, cosmic causes, both finite and infinite, retreat centrifugally, resulting in a suicide of symbolic meaning. By this route, modernity descends into the nihilism necessarily attendant on self-extinction. Without an intelligible center that purportedly lacks any possibility of being found, modernity, according to Lyotard, founders on a universal "fission of mission."[11] Yet even such self-styled "postmodernism,"' contends Dupré, constitutes but a moment within what is rightly still the modern. It remains dependent on subjectivity.[12] We will probe postmodernism more deeply in a subsequent chapter. For the moment, however, it seems safe to conclude that modernity, as still evolving, has yet to establish a final synthesis among the attenuated elements that make it up.[13]

Dupré is surely right to diagnose modernity's distinctiveness in the dichotomized triumph of human creativity over the subject's merely

---

Future of Reason (New York: W. W. Norton, 2004), chaps. 1–2; Richard Dawkins, *The God Delusion* (New York: Bantham Press, 2006), chaps. 5–9; Christopher Hitchens, *God Is Not Great: How Religion Poisons Everything* (New York: Atlantic Books, 2007), chaps. 13, 15–16.

10. Dupré, *Passage*, 250.

11. Kenneth L. Schmitz, "An Addendum to Further Discussion," *American Catholic Philosophical Quarterly* 73 (Spring 1999): 277–90, at 280; Jean-François Lyotard, "The Sign of History," in *The Lyotard Reader*, ed. Andrew Benjamin (Oxford: Basil Blackwell, 1989), 393–411, at 409–10.

12. Dupré, *Passage*, 250.

13. Ibid., 252.

mimetic response to its intuition of worldly form. If any quarrel arises with him, however, it concerns where to locate the roots of this distinctiveness. For their part, the fourteenth-century humanists who clearly embody it inherited a world in which subject and transcendence had already become significantly disjoined. Previously set in motion, this attenuation allowed the stridency of mind, freer from countervailing resistance, to become emboldened. For this reason, the origins of modernity are to be found squarely in the West's recovery of the agent intellect that eventually rendered Augustinian illumination redundant. As we have seen, this recovery put the post-Nicene Platonic synthesis of nature and grace in its coffin, even as Bonaventure endeavored to breathe fresh vigor into it. It simply could not survive Aquinas. The Aristotelian revival therefore constitutes a crucial pivot in the West's development. It caused a decisive break with the previous millennium while constituting the condition for the possibility of modernity. We currently tread the water of its wake.

Seckler and Modernity

Let us now look again at Seckler's position in order to assess its ability to address the modern problem.[14] In the first place, we have seen that central to modernity is the premium it places on the spontaneous creativity of the human person. This is precisely Seckler's point of departure. It focuses on the instinct of faith, the divine impulse that prompts us to believe. Seckler locates this in the "cradle" of nature as an anthropological *a priori*.[15] As the fecund source of intellection and volition, the instinct generates a range of psychological phenomena, such as wonder and questioning, the seed beds of novelty (52). The instinct in Thomas, says Seckler, grounds human religiosity (53). It intrinsically links divine

14. This sentence begins a section previously published within Stephen M. Fields, "*Ressourcement* and the Retrieval of Thomism for the Contemporary World," in *Ressourcement*, ed. Flynn and Murray, 355–71, from 364–67.

15. Max Seckler, *Instinkt und Glaubenswille nach Thomas von Aquin* (Mainz: Matthias-Grünewald-Verlag, 1961), as discussed by Edward Schillebeeckx in his *Revelation and Theology*, 2:30–75, at 53. Schillebeeckx is cited in the text.

and human creativity, such that human freedom, even while contingent upon divine freedom, retains its own integrity.

This link between human and divine that Seckler finds in Thomas is doubly justified. On the one hand, the instinct lodges within the divine continuum of creation and redemption. This integral act ensues from God's primordial decision. While historically extroverted, this decision is made in free love from all eternity. The instinct harnesses the emanation of creation to its redemptive return. As such, the instinct discloses nature to be a redemptive vocation that awaits a fulfillment that cannot be deduced. On the other hand, the instinct does not compromise human freedom. Just as no necessity obtains in revelation's being given, so none obtains in its being accepted. Free human choice can either fulfill the instinct by accepting Christ as the supreme value, or it can seek satisfaction in a host of secondary goods (or evils). The acceptance of revelation becomes the highest act of creativity that the human person can effect. Intellection and volition become moments within the circumincession of nature's *a priori* and the free response of the person to grace perceived as a value. Freedom thus binds the *a priori* and the response into an aesthetic whole. It establishes a new synthesis that bears the marks of the Angelic Doctor's definition of beauty: the intrinsic symmetry and harmony of form that structure the possession of truth and goodness (see *ST* I, q. 39, a. 8; II-II, q. 142, a. 2). In the wedding of divine and human freedom, grace perfects the form of human nature that it has, from the outset, prepared to be perfected.

The link established by Seckler's anthropology between divine and human freedom is fused by understanding grace itself as an analogy. Reaffirming Thomas, Seckler claims that "one and the same grace both calls and justifies" (52, citing *ST* I-II, q. 113, a. 8, ad 2). It therefore follows that prevenient and sanctifying grace are integrally distinct, not equivocally disjoined. Whereas only sanctifying grace justifies, still prevenient grace is oriented to sanctifying grace as its proper end, goal, and perfection. Commingled with nature, prevenient grace embraces human freedom even as freedom embraces grace. Furthermore, if grace is analogous, then nature must be analogous. As the subject of prevenient and sanctifying grace, nature serves as the substratum of grace's analogy. Moreover, it follows that nature and grace, as such, must be analogous. Both originate in the Logos, who is the selfsame source of their similarity and distinction. Echoing the prologue of John's Gospel, for instance, Irenaeus of Lyons says that the Word, through whom all things come to be, "in an invisible manner contains all things created, and is inherent in the entire creation." As Word, he "governs and arranges all things." As incarnate, the Word recapitulates or "sum[s] up in Himself all things" in heaven and on earth.[16] Created, presided over, and incarnated by the Logos, nature cannot be absolutely alien to the life of grace. The Word refashions from within what he himself primordially fashioned and conservingly guides.

The fundamental difference between nature and grace turns on nature's radical otherness to God.[17] Nature is finite, contingent, dependent on time and space, and historical. On this account, the Council of Nicaea posits no intermediary between divinity and creation except God's intelligent freedom. Brought forth *ex nihilo,* nature possesses no entitlement, of itself, to the life of grace.[18] Hence, as Seckler observes, a formal distinction obtains between the natural desire for God and the instinct of faith, even though they are materially the same (58). Although formally distinct, they nonetheless possess the same supernatural object. This claim entails no contradiction. As Blondel shows, a purely philosophical analysis of the natural desire warrants humanity's supernatural end, however impotent philosophy finds itself in further trying to specify it. From its perspective, theology can assert that the natural desire is an instinct for the faith that reveals the beatific vision as the person's end. Preveniently graced from the outset, nature has been rendered capable of being sanctified and justified in the continuum that embraces both creation and redemption.

Accordingly, human freedom can be seen as oriented toward its single supernatural end. Limited by finitude and flawed by sin, na-

16. Irenaeus, *Against the Heresies,* 546–48.
17. See Balthasar, *Theology of Karl Barth,* 267.
18. See Louth, *Origins of the Christian Mystical Tradition,* 75–77.

ture nonetheless implicitly participates in grace from the beginning. Precisely where, in the existential and psychological order, nature becomes an instrumental cause of grace capable of effecting humanity's final end can never be specified. Trent's decree on justification squarely refuses to do so. Despite its problems, so rightly does the supernatural existential. "Our actual nature is *never* 'pure' nature," claims Rahner.[19] "No slice of 'pure nature' exists in this world," echoes Balthasar.[20] One may just as well ask where in the waters of baptism the physical cleansing ends and the spiritual character begins. As our previous discussions have shown, the instrumental cause does not forfeit its formal power of the instrument when it becomes an instrumental power. Nor, then, does human freedom.

In sum, Seckler addresses the modern problem by developing a sacramental model of nature and grace. As grace's intrinsic symbol, nature gives grace a medium for its action. For its part, the instinct of faith, the meeting point of the two orders, posits in value a cause for the dynamic release of the human subject's existential potential. Where freedom flourishes, there results the spontaneity of human action in history, whose novelty cannot be anticipated or predicted. The wedding of human and divine freedom obtains through instrumental causality; it explains nature's creativity, even as it respects nature's distinctiveness. In thus linking humanity's pursuit of value to the God of grace, Seckler fuses into a harmony two of modernity's estranged elements: the subject who can fashion the cosmos and the transcendence that constitutes finite action's source and goal. By orienting the person to a single supernatural end that alone can consummate action, Seckler squarely lodges nature within the graced order. Nevertheless, because he understands this lodging analogically, the two orders are appropriately differentiated within their unity.

Seckler thus speaks a prophecy for the future based on his retrieval of the Thomist past. Mind's strivings originate in the religious vocation of its nature and they yearn for fulfillment in a historical value that only

19. Karl Rahner, "Nature and Grace," in *TI* 4:165–88, at 183.
20. Balthasar, *Theology of Karl Barth*, 288.

transcendence can gratuitously effect. Now situated in a paradox of its own making, modernity's confident creativity is heading full-throttle into solipsism. Accordingly, it risks foundering on the shoals of skepticism, secularism, and nihilism. If this consequence is to be avoided and modernity realigned with anything akin to its Baroque paradigm, then first and foremost mind must accurately assess itself. Subsequent chapters will contribute to such an assessment, as well as consider what, according to Dupré, constitutes the third of modernity's estranged elements: the extra-subjective cosmos. For our present purposes, however, the remainder of this chapter will further develop the sacramental model that Seckler is helping us to fashion.

Creation and Redemption

We have seen that Seckler understands the instinct of faith as the meeting point of nature and grace. These orders, although distinct, form a unity in God's primordial decision. Because grace calls nature to faith and justifies nature in faith, the instinct can be defined as a tendency of the human spirit that, as a grace inviting us to believe, initiates the entire act of faith. The single end of the human spirit, the beatific vision pledged in Christ, is thus anticipated in creation. As a promise of sanctifying grace, the instinct harnesses the emanation of creation from God to its redemptive return in God. The thesis that creation and redemption constitute a continuous and reciprocal divine action is crucial to Seckler's position. It grounds both the gratuity of grace and nature's finite otherness to God. In other words, if God is infinitely good and infinitely self-present, then his free intention to create, foreseeing the Fall, includes the free intention to redeem. As a result, the single supernatural orientation of the human person entails no compromise of the divine freedom or sovereignty over nature. Because of the importance of this thesis, a fuller development of it is needed. We will tackle this task by drawing on Rahner's metaphysics of the *Realsymbol*. This was briefly mentioned in chapter 2. Now we will explain it more fully and then mine it for profit.

By the *Realsymbol*, Rahner means that all modes of being necessarily express themselves in order to constitute their own essence or nature.[21] This self-expression is structured by the movement of emanation and return.[22] It means that being posits itself in its own "other." This other thereby becomes being's own mediating vehicle in and through which being signifies itself. Through this signification, being constitutes itself as a concrete reality.[23] But being is not realized until it returns through its self-signifying other to itself. This return brings being to the perfection and consummation of its essence (234). The emanation and return that constitute being entail a dynamic, intrinsic, and reciprocal causality. It is dynamic because being emanates its own other and returns through it. It is intrinsic because being causes its own unity by causing its own other. It is reciprocal because being constitutes itself only by returning through its self-caused other. The dynamic, intrinsic, and reciprocal causality of emanation and return means that all beings consist of three aspects: an original unity, a medium or an other, and a perfected unity (229). These are best explained by showing how Rahner interprets a doctrine of realist metaphysics called hylomorphism, which defines all finite substances as matter structured by form.

All too often, according to Rahner, the relation of form to matter has been viewed in terms of efficient causality. This view contends that form works on matter from the outside, externally as it were, in order to bring about in matter an effect alien to it. For Rahner, this view fails to understand the dynamically unified nature of beings. Form is emanated in matter, thereby giving "itself away" to matter (231). Form and matter must be understood as ontologically congenial: they constitute an original unity as the source of their difference. Because this unity obtains prior to matter's being informed, form and matter constitute

21. Karl Rahner, "Theology of the Symbol," *TI* 4:221–52, at 224. Cited in the text.

22. These terms, familiar from their use in Neoplatonic philosophy, are translations of *erfliessen* and *ausgehen* and of *reditio completa in seipsum*, a Thomist adage that Rahner uses to explain the *Realsymbol*. See "Theology of the Symbol," 229, 233, and "Zur Theologie des Symbols," in vol. 4 of *Schriften zur Theologie* (Einsiedeln: Benzinger, 1960), 275–312, at 284, 288.

23. Rahner, *Foundations of Christian Faith*, 120–22.

a unity-in-difference as the condition for the possibility of any being. This unity-in-difference is abstract: it is yet to be concretely realized as an individually existing substance. This realization obtains when form structures matter, thus constituting matter as its own other by giving matter meaning and intelligibility. Because matter incarnates form, it manifests and reveals form in and through itself. The emanation of form in matter is insufficient, however, to cause the perfected realization of a substance. According to Rahner, form must return to itself through its material emanation in order to render any substance a concrete entity (231–32). This return is necessary since, as a dynamic principle, form is not complete until it is united with itself after its emanation. This return completes a finite substance that, as a *Realsymbol*, intrinsically manifests the intelligibility of its form (231).

Because a being is *Realsymbolic* in its hylomorphism, Rahner contends that it posits its medium primarily for a being to become realized. The medium exists only secondarily so that others can know the being (225). Precisely because a being's appearance in its medium is intrinsically related to its reality, the mediation of matter in a being is not an obstacle to the immediate revelation of a being's inner reality. This "mediation of immediacy" means that the substance's reality is grasped precisely in and through its material medium, which incarnates and expresses the substance's formal intelligibility (244).[24]

As an illustration of a *Realsymbol*, Rahner cites the human person as a hylomorphic unity of body and soul. The body should not be conceived, he claims, as ontologically pre-existing the soul. Nor should the soul be conceived as the body's efficient cause that imposes itself on the body, thus animating it and rendering the person a substance. Although the body constitutes the matter, the substrate, in which the soul dynamically expresses itself, it is the soul that, emanated in the body, informs it, thus constituting the person as a spirit-in-the-world. As a synthesis of spirit and matter, humanity is essentially an ambivalent substance, capable of rendering intelligible a world of sensible

24. See also ibid., 83–84.

forms even while intrinsically conditioned by them.[25] The person is able to think, to will, imagine, and feel only because the soul is mediated to itself in and through the body (232–33). As a *Realsymbol,* the person achieves perfection only through the body, with which the soul enjoys an ontological affinity (246–47).

Rahner uses the *Realsymbol* to explain the relation between creation and redemption, nature and grace. As we have seen, being is structured by an original unity that emanates itself into its own other, through which it returns to render itself a perfected unity. Accordingly, creation and redemption constitute a unity-in-difference that originates in God's primordial "absolute decision." In other words, they are the object of his "unconditioned and all-powerful" will.[26] From within the divine freedom, the order of redemption exercises a certain priority over creation, analogous to that exercised by form over matter. Just as de Lubac affirms that grace calls into being spiritual creatures to receive it, so for Rahner God's free choice to redeem emanates the created order, which consequently inheres in the redeemed order. Because the Word of God has become an incarnate creature, nature belongs to grace as its presupposition. It is distinct from redemption, even as matter, in its unity with form, retains its distinctness. Moreover, just as the soul infuses the body with intelligent meaning, so grace charges nature with its life. Nature might thus be termed grace's own other, which redemption fashions for itself in order, by means of it, to become itself. Grace becomes itself when it realizes its end, which is effecting its saving action precisely in history. The beatific vision pledged by the incarnation consummates creation. Grace returns history, together with itself, to God from whom both come (*CC,* 49). As fallen, nature is not *ipso facto* justified; but it is oriented to justification. Sin, however calamitous, cannot triumph over the primordial unity of nature and grace in the infinite goodness of God's freedom.

25. Rahner, *Spirit in the World,* 406–7.

26. Karl Rahner, *The Christian Commitment: Essays in Pastoral Theology* [hereafter "CC"], trans. Cecily Hastings (New York: Sheed and Ward, 1963), 53. Cited in the text.

Yet for Rahner the relation between creation and redemption needs further to be nuanced. If the redemption exercises a priority over creation, it is equally true that creation exercises a certain priority over the redemption. In becoming flesh, the Word of God performs the highest act of the creation that, only through him, can come into being (*CC*, 49). Precisely because in the incarnation creation reaches its perfection, grace could be said to subsist in nature, penetrating it and incorporating all its abiding differentiations into Christ (*CC*, 39). The incarnation brings everything that exists externally to God within God, who has emptied himself into what, from nothing, he has emanated as other. As a result, the created order becomes charged with a gratuitous supernatural finality (*CC*, 49). Gerard Manley Hopkins captures this finality in his poem "As Kingfishers Catch Fire":

> Christ plays in ten thousand places,
> Lovely in limbs, and lovely in eyes not his
> To the Father through the features of men's faces.[27]

These lines reiterate how the communication of idioms discussed in chapter 1 obtains between nature and grace. What pertains to humanity belongs equally to God in Christ, and vice versa. Because creation and redemption signify each other, reciprocal predications are allowed between them, so long as God's sovereign freedom over creation is affirmed through the qualifications that we have made throughout our considerations.

The *Realsymbol* advances our understanding of the sacramental relation between nature and grace. Up to this point, our reflections have shown that this relation centers on nature as grace's intrinsic symbol. At the heart of this symbolism, instrumental causality explains how human freedom does not lose its integrity when it becomes an intrinsic medium of grace. Trent, for instance, shows us that, with the person's free consent, baptism harmoniously brings nature to a justified finality. Similarly, John Paul II shows us how the eucharist effects the

27. Gerard Manley Hopkins, *The Poetical Works of Gerard Manley Hopkins*, ed. Norman H. Mackenzie (Oxford: Clarendon Press, 1992), 141.

freedom that it signifies. When this sacrament is received, the person joins his own will with the freedom of Christ, whose loving sacrifice constitutes the heart of the eucharist. Furthermore, Seckler, in rejecting the theory of pure nature, demonstrates, along with de Lubac, Rahner, and Balthasar, the impossibility of specifying precisely where nature and grace existentially meet in realizing their common end. The important point shared by all these sources underscores that human freedom, as the power of the instrument, never loses its natural capabilities when grace confers on it an instrumental power.

The *Realsymbol*, for its part, subsumes instrumental causality into a broader context. Because nature and grace constitute a unity-in-difference, the redemption is mediated immediately in creation, and vice versa. Hence, the union of the two orders is grounded in three continuous moments: in God as their common emanation; in their mutual mediation in history; and in their return to God as their finality. These moments mean that the *Realsymbolic* structure of nature and grace obviates the theory of pure nature. Both orders share a primordially divine origin, and neither can obtain in history without the other. By contrast, instrumental causality can only account for nature's mediation of grace as both orders strive toward a common finality. It does not ground the orders as a unity-in-difference in God as their common source of emanation. Nor does it account for their mutual mediation. The *Realsymbol* thus provides a metaphysics better suited to nature and grace's sacramentality than instrumental causality. It is no wonder that Rahner replaces it with the *Realsymbol* in explaining efficacious causation.

The *Realsymbol* also incorporates the relation between prevenient and sanctifying grace into the sacramental model. Our previous discussions have shown the need for the relation between these twin graces to be conceived analogically. For instance, neither Thomas (according to Bouillard) nor Trent works out how the prevenient grace that grounds a person's movement toward baptism participates, however indirectly, in the habitual grace that causes justification.[28] Trent sug-

28. Bouillard, *Conversion*, esp. 211–19.

gests that this participation does obtain, declaring that prevenient grace effects in the person a preparation ordered to baptism. In baptism of desire, this preparation must be able to blossom into sanctifying grace without the ritual water, although specifying where, when, and how is not possible. For his part, Seckler reminds us that in Thomas one and the same grace both calls and justifies. As a result, because grace perfects the human nature that it has, from the outset, prepared to be perfected, prevenient and sanctifying grace must be integrally distinct rather than equivocally disjoined.

Developing an analogical conception of grace begins by understanding sanctifying grace not as an efficient but rather as a formal cause. If sanctifying grace functions efficiently, then it would produce its effect outside of itself; it would not, like a formal cause, take its effect up into itself as the effect's ground.[29] As an efficient cause, sanctifying grace, avers Thomas, produces a habit in the soul of the person. A habit permanently modifies humanity's form; in turn, this modification causes forgiveness, healing, and the person's justifying elevation before God (*UG*, 332). But this conception, claims Rahner, does not do justice to the action of grace in the person's existential depths. If sanctifying grace is precisely God's *self*-communication, then only formal causality adequately expresses this action (*UG*, 330). Sanctifying grace is given from within God's essence as his own very life; it subsumes its effect, the human subject, into itself. Rahner provides some nuance here, calling the causality of sanctifying grace "quasi-formal" (*UG*, 331). This epithet does not minimize grace's divinizing effect, but it does seek to avoid the ontologism that, as in Malebranche, implies an exacted union between human nature and the divine essence.

Let us continue to develop Rahner's line of thought. If sanctifying grace constitutes God's quasi-formal self-communication to nature—and if, as Trent, Bouillard, and Seckler aver, prevenient grace constitutes a disposition for sanctifying grace—then it should follow, as Rahner contends, that the relation between sanctifying and prevenient grace be

29. Karl Rahner, "Some Implications of the Scholastic Concept of Uncreated Grace" [hereafter "*UG*"], *TI* 1:319–46, at 329. Cited in the text.

understood according to the relation between a form and the disposition for it. According to Thomas, this disposition for a form is properly a material cause. Form and matter, as we have seen, constitute a substance in virtue of their unity-in-difference. Neither exists without the other. Hence: if, as Rahner previously argues, the possibility of creation presupposes the gratuitous possibility of the redemption, then it further follows that sanctifying grace presupposes a grace in creation that orders the natural desire for God to God's formal self-communication. In other words, prevenient grace is called forth, so to speak, by sanctifying grace, just as the redemption calls forth the created order to receive it (*UG*, 333). Like creation and redemption, prevenient and sanctifying grace exercise a "reciprocal priority" (*UG*, 341). Sanctifying grace presupposes prevenient grace in which to subsist, even as prevenient grace presupposes sanctifying grace in order to subsist (*UG*, 334). In short, because grace constitutes a unity-in-difference, prevenient and sanctifying grace stand in an analogous relation.

The analogous relation between prevenient and sanctifying grace embraces the three moments that structure the *Realsymbol*. First, grace originates as a unity-in-difference in the emanating will of God. Second, like form and the material cause disposed to it, sanctifying and prevenient grace are reciprocally mediated. Third, the dual action of grace, both prevenient and sanctifying, calls the human person to, and justifies him for, the beatific vision. Grace thus returns human nature to the supernatural end for which it was created.

The *Realsymbol* has served as a tool that allows us to understand the analogous relations between creation and redemption and between prevenient and sanctifying grace. Accordingly, we have seen that nature, aided by prevenient grace, constitutes the material cause disposed toward sanctifying grace as God's quasi-formal self-communication. In light of these insights, we now need to consider more precisely the relation between nature and prevenient grace. For his part, Seckler claims that the natural desire for God and prevenient grace are materially the same. This claim seems defensible if we understand it in terms of the *Realsymbol*'s three structuring moments. We could, for instance, say that prevenient grace and nature constitute a unity-in-difference originating in the primordial freedom of God's will. We could say, furthermore, that they are reciprocally mediated in history. Nature provides the presupposition for prevenient grace, whereas prevenient grace subsumes nature into the action that prepares it for sanctifying grace. As a result, we could also say that this preparation begins the process of returning nature to the beatific destiny for which it is created. If nature and prevenient grace constitute a unity-in-difference, then it follows that they stand in an analogous relation. Their unity ensues from their jointly constituting sanctifying grace's material cause.

The clue to understanding the difference between nature and prevenient grace lies in Seckler's claim that, within their material identity, they are formally distinct. On the one hand, the form of grace is God's self-communication. This begins in prevenient grace precisely as it is ordered to the sanctifying grace that can be received or rejected. On the other hand, the form of human nature, the rational soul, is, unlike grace, finite and contingent. As created from nothing, its radical otherness to God precludes any right to grace. Moreover, as fallen and hence as the locus of sin, nature is unjustified. It can resist the dynamic religious vocation to which it is materially united. The formal distinction between nature and prevenient grace does not prevent them, however, from sharing a common end. If it is grace that calls forth nature, and if the redemption is the highest act of creation, then grace from the outset engenders in nature, even in the midst of its otherness to God and its resistance to grace, a dynamism to glory. This dynamism is made concretely possible when baptism confers sanctifying grace, whether by water or desire. When conferred, God's self-communication informs its material cause, which is the unity-in-difference of nature and prevenient grace.

Before proceeding, let us summarize our conclusions. According to Seckler, Aquinas grounds the natural desire for God, which is the instinct of faith, in a central thesis. The orders of creation and redemption constitute a reciprocal continuum. Rahner's metaphysics of the

Realsymbol supports and develops this thesis. The orders originate as a unity-in-difference in God's absolute freedom. They are reciprocally mediated in history, and together they return humanity to the glory for which it is created. If creation and redemption are conceived as a *Realsymbol*, then the following claims can be made. First, the two orders are sacramental: they cause what they signify. Grace consummates the nature that incarnates it. Second, as a unity-in-difference, the two orders are analogous. Third, the relations between prevenient and sanctifying grace and between prevenient grace and nature are *Realsymbolic*. As a unity-in-difference, each of these relations is analogous. Fourth, sanctifying and prevenient grace achieve in and for nature distinct but intrinsically related purposes. Prevenient grace invites human freedom to the redemption that it can reject; sanctifying grace, with the person's cooperation, renders the life of glory concretely possible. Fifth, prevenient grace and nature constitute the material cause of the sanctifying grace that is God's formal self-communication. Sixth, if grace is analogous, then so is nature in which grace subsists. Seventh, the *Realsymbol* incorporates instrumental causality into a broader synthesis that obviates the theory of pure nature.

In addition to the advantages already discussed, understanding creation and redemption as a *Realsymbol* obviates an anthropomorphism in the Christian doctrine of God. It is implied when the order of grace offered in the redemption is viewed as God's post-creation decision to rectify the catastrophe of the Fall. To understand this advantage better, let us briefly review why understanding creation and redemption as a *Realsymbol* is important. If humanity's dynamism for the life of glory lies in creation as such, then God's gratuity must be spared by avoiding giving creation an exacted claim to the beatific vision. Accordingly, God's eternally free decision to create must be seen as foreseeing the Fall and hence as including within it the intention to redeem. For this reason, creation and redemption constitute a primordial unity-in-difference that is reciprocally mediated in history. As such, the historical events of God's salvific plan do not change God's mind. As the absolute simplicity of being, God is incapable of mutation. Moreover, as we have seen, humanity's single supernatural end, when integrated into the *Realsymbol*'s three structuring moments, can be anticipated in creation without compromising the divine freedom.

The anthropomorphism in the Christian doctrine of God has been encouraged, to some extent, by a misinterpretation of Anselm's satisfaction theory of the redemption. When Christ's saving death is viewed as the cause of God's redeeming action toward humanity rather than as its effect, the divine will is made subject to time and space.[30] Anselm himself avoided this error by distinguishing between the antecedent causality of an act and the consequent necessity of a decision. He clearly avers that, strictly speaking, God cannot be the subject of any necessity antecedent to his acting. God's absolute will is utterly undetermined. Even what is true is true first and foremost because God wills it to be true. Once God acts, however, his acts are necessary, because they are consequent upon God's spontaneous choice.[31] When posited, God's acts are antecedently necessary, because God has decided to posit them. Thus, it follows that every antecedent necessity (that is, a decision to act) entails a consequent necessity (that is, the act); and every consequent necessity implies an antecedent necessity, even though the specific cause of any act cannot be deduced with certainty from it.[32]

From these considerations, Anselm avers that Christ's saving death is consequently necessary because of God's loving freedom. It is surely appropriate for theologians to inquire more specifically into the content of the antecedent necessity that causes this death. For his part, Anselm speculates that God intends the death of his Son to be a sacrifice reconciling the paradox of God's absolute justice and absolute love. But Anselm was fully aware that the results of his inquiry were hypothetical. Others, less subtle, misunderstood his doctrine of necessity. Christ's death came to be seen as the antecedent necessity (his decision to die)

30. Karl Rahner, "Salvation," in *Sacramentum Mundi*, 5:430b.

31. Anselm of Canterbury, *Why God Became Man, and The Virgin Conception and Original Sin*, trans. and ed. Joseph M. Colleran (Albany, N.Y.: Magi Books, 1969), 150.

32. Ibid., 153.

that produced a consequent necessity in God (the satisfaction of infinite justice). Not only does this misunderstanding devolve into anthropomorphism; but it divorces the redemption from the creation, whose highest act it constitutes.

Anselm does not work out a systematic theory of the relation between creation and redemption. But aware of the danger of anthropomorphism, he manifests a keen sensitivity to their intrinsic unity. He grounds this unity in the infinite goodness of God's freedom. From this ground, it follows for Anselm, as for Rahner, that if God has allowed sin in this concrete world, then the incarnation "necessarily took place ... for our redemption" (CC, 49). In other words, because God "freely committed himself to accomplish something good" (that is, the creation), his divine nature required him to persevere "in the same intention." In the redemption, he does nothing more than accomplish "what he undertook to do." Therefore, although God performed his action by an immanent exigency, we should more properly say "that he performed it by that free decision by which he committed himself to it."[33] Accordingly, it follows that creation and redemption are consequent necessities contingent on the antecedent necessity of God's eternal goodness that history cannot alter.

Although understanding creation and redemption as a reciprocal continuum avoids anthropomorphism, it does raise a question. Rahner, for instance, asks: Why does not God's primordial goodness "simply effect forgiveness ... directly at all points of time and space"? Why, in other words, does it come "from a definite historical event, which itself is the 'cause' of forgiveness"?[34] Baldly put, the question concerns whether understanding creation and redemption as a unity-in-difference renders the incarnation (and the paschal mystery that it entails) redundant. In one sense, of course, the incarnation is redundant. Assuming that our redemption, as such, is necessary, given God's infinite goodness in light of the Fall, it is still true that God's choice to effect it through the kenotic self-emptying of his Son can only stupefy us by its wondrous gratuity.

33. Ibid., 152.
34. Rahner, "Salvation," 430b.

We can safely assume that God's simple intention to save a sinful humanity would have sufficed, in and of itself, to produce its justifying effect. But the incarnation is first and foremost an act of the highest love, representing an altruism of unmerited self-sacrifice. By their nature, such acts are utterly fortuitous and nobly heroic; they defy further analysis because they are spontaneous and free. Nonetheless, they provoke in us marvel, awe, and ceaseless gratitude of the deepest kind, as Ignatius Loyola in the *Spiritual Exercises* observes when guiding us through a meditation on the mysteries of our redemption.[35] If such a response is aroused toward any person who lays down his life for his friends, how much more so should it be aroused toward God in the face of humanity's deicide (Jn 15:13). In short, love alone suffices as the answer to our question.

But our previous considerations offer further insights. If the created order of history constitutes the redemption's material cause, then history possesses an innate yearning, propensity, and disposition for a supernatural form that only God's self-communication can satisfy. Blondel shows us that history demands a supernatural complement that it absolutely cannot provide for itself. As Paul avers, history remains "groaning in labor pains" while awaiting its full deliverance (Rom 8:21–22). Because time and space quake in expectation of an unknown messiah, the human person tends toward a supernatural end that, as de Lubac claims, calls nature into being. If therefore our redemption is to obtain, an event that consummates history would constitute its compellingly probable cause. This event, God's gracious self-communication in the Word made flesh, allows us to contemplate God from within himself. Without this communication, history would stay, at best, in something of a limbo: outside the divine, where nature's desire could not happily find surcease. Moreover, if the Logos is the agent of creation, and if creation and redemption constitute an ontological continuum, then the redeeming recapitulation of creation by the Logos is not only appropriate, but antecedently probable. The incarnation must be understood as proleptically anticipated in creation. It seems fitting to identify this

35. Loyola, *Spiritual Exercises*, 101–2.

prolepsis with the prevenient grace that calls all humanity, whether before or after the incarnation's historical occurrence, to baptism, whether by desire or water. This call, a testimony to the intrinsic unity of God's salvific economy, does not make the incarnation redundant any more than love is redundant. Nature's call in grace obtains only because God has freely chosen to effect it through the incarnation.

Nature as Analogous

We have seen that one of the problems arising from the rejection of the theory of pure nature concerns the potential diminishing of nature's theological significance. The supernatural existential, for instance, risks dissipating nature within the one concrete order of grace. Conceiving nature and grace as a *Realsymbol* preserves nature's integrity as grace's intrinsic, sacramental medium. This preservation results from the *Realsymbol*'s analogous understanding of nature. We have already explained one aspect of nature's analogous structure. Nature provides the necessary substratum for both prevenient and sanctifying grace, which are themselves analogous. Nature, therefore, subsists with grace in a continuum of two discrete moments. On the one hand, the instinct of faith represents nature's call to the sanctifying grace that, on the other hand, alone justifies. Because this call can be heeded or rejected, justification is by no means necessary in any human person.

Let us now delve more deeply into nature's analogous structure. As we have seen, nature obtains in a union with grace precisely as a difference. Accordingly, the *Realsymbol* affirms that nature is grace's "own other," called into being so that grace can effect its saving purpose. As grace's own, nature harmoniously functions in tandem with prevenient and sanctifying grace. As grace's other, however, nature possess of itself no claim to grace. On the contrary, it is finite, contingent, dependent on time and space, and fallen. Two important issues need addressing if we are to retain nature's theological significance as grace's necessary medium. The first concerns nature's ability to resist grace. Nature is not merely grace's passive substratum that simply allows grace to seize and use it for its own ends. On the contrary, nature's own exigency can actively impede grace's ends. The second issue concerns the extent to which, despite its concupiscence and sin, nature can be deemed to act for its own good ends. If we assume that no slice of pure nature exists in this world and that therefore nature's origins are charged with grace, must we then assume that whatever good ends nature achieves are due only to grace? If we do, then nature seems to lose the integrity that Trent accords it when the council teaches that grace does not deprive human beings of some responsibility for their salvation. In sum, we need to consider how nature, as the "other" that mediates grace, both resists grace and cooperates with it. We need to consider, in other words, how nature, as distinct from grace, is itself analogous.

Let us begin by developing a clue found in the Gospel of John, so influential, as we have seen, in Benedict XVI's *Deus Caritas Est.* More clearly than any other New Testament writer, John articulates the nuanced tension between realized and future eschatology. His adage, for instance, that "the hour is coming and now is" (Jn 4:23, 5:25) crystallizes the paradox of the Christian life. On the one hand, within the post-resurrection church, true worship is given to God in Jesus, because the hour of the Spirit's indwelling has arrived. On the other hand, Jesus's messiahship is not yet fully realized. Our worship in and of him, although authentic, still but anticipates the consummation of worship in heaven, whose earthly sacrament our worship is.[36]

Accordingly, the Christian must own a dual vocation: to live for Christ *in* this age and *for* the age to come. A disciple cannot feed on the flesh of the Son of Man and become in any way an autonomous prisoner of history.[37] To be sure, the mandate of Holy Thursday must be obeyed: feet must be washed here and now. But for John, the grafting of disciples on to Christ as the living vine gives them a share in the redeemer's ascent through an obedient death to the glory of the

36. C. K. Barrett, *The Gospel According to St. John: An Introduction with Commentary and Notes on the Greek Text* (Philadelphia: Westminster Press, 1978), 68.

37. Ibid., 69–70.

Father.[38] Both given and pledged, this glory inspires Christians in this world "to endure injustice patiently," while yet also working "unceasingly for justice."[39]

The Christian's dual vocation presupposes a nature recalcitrant to the grace with which it is charged. Although nature realizes grace and anticipates its fullness, nature's finitude, contingency, and propensity for evil impose limits on grace's activity. Rahner observes that, even when grace seems to shine through nature, it seems unable "to achieve anything final in the world but seems subject to the world's stronger law" (*CC*, 60). For his part, Pope Benedict reminds us that nature's limits can be sensed most forcibly in humanity's struggle with its innate imperfectability. Grounded in traducianism, this struggle is lodged in the heart of every Christian's life of grace. In the here and now, concupiscence and virtue daily vie for mastery. Until the full fruition of the eschaton, history will ever demand a conversion, a metanoia, a change of heart within individual persons.[40] For this reason, Benedict, as we have seen, remains deeply suspicious of utopian visions of social justice, even those based on universal charity. These offer only mythic delusions for any historical consummation. Whereas justice must finally give way to charity, charity, for its part, "can be realized only in the concrete form of brotherly love."[41] Ever faithful to the principle of subsidiarity, Benedict sees this love's taking shape in pockets of small units of care, compassion, and concern grounded in, and molded by, the eucharist.[42] In short, grace purifies human freedom by plunging it deep into inward conversion.

Purification is central to Benedict's theology of nature. Unless in the first instance humanity accepts God's gracious offer of friendship

38. Ibid., 84.

39. D. Vincent Toomey, "The Mind of Benedict XVI," in *Claremont Review of Books* 4 (Fall 2005): 66–71, at 69.

40. Joseph Ratzinger, *Principles of Catholic Theology: Building Stones for a Fundamental Theology*, trans. Sister Mary Frances McCarthy, SND (San Francisco, Calif.: Ignatius Press, 1987), 51–52.

41. Ibid, 54.

42. Ibid.

to which it is oriented, even the best and most humane of solidarity movements will "succeed only in miring man more deeply in his tragic situation."[43] The path of conversion and "the path that draws [humanity] together [into communion] are [thus] not in conflict; on the contrary, they need and support each other."[44] Grace also purifies the practice of human virtue. Even when acting in accord with ends deemed good by reason, virtue still needs further guidance.[45] Of paramount importance, the justice that grounds the social order needs purifying by love. To be effective, justice must spring from love and lead to love. Furthermore, the prudence that Thomas sees as the regulator of the moral life requires purification.[46] This is supplied by counsel, a gift of the Holy Spirit. For Thomas, counsel inspires an intuitive sense of truth that transcends prudence's skilled ability to assess options for action.[47] As Benedict himself says: "Faith enables reason to do its work more effectively and to see its object more clearly."[48]

Benedict's theology of purification is both dialectical and synthetic. These characteristics mean that the church stands in opposition to the secular order, even as it offers the means of reconciling the tension between them. In developing his thought, the Pontiff outlines a public role for the church as the medium of grace in a world functioning, in the main, without directly adverting to it. Following Ambrose, Benedict believes that the loving transformation of justice obtains in the church. Its redemption of individuals leads in turn to the saving of the wider society.[49] As dialectical, the church gives witness to the divine communion of love that constitutes both the basis for, and

43. Ibid., 53.

44. Ibid., 52.

45. Pope Paul VI, *Humanae Vitae*, Encyclical Letter, July 25, 1968, par. 40; all English translations are drawn from www.vatican.va.

46. Pieper, *Four Cardinal Virtues*, 7–8.

47. Anselm Stolz, *The Doctrine of Spiritual Perfection*, trans. Aidan Williams (New York: Crossroad, 2001), 187, expounding Aquinas, *ST* I-II, q. 52, a. 2 and q. 68, a. 2.

48. Pope Benedict XVI, "*Deus Caritas Est*," Encyclical Letter, December 25, 2005, par. 28; all English translations are drawn from www.vatican.va.

49. John P. Langan, "What Athens Says to Jerusalem," in *The Faith That Does Justice*, ed. Haughey, 152–80, at 160.

the finality of, the secular order's promotion of justice.[50] Without the church's eschatological prophecy, the ensuing "loss of transcendence" will evoke, according to Benedict, the flight into fanciful ideology.[51] As synthetic, the church draws the prudence of worldly consciences into its own vision. It encourages them to a self-sacrifice that transcends justice. Consequently, the church is able to implicate the secular order in its own mission, even while respecting the secular's appropriate sphere of influence. Benedict is thus aware that an outright divorce between church and state would compromise the harmony between nature and grace. But the church's public role does not consist in direct political involvement. It consists in robust preaching and educating.[52] These evangelical activities change the hearts that in turn can launch Christianity's assault on unjust social structures.

Benedict's dialectical and synthetic understanding of the relation between church and state hearkens to Augustine's *City of God*. Here the church embodies the divine city as its sacramental image placed squarely in the midst of the secular city marred by traducianism. [53] The church stands as an uncompromising alternative to an alien and hostile world and as a refuge from it.[54] Nonetheless, Augustine envisages a salutary traffic between nature and grace. Members of the human city, despite their sin, can occupy positions in the church and rightly order it. Conversely, sanctified members of the church can perform the same function in the human city.[55]

Similarly, for Benedict, the relics of original sin are ubiquitous, strewn even throughout the church, which nonetheless offers the means of conversion. Converted people, justified before God and availing themselves directly of the means of grace, can strengthen the vestigial

50. David L. Schindler, "Charity, Justice, and the Church's Activity in the World," *Communio: International Catholic Review* 33 (Fall 2006): 346–76, at 360.

51. Toomey, "Mind," 69.

52. Ibid., 71.

53. Augustine, *City of God*, especially book 19.

54. R. A. Markus, *Saeculum: History and Society in the Thought of St Augustine* (Cambridge: Cambridge University Press, 1970), 106.

55. Herbert Deane, *The Political and Social Ideas of St. Augustine* (New York: Columbia University Press, 1963), 31.

presence of God in the worldly city. But ultimate love lodges in the church as the representation of the heavenly city, whose fullness we yet await. Following de Lubac's seminal work that Vatican II incorporates, Benedict posits the church as the prime sacrament that vivifies the seven sacraments as channels of the grace that leads to glory.[56] Individuals fortified by it are thus able to elicit the secular city's virtue, leading it ever more to approach the sanctification mediated in the church.

In sum, in situating nature squarely within the Johannine tension between realized and future eschatology, Benedict constructs an analogous view that gives nature a dynamic adaptability. Here and now, even in this world of realized eschatology, nature asserts the independent muscularity of its otherness to grace. Nature's traducianism and recalcitrant imperfectability ground its struggling enmity to grace. Capable of spurning grace outright, nature means that "the world [will] hate you [even as] it has hated me" (Jn 15:18). Yet nature is innately capable of being purified by grace. It thus clearly manifests a potential for improvement under grace's influence. In its positive openness to grace, we also sense nature's otherness to grace. In it we can discern nature's willing capacity to cooperate with the grace that harnesses it for transcendent ends. Rahner claims that nature, pure and devoid of grace, is merely "guilt-laden … closed, to its own undoing, against grace" (CC, 51). This claim, Benedict shows us, is only partially true. As analogous, "pure" nature, if never actually found without grace, is, as such, both closed to grace and open to it. It is not merely the locus of sin, but the ground of some personal responsibility for salvation.

Benedict develops a further aspect of nature's analogous structure. Because grace purifies the practice of human virtue, Benedict implies that nature can function according to ends that are good in themselves. Nature consists of more than a passively free openness to grace. If we are to hold this thesis, however, and at the same time reject the theory of pure nature, then we must make a crucial distinction. To claim that nature operates for its own good ends does not thereby deny that these

56. Ratzinger, *Principles*, 47, citing de Lubac, *Catholicisme*, 50–51; and Vatican Council II, *Lumen Gentium*, pars. 7, 48.

ends can obtain only under grace's influence. As we saw previously, Thomas affirms that human persons are capable of the good of utility. This results from works pursued according to ends deemed rightly appropriate by reason without any necessary advertence to faith. If these works are done outside of baptism's sanctifying grace, they are not meritorious of salvation. But this claim does not rule out that these works are done under the influence of the prevenient grace that subsists with nature as a primordial unity-in-difference. We have already discussed at some length how natural ends and graced ends can collaborate even as the integrity of both is respected. The human liver, for instance, functions according to ends specific to it; but these ends are achieved precisely because the soul informs the body. Without the soul as its formal cause, the liver, as a material cause, will cease to realize its ends. Similarly, under the influence of prevenient grace, the entire created order can achieve good ends that are nonetheless intrinsic to it. When such works are blessed by the sanctifying grace to which prevenient grace is ordered, they become salvifically meritorious.

Even when nature is incorporated into the kingdom of God by the church's sanctifying mediation, nature, according to Benedict, requires further growth and development. While yearning for the fullness of its future transcendence, nature expands under the influence of the moral virtues and gifts of the Spirit. Accordingly, as we have seen, the promotion of justice remains inseparable from the prudence that can dilate into counsel. Just so, justice must spring from love and lead to love. In its unity with grace, both prevenient and sanctifying, nature exhibits a plasticity. Under grace, it grows toward its consummation; under the riddling influence of sin and its stubbornly corrosive effects, it retreats into willful closure. Benedict shows us that the exigency of nature is to be discerned in the analogous tension of its struggle with the grace that supports it and calls it to perfection. Whereas grace is dialectically "other" to nature, this is not the "wholly" other of Barth that crushes nature. On the contrary, nature's otherness to grace exists so that grace, in respecting nature's subsistence, can more thoroughly synthesize it with divinity.

We have seen that Benedict, in laying out an analogous understanding of nature, frames a theory of the church's relation to the state. Let us continue to develop this relation by now examining the thought of the twentieth-century American Jesuit theologian John Courtney Murray. Like the Pontiff, he demonstrates the consequences that ensue when nature's ability to act for its own intrinsic ends is compromised.

According to Murray, the church, in purifying the state, guides its "processes and structures" toward "their inherently secular ends."[57] The church, he claims, "does not aim to alter the finality of the state, but to enable the state to achieve its own finality as determined by its own nature."[58] Sentiments such as these, which underscore nature's having an intrinsic end, encourage one commentator to diagnose "Gelasian dualism" in Murray.[59] David L. Schindler critically elaborates on what he assesses as the deleterious consequences of this dualism. On the one hand, Murray's Thomism would acknowledge that all human acts are grounded in God.[60] On the other hand, Murray posits that the state should remain neutral toward religion. Neutrality toward God, Schindler claims, is a far cry from positive openness to God. Mere neutrality leads inevitably to a society indifferent to the transcendent. Such indifference devolves all too easily into the privatization of religion. This, in turn, falls quickly into secularism.[61] Consequently, not only does "Murray's position ... not provide any principled protection

57. John Courtney Murray, "The Declaration on Religious Freedom," in *Concilium* 15 (New York: Paulist Press, 1966): 3–16, at 10; in David L. Schindler, "Religious Freedom, Truth, and American Liberalism: Another Look at John Courtney Murray," *Communio: International Catholic Review* 21, no. 4 (Winter 1994): 696–741, at 731.

58. John Courtney Murray, "Government Repression of Heresy," in *Proceedings of the Catholic Theological Society of America* (1948): 26–98, at 65–66; in Schindler, "Religious Freedom," 731.

59. J. Leon Hooper, "General Introduction," in *Religious Liberty: Catholic Struggles with Pluralism/John Courtney Murray*, ed. J. Leon Hooper (Louisville, Ky.: Westminster John Knox Press, 1993), 11–48, at 25; in Schindler, "Religious Freedom," 730.

60. Schindler, "Religious Freedom," 721.

61. Ibid., 718.

against ... atheism," but "it provides an exact theoretical foundation for" it.[62] Murray thus effectively joins Puritanism and Deism in their sympathy for American secularism. All of them together share "a conception of God as first distant and hence separate from the world."[63]

In responding to these criticisms, let us first assess what Murray means by "the ends of the state." Surely it cannot be denied that the state operates according to goals really intrinsic to it. These include, as the preamble to the U.S. Constitution specifies, forming a more perfect union, establishing justice, insuring domestic tranquility, providing for the common defense, promoting the general welfare, and securing the blessings of liberty. The state's ends are achieved successively, individually, and discretely. Civic processes come to completion in the midst of other processes that are still striving toward their purpose. That the state operates for its own intrinsic teleology does not therefore compromise the simultaneous action of history's one supernatural finality in Christ. The state's functions, as Blondel has shown us, even were their entire manifold ultimately able to be accomplished, could never give history a lasting surcease. Moreover, as we have also seen, the goals of nature can operate according to their own integrity within the one immanent and transcendent end of grace.

Indeed, a closer reading of Murray shows that the putative dualism between church and state diagnosed by his critics constitutes, not their equivocal separation, but their analogous unity in-difference. In a nuanced passage, Murray writes:

> As the harmony of nature presupposes [the] enduring distinction [between nature and grace], so the harmony of [church and state] is conditioned by the fidelity of each to its own [exigency.... Church and state] complete one another, not so that one assumes the other's functions, but so that each favors the performance by the other of the other's own functions, the favoring being done by each [according to its own mode of proceeding].[64]

62. Ibid., 723.

63. Ibid., referring to Will Herberg, *Protestant—Catholic—Jew* (Chicago: University of Chicago Press, 1955).

64. Murray, "Government Repression," 57; in Schindler, "Religious Freedom," 729–30.

Although Murray thus understands the relation between church and state to be derived from the relation between nature and grace, he is shrewd enough to know that these two sets of relations are not totally congruent. The work of the church is no more equal to the entire order of grace than the work of the state is equal to the entire order of nature. God's salvific purposes operate outside the juridic borders of the institutional church, both as the prevenient grace that gives all human beings an instinct of faith and as the baptism of desire that, in addition to the usual water, can also justify. Furthermore, like Benedict, Murray knows that both church and state function in history that is still awaiting its fulfillment in Christ. Even as the ordinary medium of grace, the church now only partially realizes a future pledge of glory. It follows, therefore, that church and state both can act according to differentiated ends that are embraced within the one concrete order of grace. The key question raised by this passage therefore concerns the relation between church and state in the here and now, while they both yearn, within grace, for their common consummation.

According to Murray, whereas church and state each has its own ends, these ends are completed by each other according to the modes appropriate to each. For instance, in establishing justice and promoting the general welfare, the state provides the necessary conditions for the church to function in equanimity. Just so, the church, in preaching the Gospel and administering the sacraments, can purify nature by calling it away from sin and to the virtue that constitutes the integrity of nature's own intrinsic ends. This mutuality shows that the work of church and state can overlap in a unity within their respective diversity. Where there is a unity-in-diversity, there obtains an analogy. Without an analogous conception of church and state, precarious consequences can follow. When each is not understood to operate, under grace, according to its own intrinsic ends, the distinction between what is God's and what is caesar's can be blurred to disappearance. The result will surely entail the secularism for which, ironically, Schindler finds Murray's putative dualism responsible. If, as Schindler says, Murray makes God too distant, then we might ask what could obtain if grace is made too close—if, in other words, the ends of nature are not sufficiently differentiated, within the order of grace, from those of the church.

In answering this question, let us recall Dupré's understanding of secularism. It grows and thrives when the dialectical tension between the sacred and the profane is lost. The profane defines all spheres of experience not considered holy, divine, graced-laden. Secularism obtains as the bland homogenization of experience when nothing is considered either sacred or profane. It can develop when the sense of the sacred is lost in one of two ways. On the one hand, the cultivation of a religious attitude toward reality can cease. In this case, the meaning of the sacred sinks into the profane. On the other hand, the profane itself can lose meaning. If everything becomes sacred, then effectively nothing is sacred. If nothing is sacred, then the profane evanesces and secularism ensues. This scenario has rightly caused the Christian history of the West to judge theocracy as a general failure. John Henry Newman, for instance, deplored the Erastian establishment of the Anglican church in the United Kingdom. The callous suppression of dioceses by a Parliament eager to balance a budget precipitated John Keble's 1833 sermon on "National Apostasy" that, in turn, initiated the Oxford Movement.[65]

The upshot is that secularism can be kept at bay only by maintaining the creative opposition between sacred and profane, church and state. In turn, this opposition can be accomplished only by attributing to nature its rightful ends, even as, within grace, these ends can appropriately dovetail with those of the church. That nature can be considered profane does not therefore mean that it is devoid of grace. It means that nature is finite, contingent, and sinful. It also means that, despite these qualities, nature can function for purposes whose rationality can be apparent without conscious advertence to revelation. The church, then, does not suffer from the healthy viability of the profane. On the contrary, it feeds and thrives upon it. The church suffers when, in a misguided effort to consecrate the profane, it inappropri-

65. Newman, *Apologia*, 152.

ately encroaches upon nature's distinct purposes. For this reason, Murray's insistence that the church must respect the integrity of the state's ends not only protects the prerogatives of the church. It also protects religious liberty in a pluralist commonwealth like the United States. Let us explore this claim.

According to Schindler, Murray's interpretation of Vatican II's *Declaration on Religious Freedom* means that the state should exercise no coercion in religious matters. Bound by the natural law, the state must respect the dignity of human persons to accept responsibility for acting on their own initiative.[66] The state's silent or implicit openness to God guarantees all religions the equal status before the law that permits their diverging religious claims to thrive in peace.[67] But this interpretation of Murray's betrays, for Schindler, a fundamental error. It permits the state to delay the question of God, whose existence cannot be delayed, because it is the ground of authentic freedom. Schindler relies on de Lubac's thesis that, rejecting the theory of pure nature, posits grace as the co-condition of freedom.

Two key distinctions may assist our exploration. The first concerns the difference between God and religion. With Schindler, we might argue, for instance, that the state should not be neutral toward, or postpone, the question of God. If, as Murray rightly argues, the state is bound by the natural law, then the state should exercise a positive disposition toward the divine. After all, according to exponents from the apostle Paul to Rahner and from Cicero to Jefferson, right reason asserts God's existence. The natural law, however, is wary of filling with too much content the definition of the God that it knows. Perhaps as the U.S. Declaration of Independence avers, a claim from natural reason can be made for God as creator, guarantor of inalienable rights, and supreme judge. But any civic effort to over-define God risks giving official privilege to one positive religion over another. Just how much

66. John Courtney Murray, "The Declaration on Religious Freedom," in *Vatican II: An Interfaith Appraisal*, ed. John H. Miller (Notre Dame, Ind.: Associated Press, 1966), 565–76, at 571–72; in Schindler, "Religious Freedom," 716.

67. Schindler, "Religious Freedom," 721.

content should be accorded the definition of God should emerge according to what Murray calls the efficacy of America's public argument. By public argument, he means the continuing debate about the consensus that grants America's forms of civic order their legitimacy.[68] By efficacy, he means that public conversation is oriented toward a resolution and not merely process-driven. Resolutions may not embrace universally-shared conclusions. But they should at least be able to express those differences that can be tolerated and why, and those that cannot, and why not.[69]

If the state should therefore favorably dispose itself toward God, it should nonetheless remain neutral toward religions. Such a disposition may mean that atheists and aggressive secularists will experience some disquiet living in a body politic based on a claim that they reject. But because the state faces a duty to the natural law, its disposition toward God entails no injustice to such individuals, so long as the state compels no one's conscience. Section 2 of Vatican II's *Declaration* says: "All are impelled by their own nature and are bound by a moral obligation to seek truth, above all religious truth.... But people are only able to meet this obligation in ways that accord with their own nature, if they enjoy both psychological freedom and freedom from external coercion."[70] The document thus draws our second important distinction. The obligation to seek the fullness of truth rightly devolves upon the individual, not upon the state. It is human beings, not the state, who, as Pascal's wager warns us, postpone the questions of God and religion to their eternal jeopardy.

In light of these two distinctions, let us consider how Schindler's view contrasts with Murray's. Schindler's advocates that a sense of divine obligation should be incorporated into the functioning of freedom in civil society.[71] If this means more than the state's discharging

68. John Courtney Murray, *We Hold These Truths: Catholic Reflections on the American Proposition* (New York: Sheed and Ward, 1960), 9.

69. Ibid., 13.

70. Vatican Council II, *Dignitatis Humanae*, in *Decrees*, ed. Tanner, 2:1001–11, at 1003.

71. Schindler, "Religious Freedom," 726, quoting Pope John Paul II, *Redemptor Hominis*, par. 12.

its debt to the natural law, then we might well worry that his position would plant the same seeds that sprouted in Calvin's Geneva and in other attempts to grow the Erastianism that troubled Newman. Although Schindler does not advocate theocracy, he does realize that his use of de Lubac initiates a momentum in that direction.[72] Nonetheless, let us suppose, for the sake of argument, that the state, instead of being neutral toward positive religion, were to express a disposition toward it, not merely toward the God of right reason. We might then happily rejoice that those who would deny or privatize religion are now decisively stripped of the ability to privilege their irreligion over the religion that, arguably, shaped the Constitution's original intent.[73] Surely, however, our short-term elation would soon give way to long-term distress. Inevitably, rendering the irreligious socially marginal would unhappily alter the combatants in the so-called culture wars. Religious people united against the irreligious would give way to religious people feuding among themselves. It seems far preferable for Catholics, Christian fundamentalists, and other religious practitioners to stand united against the irreligious in the pluralist debate than to be pitted against one another in the internecine struggle that would otherwise inevitably arise. Ensuing questions about how to interpret the Constitution's favorable disposition toward positive religion would coerce particular religions to seek an advantage for their own content.

In short, therefore: if religion thrives on the profane, then the future of religious liberty in America has a vested interest in keeping precisely the opponents of religion fully active in the public square. Ironically, they can serve to purify and nourish religion. Spurring religion on more zealously to convert hearts, they can indirectly help to draw civil society more closely into those virtues that enable it to realize its own appropriate ends.

72. Ibid., 735.

73. See Gerald Bradley, "Beyond Murray's Articles of Peace and Faith," in *John Courtney Murray and the American Civil Conversation*, ed. Robert P. Hunt and Kenneth L. Grasso (Grand Rapids, Mich.: Eerdmans, 1992), 181–204, at 191; in Schindler, "Religious Freedom," 711.

Let us consider a final dimension of the theology of nature that is important for our model: the relation between original sin and prevenient grace. Original sin can be defined as the radical diminishment of humanity's intellect and will from its integrally created nature, for which humanity bears responsibility, and which results in a vitiated nature alienated from God's justice. Accordingly, as the theological tradition has often taught, it would seem to follow that vitiated nature entails not only a wounding of our primordial powers but also a deprivation of any gifts of grace (*spoliatio in gratuitis*).[74] Following this tradition, Thomas avers that humanity possessed sanctifying grace in its integral nature and sacrificed it with the Fall (*ST* I, q. 95, a. 1). Consistent with this position, Suárez, as noted in chapter 2, stresses that postlapsarian nature, now unjustified because devoid of grace, can achieve only a purely natural end.[75] They thus draw a distinction between the formal and material effects of sanctifying grace. The formal effect gives human nature a supernatural end as opposed to a purely natural end. The material effect makes meritorious good works possible.

In contrast, our model claims that prevenient grace, suffusing nature from the moment of creation, endows nature with its supernatural end. This end, neither exacted nor required, gratuitously permits nature to attain a goal transcending its innate potential. It may be objected at once that prevenient grace is insufficient to bring about an effect in nature with which prevenient grace is not itself proportionate. In other words, because prevenient grace is not, like sanctifying grace, the very life of God, it cannot give humanity a claim to the beatific vision. But this objection implies an equivocal separation between prevenient and sanctifying grace alien to our analogous model. Because prevenient grace is intrinsically ordered to sanctifying grace, our final end can be proleptically conferred at creation without, at the same time, making this end inevitably achieved. As contrasted with Thomas and Suárez, therefore, our model nuances the formal effect

74. Duffy, *Graced Horizon*, 16.

75. Francisco Suárez, *De gratia*, prolog. 4, c. 1, n. 5, in *Opera Omnia*, vol. 7 (1857), 18; cited in de Lubac, *Mystery of the Supernatural*, 89.

of sanctifying grace, understanding it as implicitly anticipated in the prevenient grace that is ordered to sanctifying grace. Nonetheless, our model does agree with them in affirming that justification, conferred only with sanctifying grace, constitutes the means needed for every person to be saved. Our model also differs with Thomas and Suarez in its conception of the Fall. In ours, humanity turns away from prevenient grace, causing a cataclysmic sin that does not, however, alter grace's formal effect—our supernatural end. Nor does original sin strip us of the ubiquity of prevenient grace, which remains always available to aid and assist vitiated nature.

These two claims are reasonable when considered in light, for instance, of the teaching of the recent *Catechism of the Catholic Church* on the relation between mortal sin and sanctifying grace. According to this source, justifying grace produces a permanent condition in human nature (§ 2000). As the gateway into this condition, baptism produces a "character" on the soul: an indelible, accidental change (§ 1121). Because concupiscence remains even after regeneration, mortal sin likewise remains a possibility for everyone. Whether integral or vitiated, human freedom can always reject grace or cooperate with it. It therefore follows that, although a baptized Christian may forfeit the state of sanctifying grace, he never gives up his ontological orientation to the beatific vision.[76] Nor does he ever stand bereft of grace, because sanctifying grace can always be restored through the sacrament of penance worthily received. Therefore: if mortal sin does not entail the loss of our final end nor the availability of grace, it seems reasonable to affirm that original sin does not forfeit our final end nor the domain of prevenient grace given with nature at creation.

For these reasons, our model argues that, before the Fall, humanity did not need sanctifying grace to attain its last end. Prevenient grace was sufficient because we were sinless. Accordingly, our model poses another contrast with Thomas, who claims that, before the Fall, we needed sanctifying grace, not to do the works of the law, but to do

76. In support, Thomas affirms that mortal sins prevent but do not change our last end (*ad adversionem ab ultimo fine*) (*ST* I-II, q. 72, a. 5).

them with the requisite spirit of charity (*ST* I-II, q. 109, aa. 2, 4). We would argue that the grace needed was prevenient, not sanctifying. Nonetheless, we would maintain that the unrighteousness resulting from the Fall creates in us a justifying need for sanctifying grace. Precisely because after the Fall we now are joined to God by his own very life, it follows that the incarnation elevates vitiated nature qualitatively higher in value above its integral state. In the position of Thomas and Suarez, Adam's *felix culpa* seems only to restore our *status ante quo*, and so seems to underappreciate the unique effects of the divine kenosis on the human nature it assumes.

Let us now conclude this section of our argument that focused on developing a theology of nature. We have been concerned with maintaining nature's significance in light of the demise of the theory of pure nature. Accordingly, we have argued that the *Realsymbol*'s conception of nature as grace's "own other" lays the groundwork for an analogous understanding of nature as the sacramental medium of grace. As grace's "other," nature, while never existing without grace, can nonetheless be discerned in its resistance to grace on the one hand and in its willing openness to cooperate with grace on the other. This analogy is enriched, however, because nature is grace's "own" other. Accordingly, under grace's influence, nature can function according to its own intrinsic ends. Nature's relation with grace is thus dialectical and synthetic. It struggles against grace, it is freely disposed to grace, and it is purified by grace, thus allowing its own ends to be incorporated into those of grace. It bears repeating, by the way, that asserting nature's intrinsic ends does not mean that these ends can function apart from grace. Nor does it entail that nature possesses two ends. As de Lubac, following Blondel and Aquinas, has shown us, the human person, precisely as a spirit in the created world, is defined by a supernatural end not proportionate to created nature. This end, we have posited, results from the prevenient grace whose availability perdures through integral and vitiated nature.

For his part, Benedict XVI lodges nature's analogy in the tension between realized and future eschatology. There it exercises a dynamic plasticity in tandem with grace. Like Benedict, John Courtney Murray models a relation between church and state on nature's analogy. He shows us that, if grace's co-conditioning of freedom is not to result in theocracy, then church and state must appropriately favor the performance of each other's ends. On the one hand, the state favors the church by affirming the God of right reason and by creatively nourishing the dialectical tension between the sacred and profane. On the other hand, the church favors the state by converting hearts, and thus purifying the public square, so that the intrinsic ends for which civil society strives may embody the virtues fittingly suited to it.

Conclusions

This chapter set as its goal to develop a model of nature and grace based on the results of the first three chapters that selectively probed the history of their relation. The model that has emerged represents a synthesis of three elements: Seckler's analysis of the instinct of faith in Aquinas, as this has developed under the influence of Blondel and de Lubac; Rahner's view of creation and redemption as a *Realsymbol*; and Benedict XVI's and John Courtney Murray's analogous conceptions of nature. Let us briefly summarize our findings.

A sacramental model of nature and grace begins in the instinct of faith. It is the meeting point in the human person of these two orders. It posits in value a cause for the dynamic release of humanity's existential potential. As nature and grace's meeting point, the instinct links human and divine creativity while respecting their integrity. Moreover, precisely as the meeting point, the instinct is lodged within the one continuum of creation and redemption. As created, the instinct is rightly called the natural desire for God; as preveniently graced, it is properly the instinct of Christian faith, which represents a call to sanctifying justification. The natural desire and the instinct are formally distinct but materially the same. As formally distinct, they still possess the same supernatural object. Unaided reason alone can demonstrate that history's creative exigencies demand a supernatural end, however impotent reason might be further to specify this end or to bring it about. The order of grace alone can claim this end as the beatific vision effected through the free action of God in Christ.

The continuum of creation and redemption that grounds the instinct of faith obtains as a *Realsymbol*. These twin orders originate as a unity-in-difference in God's absolute freedom; they are reciprocally mediated in history; and together they return humanity, vitiated by the Fall, to the glory for which it is created. It thus follows that the two orders cause what they signify. Grace consummates the nature that incarnates it. Understood as a *Realsymbol*, the two orders, structured as a series of interrelated analogies, synthesize prevenient and sanctifying grace with nature, whose theological significance they preserve. In addition, the *Realsymbol* helps to purify the Christian doctrine of God of a lingering anthropomorphism.

We have also assessed how the sacramental model of nature and grace developed in this chapter handles the problem of modernity. As the link between humanity's creative pursuit of value and the God of grace, the instinct of faith joins into a harmony two of modernity's estranged dimensions: the subject whose initiative can fashion the cosmos on the one hand and the transcendence that constitutes the source and goal of human action on the other. In the next chapter, we will continue our discussion of modernity by developing a claim previously asserted in chapter 2: that aesthetics will always provide a basis for the living synthesis of nature and grace.

PART 3

EXPLORING ANALOGY

Chapter 5

AESTHETICS, ANALOGY, AND GOD

Method

We have developed a sacramental model of nature's relation to grace. As grace's "own other," nature incarnates grace in order for grace to realize its saving purpose. Because the redemption presupposes the created order for its own subsistence, nature cannot be conceived without its graced finalization. Grace, as we have seen, calls nature into being precisely so that grace can charge nature with its life. Drawing out the implications of this model, chapters 5 and 6 will now explore the following issue: if nature is never pure, but always obtains with grace as a unity-in-difference, then those data that belong to grace should be able to broaden our understanding of those data usually considered to fall under nature. In other words, the revealed doctrines of faith should be able to nourish philosophy without this discipline's losing its appropriate autonomy. In support of this claim, John Paul II in *Fides et Ratio* argues, for instance, that "without the stimulus of the word of God, a good part of modern and contemporary philosophy would not exist."[1] Kant, in a similar vein, affirms that positive religion "quickens" humanity's discovery of rational truths.[2] Hegel says that "philosophy cannot

1. John Paul II, *Fides et Ratio*, par. 76.

2. Kant, *Religion Within the Limits of Reason*, 11; also *Critique of Judgment*, trans. J. H. Bernard (New York: Hafner Press, 1951), 157, 160.

exist without religion."[3] If nature therefore constitutes grace's intrinsic symbol, then plunging more deeply into the meaning of grace should provide us with a concomitantly deeper understanding of nature.

This claim reverses the so-called method of correlation, the order of the relation between Christianity and philosophy that often prevails. According to it, philosophy is used to conduct a religiously independent investigation of the structure of reality. On the basis of the data that this investigation assembles, the theologian, appealing to scripture and tradition as normative authorities, then works to show that the object of faith answers and even grounds the questions raised by these data.[4] Reversing the order and endeavoring to evince philosophical insights from the data of grace entails an important presupposition that needs warranting. Having received religion's content, philosophy must respect the transcendence of this content to human reason. The work of Paul Ricoeur on the symbolism of the religious myth offers us an initial insight into how this transcendence can be maintained.

According to Ricoeur, the religious myth originates in humanity's need to address a fundamental enigma of its existence: the discordance between humanity's highest yearnings and its pitifully fractured efforts to realize them. Because human reason cannot find a logical nexus that adequately explains this discordance, narrations emerge that seek to resolve it. As narrations, myths are creative forms of the imagination that tell stories. But these stories embody a content richer than their imaginative form. The myth contains a transcendent content derived from reason's intention to solve a problem that ultimately surpasses its finite power. Although reason has the ability to grasp the fundamental enigma of human existence and dimly to perceive its resolution, reason lacks sufficient power exhaustively to understand it. As a result, the

3. Hegel, *Enzyklopädie der philosophischen Wissenschaften*, 2nd ed., in *Werke* VI, ed. Marheineke and Bauer (Berlin, 1840), second preface, xxi; in Emil L. Fackenheim, *The Religious Dimension in Hegel's Thought* (Boston: Beacon Press, 1967), 116.

4. See Hans W. Frei, *Types of Christian Theology* (New Haven, Conn.: Yale University Press, 1992), esp. 30–38.

myth more often conceals rather than reveals its transcendent content.[5]

Because myths express truths only partially discernible by reason, the rational content embodied in their imaginative form endows them with a surplus of signification.[6] This constitutes religious myths as symbols of the truth that transcends reason's discursive expression. As forms of human expression needed for reason to posit its transcendence, symbols cannot be eliminated as naive pseudo-explanations by any set of hermeneutics.[7] For instance, the story of the Fall in the first chapter of Genesis uses an apple, a snake, and various anthropomorphisms to speak about God, humanity's relation to God, and the nature of evil and temptation. The surplus of signification embedded in these images needs to be teased out by repeated interpretation. Because concepts fail to exhaust the meaning of the images, in religion the imagination can assume a priority over reason. Images give rise to concepts. Accordingly, because myths must be interpreted in order for reason to clarify their surplus of signification, they become the soil that generates and feeds philosophy.[8]

In what sense then can Christian revelation, as a departure point for philosophy, be considered to posit symbols bearing a surplus of rationality that reason cannot fully articulate? In order to answer this question, we must add a first qualification to Ricoeur. Understanding religious myths as symbols of rational transcendence is not opposed to understanding them as historical data. The life, death, and resurrection of Christ, for instance, may be affirmed as both historical and mythic. Vatican II's *Dei Verbum*, we will recall, teaches that God's revelation is not first and foremost communicated in images, words, and concepts,

5. Joseph Kockelmans, "On Religious Myths," in *The Challenge of Religion: Contemporary Readings in Philosophy of Religion*, ed. Frederick Ferré et al. (New York: Seabury Press, 1982), 213–33, at 228–29; citing Paul Ricoeur, *The Symbolism of Evil*, trans. Emerson Buchanan (New York: Harper and Row, 1967), 3–9, 161–71.

6. Kockelmans, "Myths," 220.

7. Ibid., 229

8. Ibid., 229–30, citing Ricoeur, *Symbolism*, 347–57. See also G. W. F. Hegel, *Einleitung in die Geschichte der Philosophie*, ed. Johannes Hoffmeister and Friedhelm Nicolin (Hamburg: F. Meiner, 1959), 173–75.

but in the person of Christ.[9] For this reason, we argued in chapter 1 that the symbolism of religious language is ultimately derived from the symbolism of the Son, the historically incarnate image of the Father. Nonetheless, the events of Jesus's life, even as acted out in time and space, are mythic: their memory has been sustained in a community whose faith and worship have interpreted them in fidelity to the apostles and disciples who witnessed them. In the history of this community, a series of narrations has emerged that embody the community's deepened understanding of the events. These narrations are found in the scriptures and in the oral and written tradition that both precedes and succeeds them. For their part, the Gospels are products of a seminal tradition of theological reflection; they are cast in an imaginative form that presents their message in the description of events. The inner meaning of their imaginative form is interpreted over time by the community. As a result, doctrines are forged, such as those posited by the Councils of Nicaea (325) and Chalcedon (451). These have resulted from the community's using philosophy as its principal hermeneutics to interpret the inner message of the Gospels.

We thus return to a key insight of Johann Adam Möhler's: doctrines are symbols. They interpret an oral and written tradition that itself interprets the enfleshed image. As symbols, they make no claim exhaustively to disclose the identity of Christ. Although they make statements about his identity that are neither revocable nor revisable, they do not replace the scriptures, even as these do not replace the incarnation. They derive their life from the imagery of the Gospels to which they remain subordinate. Moreover, although doctrines definitively interpret the Gospels, they nonetheless become the basis for further interpretation. The discipline of theology must therefore continually return to Gospel imagery for fresh insights. In short, doctrines embody a religious truth that, grounded in history and transcending human reason, continually presents reason with a source of insights that renew reflection.

9. Vatican Council II, *Dei Verbum*, chap. 1, par. 2 (2:971–81). Cited in the text.

Let us add a second qualification to Ricoeur's understanding of the religious myth. Just as its symbolism can be historical, so also can it be divinely inspired. In chapter 1, for instance, we referred to *Dei Verbum*'s assertion that in the scriptures divine inspiration has "taken on the likeness of human speech, just as the Word of the eternal Father, when he assumed the flesh of human weakness, took on the likeness of human beings" (par. 13). Put another way, because God makes full use of the powers of human authors, it follows that their creative faculties, in fashioning narrations and in interpreting them, become sacraments of divine inspiration (par. 12). While maintaining their own integrity, these powers can fulfill a divine finality in and through the medium of words truly their own (pars. 11–12). This understanding of inspiration is compatible with Ricoeur's claim that the religious myth contains a transcendent content. As we have seen, this content is derived from reason's intention to solve a problem that ultimately surpasses its finite power. Narrations thus emerge in order to fill a logical nexus unavailable to reason. It might be argued that divine inspiration establishes precisely this nexus. Inspiration does not change reason's intrinsically finite nature, but it does endow reason's products with an authority that they would not otherwise possess. Accordingly, the Gospels and their dogmatic interpretations can exert a normative claim on the believer. Just so, the Genesis myth becomes not merely one account among many possible ones through which reason seeks to resolve an enigma of human existence. It can constitute an authentic doctrine of faith.

When the action of divine inspiration in history is integrated into Ricoeur's account of the religious myth, it follows that the surplus of signification of Christian myths can be seen to originate in two causes coupled into a unity: reason's transcendental constitution and the action of grace. As a result, this surplus synthesizes two rationalities, the human and the divine. As a product of a theandric marriage, the Christian myth can be used by philosophy as a departure point insofar as philosophy seeks to clarify what it judges to be the content of human rationality in the myth's surplus of signification. Philosophy thus retains its autonomy, whereas the religious myth retains its divine etiology. The philosopher may freely use the methods of his discipline when interpreting the religious myth. But the Christian theologian who uses philosophy to work out a hermeneutics of divine revelation will be able to assert that the religious myth constitutes philosophy's origin and final validation.

Using these considerations as a warrant, this chapter and the following one probe Christian revelation in order to discover philosophical insights. Chapter 5 considers the theological aesthetics that Hans Urs von Balthasar has recently brought to the fore. It will discuss how a central Christian image, the crucifixion, can constitute the paradigm of beauty. Intimately related to truth, goodness, and unity, beauty forms an irreducible structure of reality. We will discover that the crucifixion, precisely as a object of revelation, entails fresh insights for philosophy's analogical conception of the relation between divine and contingent being. Fresh insights into analogy will also be unveiled in chapter 6. It will use as its starting point the prayer with which Ignatius Loyola closes the *Spiritual Exercises*. Within its grace-inspired imagery, we will discern the philosophy of love that grounds the events of the cosmos. Both of these chapters will reflect on the doctrine of God and continue the dialogue with modernity that has elsewhere occupied our study. Finally, chapter 7 will bring our argument to a close by considering analogy's role in mediating between Christianity and other religions.

Christian Beauty

When in chapter 2 we last discussed beauty as a divine quality, we contended that the self-expression of the Logos in history constitutes its prime object and paradigm. The principal work of divine revelation is Christ's passion and death as the necessary prelude to his resurrection. If this is the case, then it poses a serious challenge to the central analogy of Christian aesthetics. This analogy is expressed by Basil the Great when, at the end of one of his important works, he writes: "From the beauty of created things, the nature of the creator is correspondingly inferred."[10] How can the Christ, we might ask, suffering innocently in degradation and agony, be considered a revealed icon of a beautiful God? To begin resolving this paradox, let us turn to Hans Urs von Balthasar.

Balthasar first distinguishes "theological aesthetics" from a "theology of aesthetics." Both entail an analogy between infinite and finite modes of being. On the one hand, theological aesthetics finds its authentic ground in God's freely uttered self-revelation.[11] Because this constitutes the norm, standard, and touchstone of beauty, it draws us more and more into the glory of the living God. On the other hand, a theology of aesthetics gives priority to worldly standards of beauty, from which it then draws inferences about God. As a result, it risks dragging us more and more into sentimentality and its related problems of nominalism and solipsism (1:79).

In asserting the objectivity of theological aesthetics, Balthasar strongly opposes the Enlightenment view that shifts the foundation of beauty to the subject's perception (1:22). For Balthasar, beauty is not in the first instance a function of the individual's judgment of taste. It results from the person's response to the form of the reality perceived (1:19–20, 26). Thus returning us to pre-modern criteria, he affirms, with Socrates, that form accounts for the intelligibility of any existent. With Aristotelian realism, he holds that form radiates the clear light of being (1:19). With Bonaventure and the Augustinian tradition, he emphasizes that form, by definition, possesses a self-expressive power.[12] Radiating its intelligibility outward, form makes itself perceptible, understandable, nameable, and loveable (1:20). Accordingly, beauty is nothing less than the shining knowability of being, whose truth in turn causes delight in the judgment of the perceiver. This delight is a consummate good in all senses—ontologically, morally, sensuously. As transcendentals, being,

10. Basil of Caesarea, "Letter 8," in *The Letters*, trans. Roy J. Deferrari (London: W. Heinemann, 1926), 1:47–93, at 93.

11. Balthasar, *GL* 1:29. *GL* is cited in the text by volume and page.

12. Balthasar, "Bonaventure," in *GL* 2:260–362, at 335.

truth, goodness, and beauty are common to all existents and hence embrace all particularity in their universal necessity.[13]

Importing the identity of the transcendentals into theology, Balthasar affirms that form constitutes the very substance of Christianity (1:28). While it is true that God is infinite Spirit and has no material form, nonetheless Christians profess belief in the Trinitarian structure of the one God. The Father utters himself in his Word who, breaking the divine silence, speaks both in the creation of the cosmos and in the incarnation. By embracing a flesh-form, the Word-form empties itself in a sublime kenosis that, in a luminous paradox, expresses divinity to the eyes of faith (Phil 2:7). The Christ-form thus becomes the unique sacrament of God's real presence, such that "he who sees [him] sees the Father" (Jn 14:9). Precisely to protect revelation as form, the early church condemned Gnosticism and Arianism. These undermined both the immanent structure of the Trinity and the economic structure of the creating and redeeming Word. As heresies, they would have immunized God from form and hence from beauty.

If the intrinsic structure of reality is radiated forth in the incarnation, then all deeds and words of the particular Jewish man Jesus must reveal, *a priori*, the divine standard of beauty (1:28). In other words, if God is beautiful by definition, and if Christ is God, then the acts of Christ must set the first principles of authentic aesthetics. It follows that Christ's beauty must accordingly judge, or cast into a shadow, the beauty of all other created forms. It must manifest the aesthetic inadequacy of the finite (and sinful) order (1:34). If, however, Christ's saving passion and death are the summit of beauty, then our common understanding of beauty would seem to crumble. Let us consider this irony more deeply.

In one sense, Christians have grown accustomed to thinking of the crucifixion as aesthetically pleasing. It is the subject of numerous works of art and is commonly displayed in homes and churches. However laudable this pious custom may be, from a theological perspective it needs

13. Johannes Baptist Lotz, "Transcendentals," in *NCE* 14:240; for the subtleties of this identity, see *GL* 2:333.

some salutary deconstructing. It seems, for instance, to run counter to what Kant defines as the hallmark of human aesthetic experience: the "universal sense of satisfaction."[14] For Thomas, this satisfaction, as we observed in chapter 4, ensues from the delight conferred upon our intuition by the intrinsic symmetry of reality (*ST* I, q. 39, a. 8; II-II, q. 145, a. 2). It is known when we contemplate the majesty of the great panoramas of nature, such as Ireland's cliffs of Moher and Arizona's Grand Canyon. It is felt when we stand enthralled by the ingenuity of architectural forms like the Parthenon and Pantheon. Its expectation draws us repeatedly to concert halls and to the world's great museums, whose treasures help us to purify, elevate, and transform the otherwise quotidian routine of normal life.

But the crucifixion, by contrast, stands as a universal metaphor for injustice, torture, and death. These are among the chief moral and physical evils of the human condition that repel us in their ugliness. As evils, their irrationality, according to Augustine, results from a corresponding deprivation of an ontological reality that ought to obtain.[15] It is therefore not surprising that Paul encountered the cross as the chief obstacle to evangelization. A "scandal" to the Greeks and an "absurdity" to reason, it seems devoid of the power to delight (1 Cor 1:23). This is because it seems devoid of symmetry and intelligibility.

Grünewald's altarpiece, renowned as a touchstone of German art, is one of many works that endeavor to fill this void.[16] It confers an alluring beauty on the agony and humiliation of Christ, which it nonetheless depicts with grim realism. Commissioned before 1516 for a hospital chapel near Isenheim, the painting was intended to serve as a catharsis that would draw forth and thereby ease the pain of patients suffering from a (now rare) gangrenous disease.[17] There can only be one ethical justification for conferring delight on such a morally problematic subject: the

14. Kant, *Critique of Judgment*, 45–46.

15. See for instance Augustine, *Enchiridion* IV.13 and *City of God* IX.9.

16. Arthur Burkhard, *Matthias Gruenewald: Personality and Accomplishment* (New York: Hacker Art Books, 1976), 42.

17. Ruth Mellinkoff, *The Devil at Isenheim: Reflections of Popular Belief in Grünewald's Altarpiece* (Berkeley: University of California Press, 1988), 1.

subject's intrinsic beauty. But once we accept this beauty in faith, once theological aesthetics takes as its measure the ignominy of the death of God's absolute Word, then we face a problem opposite to that posed by Basil. We are led to wonder whether the Grand Canyon, the Pantheon, and Grünewald's altarpiece are, in fact, authentically beautiful.

Yet this cannot be the case. If, as we previously observed, the beauty of the Trinity vestigially animates all created forms, even after the Fall, then what is normally called beautiful according to worldly aesthetics must in some measure overlap with theological aesthetics. Much of what the world calls beautiful is an implicit recognition of the divine artisan's primordial creativity. If God made the world from nothing *sui et subjecti*, then God must be the exemplary cause of all that is and can be. It follows that finite existents constitute images patterned after archetypes immanent in the divine intelligence.[18] God's beauty, "at once so ancient and so new," is channeled into the finite cosmos by means of God's free intention to create.[19] In short, however much the cross of Christ sets the standard of beauty, it cannot be understood to destroy the integrity of worldly aesthetics. On the contrary, it must give this integrity its center.

Aware of this problem, Balthasar contends that his theological aesthetics wishes to posit no "definitive caesura" between God's revealed beauty and "intramundane aesthetics."[20] Concerning the term beauty, Balthasar wants to tread solidly down the middle path of analogy. On the one hand, he eschews a univocal understanding of beauty that would posit the identity of divine and intramundane aesthetics. On the other hand, he eschews an equivocal understanding that would juxtapose them as contradictory. A univocal understanding would sacrifice Christianity's conception of the divine transcendence. An equivocal understanding would undermine the vestigial theology of Trinitarian nature inherited from Fathers like Basil. As analogous, God's beauty and intramundane aesthetics must enjoy, as we know from previous

18. Aquinas, *ST* I, q. 14, a. 8, and q. 15, a. 1; see also *Summa contra Gentiles* II, chaps. 45–46; *De potentia* q. 3, a. 1, ad 12.

19. Augustine, *Confessions* X (231).

20. Louis Dupré, "Hans Urs von Balthasar's Theology of Aesthetic Form," *Theological Studies* 49 (1988): 299–318, at 302.

discussions, marked differences within an authentic similarity (1:35).

The need to work out a consistent analogy constitutes the central problem in Balthasar's theological aesthetics. However much he shows an awareness of it, Balthasar does not systematically address it. If we were to appeal to Isaiah Berlin's famous metaphor for great thinkers, Balthasar would more resemble the fox than the hedgehog. He digs his intellectual burrows in a seemingly scattered fashion rather than linking them by well-connected tunnels.[21] To make full sense of Balthasar the fox, we must become a hedgehog for him, burrowing our way through his thought so that his seminal genius can become more apparently coherent. The secret of this coherence, we wish to argue, lies in an innovative interpretation of Thomas's doctrine of analogy. Chapter 1 initiated a discussion of this topic in the Common Doctor. Now let us comment on how Aquinas skillfully integrates the analogy of proper proportionality with the analogy of intrinsic attribution.[22]

Beauty and Being

In the analogy of proper proportionality, the same quality is predicated of different subjects, because this quality belongs intrinsically to each subject, although in a manner appropriate to each. Thus, as Aristotle observes, soul is properly predicated of humanity, animals, and plants, although in differing levels of potential.[23] In intrinsic attribution, a quality is predicated principally of one subject (the prime analogate) and then of other subjects, because these bear a relation to the principal subject. Thus, health is properly predicated of human beings and only secondarily of medicine, food, and blood, because these enhance human health.[24]

21. See Isaiah Berlin, *The Hedgehog and the Fox: An Essay on Tolstoy's View of History* (New York: Simon and Schuster, 1970).

22. Étienne Gilson, "Cajétan et existence," *Tijdschrift voor Philosophie* 15 (1953): 267–86; in George P. Klubertanz, *St. Thomas Aquinas on Analogy: A Textual Analysis and Systematic Synthesis* (Chicago: Loyola University Press, 1960), 13.

23. Aristotle, *De anima* 414e28.

24. Frederick Ferré, "The Logic of Analogy," in *Challenge of Religion*, ed. Ferré et al., 104–13, at 106–7.

As chapter 1 began to show, Aquinas's doctrine of analogy is concerned with the attribution of the transcendentals: being, truth, goodness, and beauty that, as mentioned earlier, determine finite realities but do not, in and of themselves, admit of any finite determination. Consequently, they are also often called perfections. In proper proportionality, the transcendentals intrinsically inhere in both infinite and finite modes of reality. In other words, God may be said to be good in his own right, and so may all finite realities simply because they exist. In intrinsic attribution, God, as reality's infinite mode, is the prime analogate or principal subject of the perfections. As the unique being whose essence is infinite existence, God realizes the transcendentals in no determined sense. By contrast, finite modes of being embody the transcendentals according to their specifically determined essences. Thus, although a perfection inheres intrinsically in a finite essence, this essence embodies the perfection only as an imperfect image or likeness of the divine archetype.[25] Aquinas denies that we can conceive any adequate notion of the divine perfections, although we can attribute them to God once God's infinite existence is known. According to the analogy of intrinsic attribution, any determined instance of a perfection implies the existence of its unlimited prime analogate.[26]

In light of Thomas's doctrine, we can see more clearly why Balthasar's notion of beauty appears to contradict both types of analogy. It seems inconsistent with proper proportionality, because the revelation of Christ's passion and death patently conflicts with intramundane beauty. It appears to run against intrinsic attribution, because no similarity seems to obtain between philosophical aesthetics and the revealing God who is beauty's prime analogate. The key to Balthasar's analogy lies in properly understanding the relation between beauty and being. In turn,

25. For Aquinas's treatment of the relation between intrinsic attribution and the metaphysics of participation, see *De potentia* q. 3, a. 5; q. 7, a. 7, ad 2; *Summa contra Gentiles* II, chaps. 15, 53; III, chaps. 66, 97; *ST* I, q. 3, a. 8; q. 44, a. 1; q. 47, a. 1, q. 75, a. 5, ad 1 and 4; q. 79, a. 4; *In Joann. Prol.*; *Quodl.* 2.2.1; citations in Klubertanz, "Analogy," *NCE* 1:464, and in *Aquinas on Analogy*, appendices I, II.

26. See especially Aquinas's analysis of the perfection "living" (*ST* I, q. 4, a. 2); in Klubertanz, "Analogy," *NCE* 1:465.

this relation cannot be understood apart from Balthasar's assertion that the analogy of being finds its ultimate vindication in the analogy of faith.

According to Balthasar, the analogy of faith consummates the analogy of being. In other words, when philosophy posits absolute being on the basis of contingent being, and when theology posits that this absolute being freely offers grace to sinful created beings, the concept of being used by the two disciplines is analogous. The terms "absolute being" and "contingent/created being" never meet in a univocal overlap. According to theology, the absolute being that philosophy affirms on the basis of contingent reality is analogous, because only theology knows that this absolute is the God who freely offers grace. Similarly, according to theology, the contingent being of philosophy is analogous. However much philosophy can dimly grasp the origins of finite being in the absolute, only theology knows that finite being is the subject of a freely offered revelation. It follows, therefore, that theology renders the philosophical analogy of being analogous.[27] The analogy of being can be seen as a moment subsisting within the analogy of faith, which reveals the inner nature of the absolute and the ultimate purpose of the finite order. The nature of the first is lovingly to save and that of the second is freely to be saved.[28]

What is important in Balthasar's concept of being as analogously analogous is that a double level of dissimilarity obtains within the similarity between the revealing God and the finite order that receives the revelation. The analogy of being knows the absolute as dissimilar to contingent being, and the analogy of faith knows the revealing God as dissimilar to philosophy's absolute. This double level of dissimilarity so attenuates any similarity between God and the world that at once it affirms the radical contingency of the finite order, while it establishes a basis for a novel revelation that can challenge the hegemony of intramundane aesthetics. In order for this analogy to be consistent,

27. I owe the expression "analogous analogy" to Joseph S. Costantino, "Balthasar, Tracy, and Analogy" (STL thesis, Weston Jesuit School of Theology, 1988), 98.

28. Balthasar, *Theology of Karl Barth*, 273–76.

however, a notion of the Godhead must be framed that incorporates dissimilarity within similarity. We shall begin to explore this notion by turning to Balthasar's study of a fifth-century corpus attributed to Pseudo-Dionysius the Areopagite. Known as the architect of negative theology, Pseudo-Dionysius asserts that God and the world constitute a "like unlikeness and an unlike likeness."[29]

According to Balthasar, Pseudo-Dionysius distinguishes God's self-communication, which grounds the finite order, from the reality of God who communicates. God communicates being to sensuous reality through or by means of his own being.[30] This act of self-manifestation is the bridge between infinite and finite being and the ground of the simultaneous similarity and dissimilarity between them. God's self-communication thus constitutes and establishes the analogy of being. At once, this act flows forth from God even as it creates the cosmos that, in its contingency, is radically other than God. What is especially important for Balthasar is that the source of this act lies in another perfection of the Godhead: goodness. As noted in chapter 2, this perfection, according to Pseudo-Dionysius, is equally convertible with beauty and eros (passionate love), and with light.[31] The divine act of being is mediated by these; from them, being proceeds, and in them, being subsists.[32] God's beauty and eros (and goodness and light) are thus "the cause of initiation" of being.[33] Beauty and eros constitute "the one

29. Pseudo-Dionysius the Areopagite, *De coelesti hierarchia* [hereafter "*CH*"] XV.8 (337B), in "Denys," *GL* 2:144–210, at 166, 179–80. Balthasar cites the works of Pseudo-Dionysius according to *PG* 3. For other perspectives on Balthasar's treatment of Pseudo-Dionysius, see Cyril O'Regan, "Thick Retrieval," *Gregorianum* 77 (1996): 227–60; and Georges de Schrijver, *Le merveilleux accord de l'homme et de Dieu: étude de l'analogie de l'être chez Hans Urs von Balthasar*, Bibliotheca ephemeridum theologicarum lovaniensium 63 (Louvain: Peeters, 1983), 297–306.

30. Balthasar, "Denys," *GL* 2:170.

31. Balthasar, "Denys," *GL* 2:189, referring to *DN*, chap. 4. Balthasar does not define eros in Pseudo-Dionysius, but "passionate love" is consistent with Paul's use of it in Gal 6:14, and with other classical texts, such as those by Philo. See Walter Bauer et al., *A Greek-English Lexicon of the New Testament and Other Early Christian Literature*, 2nd ed. (Chicago: University of Chicago Press, 1979).

32. Balthasar, "Denys," *GL* 2:189, referring to *DN*, chap. 5.

33. *CH* III.1 (164D); in Balthasar, "Denys," *GL* 2:196.

cause of all beings," through which flow "both being and well-being to all that is."[34]

This understanding of the relation between being, beauty, and eros in the Godhead sheds light on the two questions that the analogies of proper proportionality and intrinsic attribution pose to Balthasar. First: how can beauty be said properly to inhere in the revelation of Christ's passion and death, since these patently conflict with intramundane standards of beauty? Second: how can any similarity obtain between these standards and the revealing God who is beauty's prime analogate? As to the first question, it is clear, as we have seen, that intramundane beauty, in and of itself, has difficulty grounding a similarity between its standards and the crucifixion. Once faith perceives a similarity, however, reason can be led to see that it is not inconsistent with its own norms. This consistency can be shown when the second question is addressed. Doing so requires considering, in turn, the relation between being and beauty and the relation between being and eros. Let us begin with the relation between being and beauty.

The philosophical analogy of beauty is negated when it confronts the passion of Christ, whose crucified form does not appear beautiful. The cross fails by intramundane aesthetics because it is a revelation of absolute beauty. Intramundane aesthetics is convertible with the intramundane mode of being, as Thomas's view of the transcendentals indicates. This mode is finite. Finite being is analogous to God's being but, as Balthasar's study of Pseudo-Dionysius shows, being is mediated by the divine beauty. As a result, worldly aesthetics are analogously analogous to God's beauty. They are twice dissimilar to the inner essence of divinity. The ascent from worldly beauty to God, therefore, only reaches by a simple analogy the divine being. Only by means of a further analogy, an analogous analogy, can this ascent reach the divine beauty. As the cause of initiation of being, the divine beauty generates the divine being that, as the instrumental cause of the finite order, is the immediate ground of worldly aesthetics.

34. Pseudo-Dionysius the Areopagite, *De ecclesiastica hierarchia* I.3 (373CD); in Balthasar, "Denys," *GL* 2:200.

Because being is mediated within the Godhead through beauty, Balthasar's analogy is spared from lapsing into an equivocation between God's being and beauty that only an act of blind faith could breach. Because being subsists in beauty and flows forth through it, God can be at once the ground of intramundane aesthetics (in virtue of absolute being) and of a revealed aesthetics of the cross (in virtue of absolute beauty), even though, from the vantage of worldly beauty, the crucifixion appears scandalous. That being and beauty constitute within the infinitely simple Godhead a dissimilarity-in-similarity does not require the analogy of faith to perceive. Such a notion is rationally tenable. We shall develop this point shortly.

What does require the analogy of faith clearly to be perceptible is the similarity between the divine beauty, the crucified Christ, and intramundane aesthetics. The key to this perception is found in Pseudo-Dionysius's notion that God's beauty, as opposed to the beauty of the world, cannot be understood apart from God's eros or passionate love. Whereas worldly aesthetics appeals to the harmony and form of being, the divine beauty functions according to a higher principle. This is not merely the love of Aristotle's first cause or prime mover, to which all finite processes are drawn as their ultimate goal.[35] It is the revealed love of a person. It goes forth from itself, taking the form of a slave (Phil 2:7), laying down its life for its friends (Jn 15:13), dying even for sinners (Rom 5:8). Shining forth in the scandal of the cross, this love, grasped in faith, transforms an image assessed as ugly by intramundane norms into an icon of beauty.

In light of the analogy of faith, then, how dissimilar is the aesthetics of the cross from intramundane beauty? On the one hand, there can be no doubt that the cross judges the beauty of all worldly standards. It shows the inadequacy of using the harmony and form of being as the ultimate norms of beauty. It deconstructs their absolute universality by rendering them dependent on a deeper meaning of aesthetics. This meaning is God's passionate love that can be neither induced or deduced. It must be revealed.

35. Aristotle, *Metaphysics* 1072a18–36.

On the other hand, the beauty of the cross is not equivocal to intramundane beauty. Although it deconstructs worldly aesthetics, its revelation reminds us forcefully that worldly beauty, even when evaluated by its own standards, is analogous. To illustrate this, we need only take as an instance the Nobel laureate, Mother Theresa of Calcutta. Judged strictly by the harmony and form of worldly beauty, she was far from attractive, just as the work she undertook was far from conferring Kant's universal sense of satisfaction. And yet she allured the imagination of the world. Emerging through her personal fragility and homeliness, and through the grime of her work among dying outcasts was the beauty of a humanely loving and heroic self-sacrifice. This was appreciated not just by Christians but by diverse people of goodwill, notwithstanding their religious belief or lack of it.

If loving self-sacrifice exerts a universal aesthetic appeal, then worldly beauty is an analogy of proper proportionality. In other words, beauty inheres in the Grand Canyon, a Mozart sonata, and the Parthenon, even as it does in Mother Theresa and her work. As a result, anyone, even without the analogy of faith, can begin to understand how Christ's crucifixion can be perceived as beautiful, although only the conviction of faith can ground a firm certitude of this beauty. Balthasar's doctrine of analogy is fully consistent, therefore. No definitive caesura obtains between worldly beauty and the cross. They are properly proportional, although only the analogy of intrinsic attribution can establish this. In other words, God must freely reveal that the prime analogate of absolute beauty is his own saving love.

God's Simplicity

We have argued that God can be the analogous ground of an intramundane aesthetics and a revealed aesthetics, despite the cross's apparent scandal. As mentioned earlier, this argument depends in part on the credibility of the infinitely simple Godhead's embracing being and beauty as a dissimilarity-in-similarity. This credibility needs some further justifying, especially in light of Thomas's magisterial treatment. According to it, the divine simplicity means that God is absolute being, with which essence is simultaneous. This simultaneity constitutes pure and unlimited act, utterly uncompounded, devoid of potency (*ST* I, q. 3, a. 3; q. 4, a. 7). If, as Pseudo-Dionysius avers, God's beauty (and love and goodness with which it is convertible) generate and infuse God's being, then two principles are introduced into God, one of which is subordinate to the other. In what sense, then, can God be deemed absolutely uncompounded? There is a way of meeting this objection, but Pseudo-Dionysius's thought, of itself, does not provide the resources. For these, we turn to the thinker with whom we began, Basil the Great, one of the three Cappadocian Fathers.[36]

Basil presents us with two important insights. First, he resolves unity and difference in God by appealing to the analogy implied by the term "one." When one is predicated of God, it means that God's unity is grounded in the simplicity of his nature. By contrast, when one is predicated of finite realities, it means number, definition, subjection to the conditions of time and space, and the ability to undergo change according to these conditions. The unity of finite realities is thus always compounded. Form and matter, the principles of this compound, obtain in an ontological harmony that constitutes a substance. Nonetheless, these principles are really distinct. They are ontologically heteronomous within their unity, in the sense that form confers definition, whereas matter confers specification.[37]

Because numerous attributes are rightly predicated of God, a plurality of entities seems to inhere in him. This appearance is a concession to our finite minds that cannot objectify the essential simplicity of God. When the term one is analogously predicated of God, God's attributes, although plural, emerge as only "virtually" distinct from each other and from his nature. God's nature and the distinctions predicated of it are essentially homogeneous. Unlike the composition of form

36. For further resources in dealing with this objection, see David L. Schindler, "Is Truth Ugly? Moralism and the Convertibility of Being and Love," *Communio: International Catholic Review* 27 (2000): 701–28.

37. Basil, "Letter 8," in *Letters*, 1:53. Cited in the text.

and matter, however, the unity of the divine substance is not complex (L8:55n3). Any distinction in God, therefore, is not properly counted as a number.

In a second important insight, Basil appeals to the concept of community (*koinonia*)to specify God's oneness. The virtual distinctions in God inhere in a unity that is "continuous and uninterrupted."[38] Unlike the complementarity of form and matter that entails a real distinction, "there is nothing which intrudes itself" between the virtual distinctions. Basil asserts: "Beyond the divine nature, there is nothing which subsists that could really divide it from itself" (L38:209). As a result, a paradox obtains in God, whose distinctions constitute a "united separation" and a "disunited connection" (L38:213). God's simplicity of nature resolves this paradox, which therefore vitiates neither God's unity nor oneness.

Basil does not explicitly consider the relation in God between being and beauty (and its convertibility with love and goodness), but his insights help us to develop a model that can preserve the divine simplicity. Beauty and being can be understood as virtually distinct in God. Being emerges eternally from the divine beauty that, by impregnating being, renders being a constitutive moment within itself. As a result, the distinction between beauty and being implies no interval or void but constitutes a continuous and uninterrupted unity.

We might develop the relation between beauty and being further. We might, for instance, argue that, if beauty eternally generates being, and if beauty impregnates being, then being is the eternal image or reflection of beauty. In this case, the relation between beauty and being might be understood as an instance of the mediated immediacy that we defined in chapter 4. In other words, the divine beauty mediates itself through being. In being, beauty sees itself. It might even be said that beauty obtains its own perfection by seeing itself reflected in being. For its part, being is mediated through beauty because beauty generates it. If beauty and being thus mediate each other in God, then

38. Basil, "Letter 38," in *Letters*, 1:197–226, at 209. Cited in the text.

their relation is reciprocal. As such, they subsist in God as a community bound together in the simplicity of virtual distinctions. Consequently, neither is subordinate to the other, because each is needed for the constitution of the other. If so, then Balthasar's analogy of beauty consistently integrates dissimilarity within the divine simplicity.

Finally, Basil's notion of virtual distinctions helps us to conceptualize the interdependence among beauty, love, and being in God's essential simplicity. Because beauty is equally convertible with love, it follows that being is constituted in and by the beauty of absolute love. For its part, this love, which is the divine beauty, reaches its fulfillment in being—in what is formal, intelligible, communicable, and knowable. Where there is love, there is necessarily freedom. If the generating "heart" of God is therefore free, beauty and being are by nature intrinsically free. It is ultimately this freedom that gives form to the beauty of the cross, even as this same freedom creates, sustains, and conserves the symmetry of the cosmos. We take delight in this symmetry by our human sensibility. We take delight in the cross by the sense of our spirit quickened in prayer to love even as we are loved. The next chapter will further develop the relation in God among beauty, love, and being.

In sum, up to this point we have studied Balthasar's theological aesthetics in order to understand how a revealed datum of grace can be a starting point for deepened philosophical insight. The crucifixion of Christ asks philosophy a probing question about the ultimacy of its aesthetic standards. The Christian image suggests that reality's intrinsic symmetry and universal sense of satisfaction must yield to loving self-sacrifice. Revelation, in other words, deepens and extends worldly beauty's analogy of proper proportionality. It invites reason to see that, as an icon of beauty, human heroism trumps the wonders of nature and the artifacts of human creativity. In addition, our study of Balthasar has shown reality to be analogously analogous. In turn, this insight has shed a fresh perspective on the Christian doctrine of God. As a conclusion to this chapter, let us draw out some further implications of reality's analogous analogy and use this concept to continue our dialogue with modernity.

Analogous Analogy

Balthasar's analogous analogy helps us to clarify a lingering issue in the position developed by Seckler and at the same time to correct an error in Rahner. Previously, we stated that Seckler affirms the formal distinction between the natural desire for God and the instinct of faith within their material identity. We argued that this thesis entails no contradiction, because both the desire and the instinct can consistently claim one and the same supernatural object. Whereas the instinct of faith is directed toward the beatific vision, the natural desire, as Blondel demonstrates, is oriented toward a supernatural end that could consummate history's immanent exigency. Although unaided reason remains impotent further to specify this end, still theology, from its perspective, reveals it to be God's action in Christ. Nonetheless, however much Seckler, following de Lubac, rightly asserts the human person's one supernatural end, he remains unclear about how the absolute of philosophy and the graciously self-revealing God are correlated. For his part, Rahner posits a correlation by distinguishing between the pre-apprehended absolute of general revelation and the incarnation of categorical revelation. But as we have seen, his account, the supernatural existential, maintains the possibility of a natural end for the pre-apprehended absolute. As a result, Rahner continues to hold, however subtly, the theory of two ends for the human person, which we have seen de Lubac correctly find to be incoherent.

Balthasar's critique of the supernatural existential discussed in chapter 2 is decisive: the ends of the person asserted by general and categorical revelation appear equivocal, not correlated. Consequently, as Balthasar further maintains, any relation between natural and graced knowledge of God must be clearly analogical. In other words, when philosophy posits absolute being on the basis of contingent being, and when theology posits that this absolute being freely offers grace to sinful human beings, the concept used by the two perspectives is itself analogous. Philosophy's absolute being and grace's epiphany in Christ, albeit materially the same, do not meet univocally in a formal overlap. Positing for the absolute a distinction within identity, Balthasar's analogous analogy rectifies Rahner, even as it clarifies Seckler, with whom it nonetheless holds a single end for humanity. Analogous analogy thus lies in the core of reason's relation to faith. Emerging from a theology of beauty, it exemplifies the claim made in chapter 2 that art will always provide a living synthesis of nature and grace.

Balthasar's analogous analogy can also assist us in further understanding the relation of nature and grace to modernity. No account of this problem can be complete without reflecting on what has come to be known as postmodernity. We last mentioned this phenomenon in chapter 4 when referring to Dupré's contention that the postmodern constitutes but a moment within the modern. If modernity's defining quality consists of the premium that it places on mind's creativity in relation to physical reality, then postmodernity, he opines, remains dependent on subjectivity. The incisiveness of this critique can hardly be denied. Derrida, for instance, even while sundering the link between language and objective reference, subsumes language into writing.[39] His endeavor cannot be viewed as anything other than a quintessential act of inventive intelligence. Consequently, what one commentator calls postmodernism's "riot of diversity" does not signal the rise of a new paradigm, as modernity would stand, for instance, in relation to the classical tradition of formal mimesis.[40]

Nonetheless, postmodern thinkers can help modernity more deeply to appropriate its own tradition. This claim is paradoxical, because these thinkers are opposed to ontology, the universal science of being that for so long has grounded and sustained the western mind's self-

39. Jacques Derrida, *Of Grammatology*, trans. Gayatri Chakravorty Spivak (Baltimore: Johns Hopkins University Press, 1976), 6–7.

40. Kenneth L. Schmitz, "Postmodernism and the Catholic Tradition," *American Catholic Philosophical Quarterly* 73 (Spring 1999): 233–52, at 233.

understanding. Postmodern presuppositions in linguistic philosophy lead to a marginalization of the process in human rationality whereby the universal element in knowledge is conceptualized.[41] Yet even their deconstruction of the universal evinces an implicit appreciation of, and instinct for, the value of the singular.[42] This term does not mean the particular, which is merely the opposite of the universal. On the contrary, it means the individual existent that takes into itself "the commonality of the universal" and the "determinacy of the particular."[43] For instance, although Lyotard dismisses all "grand narratives," he does so because of their generality that, in seeking the universal, neglects the distinctive value of the individual datum.[44] Recovery of this value is seen in Derrida, not only in his "pains to reflect upon a philosophical text in such excruciating detail," but also in his commentary on "gift."[45] Similarly, however "off-side" Foucault's analyses may be, they aim at exposing hidden dimensions in specific institutions of the West.[46] Let us pursue with postmodernism this quest for the singular and then bring it into dialogue with Balthasar's aesthetics.

Postmodernism's critique deconstructs the singular based on its view of "event," a notion central in Lyotard and Foucault but also important in Derrida, Nancy, and Deleuze. Event does not mean merely "a unique and unrepeatable happening," but a necessary condition for all thinking, which is necessarily historical.[47] Because history is not guided by a universal referent, at least not in any properly determined sense, it is shot through with radical contingency. Since all thinking is perforce historical, it is also absent of a center.[48] This absence, a sum-

41. Ibid., 247.

42. Ibid., 244.

43. Ibid., 247.

44. Ibid., 244.

45. Ibid., 233. See for instance the analysis of Augustine's *Confessions* in Jacques Derrida, *Circumfession: Fifty-nine Periods and Periphrases*, in Geoffrey Bennington and Jacques Derrida, *Jacques Derrida* (Chicago: University of Chicago Press, 1993), no. 30; and Jacques Derrida, *The Gift of Death*, trans. David Wills (Chicago: University of Chicago Press, 1995).

46. Schmitz, "Postmodernism," 233. See for instance Michel Foucault, *Discipline and Punish: The Birth of the Prison*, trans. Alan Sheridan (New York: Vintage, 1979); *The History of Sexuality*, trans. Robert Hurley (New York: Pantheon, 1978–86).

47. Thomas R. Flynn, "A Reply to Kenneth L. Schmitz," *American Catholic Philosophical Quarterly* 73 (Spring 1999): 261–66, at 266.

48. Ibid.

marizing idea of postmodern thought, does not indicate merely the lack of a center to be found.[49] It is an absence without the possibility of a center.[50] Thus history for Lyotard and language for others are devoid of objective signification.[51] Following de Saussure, Derrida insists on the arbitrariness of linguistic signs. Linguistic meaning, no longer circumscribed by objective reference, ensues from a process of the progressive transference of one sign to the next.[52] As a result, writing draws "along with it all the reassuring signifieds," effectively "destroying the [objective] concept of 'sign' and its entire logic."[53] Not only does critical theory therefore deconstruct the privileged position held by the artifact. But all structures of the world—beliefs, practices, institutions, traditions—are subject to the same fate.[54]

Postmodern thinkers are thus ambiguous about the status of the singular. The process of rewriting the singular's universality is parasitic upon the very world institutions deconstructed. Moreover, this ambiguity becomes more pronounced when the question of history's radical contingency is probed. How utterly devoid of determination is the postmodern concept of event? Commenting on Jan Patocka's reading of Heidegger, Derrida "acknowledges the need for *someone* to call us to decision," to give direction to the authenticity of human endeavor, even if the voice calling lacks "any determinable identity."[55] A glimmer of teleology thus begins to appear in the postmodern conception of history. This same glimmer appears in Derrida's remark on law. Law can be deconstructed because it is a human construction. Justice, however,

49. Raman Shelden and Peter Widdowson, eds., *A Reader's Guide to Contemporary Literary Theory*, 3rd ed. (Lexington: University of Kentucky Press, 1993), 178; in Kenneth Schmitz, "An Addendum to Further Discussion," *American Catholic Philosophical Quarterly* 73 (Spring 1999): 277–90, at 280; and in Flynn, "Reply," 262.

50. Schmitz, "Addendum," 280.

51. Jean-François Lyotard, "The Sign of History," in *The Lyotard Reader*, ed. Andrew Benjamin (Oxford: Basil Blackwell, 1989), 393–411, at 409–10; see also *The Differend: Phrases in Dispute* (Minneapolis: University of Minnesota Press, 1988); in Flynn, "Reply," 262.

52. Schmitz, "Addendum," 281.

53. Derrida, *Grammatology*, 6–7; cited in ibid.

54. John D. Caputo, "Commentary on Ken Schmitz, 'Postmodernism and the Catholic Tradition,'" in *American Catholic Philosophical Quarterly* 73 (Spring 1999): 253–60, at 255.

55. Schmitz, "Addendum," 278, quoting Derrida, *Gift*, 32–33.

if it exists, cannot be deconstructed, presumably because it transcends human origins.[56] One begins to wonder whether postmodernism has not itself already initiated the deconstruction of the radical contingency with which it riddles history. If it has, then the continuing process of writing so central to postmodernism seems to be pointing its thinkers toward a richer appreciation of the singular precisely as a universal event.

Postmodernism's impetus toward this richer sense is further adumbrated when the relation between event and novelty is considered. For instance, Lyotard observes that radical contingency obtains, not only in history, but also in contemporary science. He extends the principle of uncertainty posited in microphysics to all empirical processes, whose contingency thus becomes "undecidability."[57] But as Kenneth Schmitz observes, in empirical events, the novelty of phenomena is undecidable, not because of our ignorance, but because of "a mysterious active principle within reality itself" that generates creativity.[58] Thus, to the extent that postmodernism uses undecidability in nonhuman events as a basis for positing an absent center in human events, a false analogy obtains. In historical events, novelty is undecidable because of the spontaneity of human choice.[59] Indeed, this spontaneity would seem to be the energy driving the continuous process of writing that subsumes language and establishes meaning by the repeated transference of signs. If the call to make this spontaneity authentic seems to be evoking in postmodernism a hint of teleology, then events, even by postmodern standards, seem to revolve more around a center than they subsist in a radical absence.

Developing this hint into a patent thesis, Balthasar's aesthetics shows that a rich concept of the singular addresses postmodernism's

56. John D. Caputo, "Philosophy and Prophetic Postmodernism," in *American Catholic Philosophical Quarterly* 74 (Autumn 2000): 549–68, at 565–66; citing Jacques Derrida, "The Force of Law: 'The Mystical Foundation of Authority,'" trans. Mary Quantaince, in *Deconstruction and the Possibility of Justice*, ed. Drucilla Cornell et al. (New York: Routledge, 1992), 3–66, at 14–15.

57. Schmitz, "Addendum," 277–78.

58. Ibid., 278.

59. Ibid.

maladroit account of contingency as the seed bed of novelty. For Balthasar, Christ is the unique singular, the concrete universal, in whom "the essence of event as well as doctrine is embedded."[60] Because Christ is the enfleshed wedding of historical dynamism and self-subsisting transcendence, his determined humanity intrinsically expresses the infinite reality of God.[61] Theological aesthetics thus constitutes nothing less than the shining forth of the singular in its preeminent sense. Its beauty reveals a spontaneous novelty, heretofore undetermined, that incorporates contingency.

This revelation is achieved, first and foremost, by the striking innovation of Balthasar's grounding beauty, not in a consideration of reality as abstracted from the contingency of process, but squarely in a specific historical event—the crucifixion. On this ground, his analogous analogy so distances the similarity between God and the world that it strongly affirms the finite's radical contingency on the one hand and the divine revelation on the other hand, whose novelty can appear as *tout autre* (totally other) to intramundane standards, systems, and narratives.[62] In other words, the cross deconstructs the hegemony of the delight in harmony and symmetry as the norms of beauty. It renders these dependent on a deeper meaning of aesthetics. Originating in the indeterminacy of the divine freedom, this meaning manifests God's passionate love that cannot be induced, predicted, or deduced. Yet even as the crucifixion's strange appeal casts a judgment on historical process, it does not conflict with intramundane aesthetics or compromise God as beauty's prime analogate. Its gratuity shows us forcefully that worldly beauty, even when evaluated by its own criteria, is analogous.

In short, Balthasar's development of analogy entails a more extensive conception of the singular for which some strains of postmodernism are instinctively groping. He thus gives its proponents additional reason to question whether the emergence of novelty, however spon-

60. Balthasar, *Theology of Karl Barth*, 266 (emphasis removed).

61. Ibid.

62. Caputo, "Commentary," 255, referring to Derrida (unspecified).

taneous, can ever utterly elude human knowing. Far from setting up an impasse to a deeper penetration into reality, a rich appreciation of the singular such as his shows that contingency can be the creative heart of history. By deconstructing the relativism in the postmodern view of the singular, Balthasar buttresses Dupré's claim. Postmodernity subsists as a moment within a modernity fully endowed with resources to address its concerns. As an appreciative parent, modernity should nurture its offspring out of its immaturity.

Balthasar's notion of beauty can also help us to craft a role for Christian aesthetics in the face of modernity that we currently experience. Let us begin by considering modernity's current plight in contrast with the Baroque. Chapter 1 argued that the Baroque achieved its synthesis based on a vital presupposition: it emerged from a homogeneously God-centered culture. Modernity's three composite elements—human creativity, the extra-subjective cosmos, and their common transcendent ground—were harmonized, not estranged, as they are today. Hence, a distinctive form of beauty could emerge as symptomatic of their unity. In this beauty, at once representational and fanciful, saints and incarnate angels could radiate the glow of nature redeemed. In the Baroque's dynamic aesthetics of an ever-expanding universe of light and color, grace could be imagined as decisively subduing nature prone to the corrosiveness of error and evil. Little sense of the perduring insidiousness of these finds illustration in Baroque artifacts. Nor do we often baldly confront in them a sense of nature's concupiscent recalcitrance to grace's congenial action. The archangel's lance, for instance, victoriously thrusts the satanic dragon on the facade of Munich's Michaelskirche. Similarly, vanquished heretics fall in limber disgrace from the edges of Pozzo's *trompe l'oeil* of Jesuit triumphalism in Rome's Sant'Ignazio. An exception may be found in southern Bavaria's Wieskirche, where the grisly altarpiece of Christ scourged shatters, as if by bad taste, the splendor of the domed rotunda's white and gold. But this is more rococo than Baroque.

To our own later eyes, the Baroque's anachronism, even for believers, cannot be ignored. In the present situation, one cannot help but feel that the message of Baroque genius remains naively deficient in evoking religious sentiment. It is a sad irony of history that such an achievement of the human imagination, even while unchanged in the glory of its virtuosity, should appear as superficial and unconvincing. These hallowed shrines nowadays elicit more of the museum's disinterested connoisseurship than the church's contemplative devotion. A visit, for instance, to the still active monastery of Andechs, Zimmermann's masterpiece on the Ammersee, will find many a curious sightseer from the adjacent beer garden. But rare indeed is the pilgrim at prayer. Similarly, the Gesù along the Eternal City's Corso Vittorio Emmanuele stands daily replete with photo-eager tourists. But to avoid irreverence, the eucharist cannot be celebrated during "opening hours." In short, the message that Baroque beauty once proclaimed has evanesced; the analogy that structures it currently hobbles with a contemporary limp.

We might suggest, by contrast with Balthasar's notion of beauty as a complex analogous analogy, that the Baroque emphasizes intramundane criteria of aesthetics. These presuppose a simple interpretation of Basil's adage that the beauty of the divine is inferred from the beauty of the world. The Baroque's dynamic forms, which mediate between the merely earthly and the purely heavenly, display a nature brought by grace to nature's intrinsically appropriate harmony. In a homogeneously God-centered culture, such beauty can readily confer a universal sense of delight. Even today, one can still experience an enthralled admiration for the Baroque's ingenious allegory and complex imagery, however much a modernity marked by skeptical secularism dissociates these from an active faith. Because the secular is grounded in the distance between transcendence, mind, and the physical world, depicting natural forms in their sanctified perfection does not speak to our impoverished religious attitude. On the contrary, to this attitude the sacred appears no more patent than the profane.

Nonetheless, we need not wallow in too much grief over the Baroque's passing. However effective its transient synthesis, still its aesthetics displays but one dimension of the rich interplay between nature and grace. In fact, our current situation presents Christian art with a paradox that can spur fresh innovation. On the one hand, art must evoke the sense of transcendence that a secular age has placed at such distance from the modern connoisseur. On the other hand, even as it does, art must not abandon beauty's intramundane standards. If it does, it will forfeit altogether the analogy between transcendence and the world. Christianity can ill afford such a scenario. After all, in the incarnation, God and the world are salvifically joined; the divine love comes as the utterly unexpected gift that absorbs the perfidy of a fallen creation. As Balthasar reminds us, Christ, as the universal singular, embodies a distinctive beauty that, even while positing a caesura between itself and worldly aesthetics, affirms the created cosmos. As a consequence, Christian art must stretch the standards of intramundane beauty in order to represent them as analogously analogous to the beauty of the divine.

Past achievements can present this contemporary task with guiding precedents. Let us, for example, return to the Isenheim altarpiece of Grünewald. The grim realism of its agony, combined with the gangrenous Christ, starkly, even shockingly, contrasts with the beauty of the image's color and technical genius. These representations of formal symmetry can give us a certain delight, even as their vivid display of moral and physical evil can likewise repel us. Intramundane aesthetics is thus evoked while simultaneously deconstructed. The painting embodies a caesura that limits, even rudely halts, any pleasure that it elicits. In other words, the alluring beauty of the work's sensuousness draws us into contemplating the apparent ugliness of its crucified theme. The mind is thus stimulated to ponder a paradox that the artifact, in and of itself, does not resolve. The verbal silence of the work does not explicitly teach us that God's self-sacrificing freedom constitutes ultimate beauty. Such a lesson can only emerge from the analogy of faith. Because this analogy was known—and, more importantly, lived—by the patients who visited the hospital's chapel, the altarpiece could fulfill its aesthetic end. This gave them the comfort of hope in their pain by leading them deeply into the love of God in his own.

Today, of course, secular culture's lack of ready access to the analogy of faith deprives the Isenheim image of the transparency of its ultimate purpose. Nonetheless, its aesthetic paradox can continue to speak a hushed voice. Precisely because to its contemporary beholders it now offers more confusion than comfort, the tableau provokes a wonder that can create an opening for faith. This opening is caused, ironically, by the emptiness that one might feel when gazing on it. No one, however skeptical, can finally escape the question insistently posed to the thousands who each year visit the Alsacian museum where in Colmar it is housed: what attitude could prompt human genius to render so ugly a message so beautifully? This riddle engenders in the mind a dialectic that allows the beauty of Isenheim, unlike the high technique of the Baroque, to defy the vagaries of history. Despite its late medieval provenance, the work shines forth as distinctively religious and modern, today evoking its transcendent object implicitly, precisely because it denies that the beauty of its sensuous form is sufficient to explain its full aesthetic intent.[63] The artifact's surplus of meaning lies now not so much in the religious attitude that inspired its original audience, but in the modern mind's incapacity to render it fully intelligible.

A more recent artifact rises to meet the challenges of modernity in Georges Rouault's depiction of the face of Christ. Appearing in various versions between 1912 and the 1950s, the painting continues a tradition practiced by El Greco, Domenico Fetti, Gabriel Max, and others of representing the icon of Christ attributed to Veronica's veil.[64] Like Grünewald, Rouault depicts a paradox by stretching the limits of beauty's intramundane criteria. The tableau possesses a strange symmetry, even as its color tends toward the dull and heavy. Its technical mastery does not readily dazzle. In fact, nothing handsome distinguishes the face; nor does it seem, in the strict sense, representational of human-

63. Dupré, *Other Dimension*, 185, citing Libert Vander Kerken, *Religieus Gevroel en Aesthetisch Ervaren* (Antwerp: Standaard-Boekhandel, 1947), 67, 91.

64. Mario Ferrazza, "163, Georges Rouault (Paris 1871–1958), *The Holy Face (Sainte Face)*," in *The Vatican Collections: The Papacy and Art*, ed. John P. O'Neill et al. (New York: Metropolitan Museum of Art, 1982), 247.

ity. On the contrary, Christ appears distorted, certainly idiosyncratic, and not evocative of ready sympathy. These apparent deficiencies of taste create a caesura between the image and our usual expectations of aesthetically pleasing humanity.

As with Grünewald, however, this hiatus stimulates the eye to a closer study hopeful of drawing forth the work's latent beauty. This hope results from what one commentator calls the painting's "plasticity."[65] Ironically, the image's drabness actually represents a universal humanity. Who, we find ourselves asking, does the Christ resemble? Is it, for instance, an Ashkenazi Jew, or an Hispanic Indian? An illegal immigrant? Perhaps a migrant worker, or a Polynesian fisherman. Is it a Basque shepherd, a mechanic in Milan's Fiat factory, or a Mongolian subsisting near the Russian border? Is it Joshua, or a Canaanite prince? Isaac, or Ishmael? Whatever human being one might see in this mirror of an image, it is one and the same Christ who plays in "the features of men's faces." In these, he is "Lovely in limbs, and lovely in eyes not his."[66] The beauty radiated by the artifact deepens our awareness of human solidarity. Knowing more profoundly the love of Christ in his passion plunges us more intimately into the rich panoply of the ordinary struggles of the human condition. Conversely, loving humanity in the commonness, even the vulgarity, of its quotidian routine immerses us more deeply into Christ.

In sum, the aesthetic ingenuity modeled by Grünewald and Rouault is suited to the plight of secularism. In a sense, they turn the Baroque inside-out. They resist showing us how the light of grace brings into relief the luxuriant charm of nature. On the contrary, they exploit religious themes ironically to reconstitute a sense of the profane. They do this by evoking sentiments associated with the distinctive aspects of the profane that they display. In Rouault, for instance, the ordinariness of humanity disappoints. In Grünewald, moral and physical evil repels. In both, a divinity seemingly held hostage by, even reduced to, the profane stuns and bewilders. Not represented as homogeneously redeemed, nature emerges as richly singular, eccentric, heterogeneous, and fractured.

65. Ibid.
66. Hopkins, *Poetical Works*, 141.

In fashioning this vision, these two artists endeavor to reassert the salutary dialectic between the profane and the sacred that, as we argued in the previous chapter, alone keeps the secular at bay. As we said there, that nature can be considered profane does not deny its intrinsic union with grace. It does mean, however, that nature subsists, not merely as grace's substratum and congenial partner, but also as grace's combatant. If the Baroque, in a homogeneously God-centered culture, exploits nature's assent to grace, then Grünewald and Rouault remind us of the conflicts still entailed in nature as it struggles toward the fullness of the eschaton. These maestros of the eye invite us to contemplate that nature, not altogether extricated from its tragic situation, demands the salutary purification described by Benedict XVI. Nature is disharmonious with itself even as it is disharmonious with its final beatific end. As a result, nature is analogously analogous with grace. Grace heals nature's intrinsic rifts even as it enables nature to realize its disproportionately ultimate purpose.

By recovering the profane dimension of nature, these two artists do not spurn, however, the message of the Baroque. Nature's relation to grace is not only dialectical, but synthetic. By highlighting mind's labored access to grace, together with grace's perceived distance from the world, Grünewald and Rouault seek, paradoxically, to unite modernity's three estranged components. For them, transcendence is not postmodernism's unobtainably absent center; it is rather a complex analogy embodied in the person of Christ in the event of the cross. Hence, we might argue that their work chiefly proposes to nourish and stimulate the instinct of faith. If fulfilling this instinct absorbs humanity in its highest creativity, then these painters baffle and blind the contemporary mind only to clarify and enlighten it. In reconstructing the profane, they correspondingly deconstruct the secular, and so assist the sacred to rise, phoenix-like, from its ashes. They add further support to the claim made in chapter 2 that art will always provide a living synthesis of nature and grace. Ultimately seeking to reconcile the tension that they provoke, these works of virtuosity invite today's thwarted religious attitude to hope for, and in, grace.

Chapter 6

NOVELTY, ANALOGY, AND GOD

Our argument thus far has relied on Dupré's observation that the onto-theological synthesis of the West consists of three elements: the noetic subject as the interpreter of reality; the extra-subjective cosmos; and the transcendent source of both. Dupré affirms that modernity results from mind's assertion of its creative prerogatives over against a more passive assimilation of the physical world on whose forms mind, in other respects, depends. In meeting the modern problem with a model of nature and grace, chapter 4 argued that Thomas's instinct of faith, as retrieved by Seckler, accounts for the dynamic release of the human subject's potential. Where freedom flourishes, there results the spontaneity of human action in history, whose novelty cannot be anticipated or predicted. The instinct fuses into a harmony two of modernity's estranged elements: the subject whose creativity can fashion the cosmos, and the graced transcendence that constitutes this creativity's source and goal. Furthermore, we also claimed that the modern mind's assertion of its creative prerogatives has deepened the skepticism that leads to secularism. Moreover, skepticism has been broadened by developments in the empirical sciences that highlight the spontaneous capacity of the cosmos for emergent novelty. These have further strained the link between transcendence and the knowing subject. They have made it less than obvious how the world's causation can be reconciled with absolute being.

In light of our previous findings, and the method that we are using in chapters 5 and 6, our present task entails using a datum of grace as a starting point to develop an analogy that can integrate the novelty of the cosmos into human and divine freedom. The datum that we shall use is the "contemplation to obtain divine love," the concluding prayer of Ignatius Loyola's *Spiritual Exercises.* In explicating it, we shall further develop the philosophy of God sketched in the previous chapter.

Loyola's contemplation is intended to help the person making his way through the *Exercises* to recapitulate all the other contemplations done over thirty silent days. As a grand finale, the exercitant is asked to consider more deeply the nature of the love that God has instilled and awakened in his prayer. Love, Ignatius opines, consists principally in a mutual sharing of goods. As the paradigm of love, God, he says, is a laborer who works in creation by dwelling in it, filling it with life, and conserving it in being. Brimming forth love from his infinite superabundance, God issues all blessings and gifts "as the rays of light descend from the sun, and as the waters flow from their fountains." In recompense, what more can a human being who enjoys such unmerited bounty do but make his own self-offering to the divine self-offering that he receives. "You have given all to me," the retreatant is counseled to pray, "to You I return it."[1]

Let us concern ourselves with the claim that this vision, both poetic and panoramic, purports to make on our reason. Veiled under a well-intended piety, the prayer's appeals to the commonplaces of experience, like work, light, and flowing water, contain a metaphysics both sweeping and profound. They imply that, impregnating being, a dynamic and infinite love drives the finite order towards itself in a self-transcending motion. In making this metaphysics explicit, we will begin with its claim that the finite order is dynamic. Accordingly, let us turn to the doctrine of substance, which explains the finite order's basic structure.

1. Loyola, *Spiritual Exercises,* 101–3.

Substance, Motion, and Novelty

Substance explains the process of change or "becoming" precisely as a function of being, the universal horizon that is convertible with the intelligible. A translation of the Greek term *hypokeimenon*, substance means that which "stands under" or supports a reality. The classic definitions in Western thought, following Aristotle, offer variations on a common theme: substance is that which is apt to exist in itself and not in another.[2] A substance embraces its accidents, those attributes such as quality and quantity that are apt to exist, not in themselves, but in another. A substance is thus a reality in itself, distinct from its accidents, which inhere within it.[3]

Aristotle tends to see a substance as the sum total of its component accidents and thus to underplay the active relation obtaining between the whole and its constituents.[4] Descartes imports this tendency into modern thought. Although he contends that substances need nothing except God to exist, he tends to posit substances as isolated entities that exist "by" themselves rather than "in" themselves.[5] Norris Clarke observes that this isolation causes Whitehead, the Anglo-American process thinker, to reject the notion of substance altogether, because it fails to account for the mutual engagement among entities.[6] By contrast with the inert and reclusive model that descends from Aristotle through Descartes, some recent Thomist thought aims to retrieve the incipient dynamism in Aquinas's view of substance. It seeks to understand a substance as a system within a system. Accordingly, substance, in grounding the unity of an entity through change, is intrinsically en-

2. Aristotle, *Metaphysics* 1029a1–2. Cited in the text.

3. W. Norris Clarke, "Central Problems in Metaphysics," 7–8 (photocopy, course notes, Department of Philosophy, Fordham University).

4. Ibid., 8.

5. Clarke, "Central Problems in the History of Metaphysics" (photocopy, course notes, Department of Philosophy, Fordham University), 2. See René Descartes, *Principles of Philosophy*, trans. Valentine Rodger Miller and Reese P. Miller (Dordrecht: D. Reidel, 1983), part 1, principle 51.

6. Clarke, "Central Problems in the History of . . . Metaphysics," 2.

ergetic. As such, it explains the vitality of the processes of the finite order.[7]

Rahner, for instance, uses the *Realsymbol,* a theme already familiar to us, to make an especially important contribution to the understanding of finite substances as dynamically ontological events. As we will recall, the *Realsymbol* means that substances necessarily express themselves in order for their essential nature to become constituted. Substances are symbols because their accidental qualities are the media in which the identity of substances manifests and realizes itself. In a *Realsymbol,* the reality that the symbol represents is contained within the symbol itself. Following Aristotle's hylomorphism, Rahner posits that all finite substances are constituted by matter structured by form. Form is the cause of the essence or "whatness" of any existent (983a27); matter is the cause of its individuation and potential for change (1042a25). Consistent with Aristotle, Rahner views form and matter as distinct but inseparable metaphysical co-principles. But as chapter 4 has shown, Rahner adds new life to Aristotle by interpreting matter and form as reciprocally engaged partners. The origins of this creative interpretation lie in Hegel's logic of the "notion." When Hegel posited it, the notion was a new concept knowing no counterpart in traditional metaphysics.[8] Because of the notion's importance for Rahner's contribution to our present argument, let us briefly explore it.

According to Hegel, the notion is "the very heart" of the dynamic creativity inherent in reality.[9] "Becoming" is the fundamental or primal notion that originates all other ontological dynamisms (*EL,* 132). It is becoming, not being, that constitutes and generates the real order. True to its dynamic nature, becoming emerges from the mutual en-

7. Ibid., sections 8–10, advances this understanding and lists a bibliography.

8. W. T. Stace, *The Philosophy of Hegel* (London: Constable, 1955), 223.

9. Hegel, *EL,* 232. Cited in the text. This source renders Hegel's *Begriff* as "notion," which is used here. Recent sources, however, prefer "concept." See, e.g., Hegel's *Lectures on the Philosophy of Religion, One-Volume Edition: The Lectures of 1827,* ed. Peter C. Hodgson, trans. R. F. Brown et al. (Berkeley: University of California Press, 1988).

gagement of its two constituent partners, being and nothing. Considered separately, these are not concrete realities but pure abstractions of thought; they exist only as components of the notion that embraces them. It is thus becoming, as the primal notion, that for Hegel is the first concrete thought (*EL*, 132). Nonetheless, the abstract thought of being is the origin of the dynamic becoming that structures reality. This is so because being deductively entails the thought of nothing. Because being is the highest possible abstraction, it is therefore empty of any concrete reality. As a result, it is equivalent to nothing. Because nothing is deduced from being, nothing can be considered being's "own other" into which being passes. For its part, nothing, because it is the equivalent of being, may be said to pass into being (*EL*, 127–28).

It is this reciprocal "passing into" that, for Hegel, is the defining principle of the notion. It means that one thought generates another thought that, because of its opposition to the thought from which it ensues, is equivalent to the generating thought (*EL*, 218). In their passing into each other, the two thoughts constitute a unity-in-difference. Most importantly, this dynamic unity-in-difference produces a genuine ontological advance. In their opposition, the two thoughts parent the birth of the notion, which emerges in reality as something concretely new.[10] This emergence achieves a "sublation." It represents a self-perfection or self-consummation of the reciprocal passing-into of the two thoughts that produce it (*EL*, 129). In the case of the unity-in-difference that is being and nothing, this self-consummation is becoming. Because becoming is the fundamental notion, reality is thus conceived by Hegel as dialectically driven in its core.

Concerned about the deeper cause of this dialectic, Hegel's idealism asserts that the notion is embraced by spirit. The notion is spirit's heart. Spirit, not being, is thus for Hegel the universal horizon. As we will recall from chapter 2, spirit reconciles all oppositions because it includes them in its own infinite act. Because spirit is the generating source of reality's immanent dialectic, the notion's successively eter-

10. John E. Smith, "The Relation of Thought and Being: Some Lessons from Hegel's *Encyclopedia*," *New Scholasticism* 38 (1964): 22–43, at 36–37.

nal sublations progressively disclose spirit. Accordingly, spirit fully enfolds within itself the finite order, which constitutes an accident within spirit's own absolute substance. Infinite and finite thus constitute a unity-in-difference that is fundamentally univocal.

In his use of Hegel, Rahner wants to posit the core of substances as dynamic without at the same time devolving into the univocity of reality that underlies Hegel's idealism. Before laying out Rahner's differences with Hegel, let us first appreciate his debt to the great Romantic. Especially significant is Rahner's understanding of how a substance gives birth to ontological novelty: how, in other words, a substance produces a genuine ontological advance. This originality becomes clear when Rahner's theory of substance is interpreted in light of his theory of motion, change, and becoming. In the realism of Aristotle and Thomas, motion is the transition from potency to act. It occurs when a substance concretely embodies any change that is possible for it to undergo. Traditionally, this transition has not been understood to produce any indeterminate or spontaneous novelty in the real order. In other words, change brings forth no new being. Becoming merely modifies the mode in which the substance exists. Change, in short, simply explicates those determinations already latent in the substance.[11]

Rahner finds this traditional view untenable. Because change alters the accidents of a substance, he asserts that, *prima facie*, an entity possesses a newness. Change produces increments in reality heretofore undetermined (*H*, 73). These cannot be due, he argues, to the finite substance alone. On the contrary, undetermined increments in reality emerge when substances change, precisely because substances transcend themselves (*H*, 76–77). In other words, the new increments effected in change entail that a substance exceeds the strict limits of its essence or nature. Consequently, some other cause both superior to, and independent of, the substance in motion is required (*H*, 75–76). But this cause cannot merely be another finite substance. When any sub-

11. Karl Rahner, *Hominization: The Evolutionary Origin of Man as a Theological Problem* [hereafter "*H*"], trans. W. T. O'Hara (Freiburg-im-Breisgau: Herder, 1965). Cited in the text.

stance acts on another, it too undergoes a change that produces in itself a new self-transcending ontological determination. Because an endless regress would obtain if an adequate cause is sought only among finite realities, Rahner reasonably infers that this cause must be infinitely self-subsisting (*H*, 75). In this he agrees with Hegel. But because for Hegel the dialectic of the notion is driven by spirit's infinite and all-reconciling activity, Rahner parts company with him in an important respect.

For Rahner, the infinite does not constitute finite substances as its own accidents. It therefore cannot be defined as Hegel's spirit (*H*, 75–76). On the contrary, Rahner follows Thomas in affirming that the infinite is both self-subsisting and the cause and ground of the world's unity (*H*, 50). As the world's ground, it is thus immanent in empirical processes. As self-subsisting, it is also absolutely transcendent to them. Because it exists prior to the duality of form and matter, it cannot be encountered among substances and their processes as one of them. Nor can its effects within them be categorically isolated. (*H*, 51). In other words, the differences between infinite and finite cannot be reconciled into a univocity by the infinite's immanence in the finite. These claims ground Rahner's ability to preserve between both modes of reality the two analogies discussed in the previous chapter—intrinsic attribution and proper proportionality. Analogous predications remain ontologically distinct within their similarity because the finite's sustaining source utterly self-subsists.

Concerning the mode of the self-subsisting infinite's immanence in finite substances, Rahner stresses final causality. As Aristotle affirms, an infinite final cause is necessary to draw the changes of all finite realities to completion (1072a24–25, b10–12, 28–30). Developing Aristotle's position, Rahner posits that, as a final cause, the self-subsisting infinite evokes ontological novelty in changing substances. The realization of their newly determined novelty does not emerge with any mechanistic necessity. It is not fully predicable on the basis of the substance's potential. On the contrary, Rahner asserts, it embodies genuine spontaneity. The infinite cause functions in tandem with the randomness of empirical process (*H*, 64–65, 75–76, 80). As a result, changes as such may randomly emerge in substances, but their novelty results from the transcendent infinite that draws it forth in and through random changes.[12]

Although the immanence of the infinite causes changing substances to exceed the strict limits of their essence, it should not be understood as empowering them to mutate from one essence to another. It does not effect a substantial change. It accounts for the novelty produced in accidental change, insofar as substances realize new determinations that are spontaneous increments in being.

Novelty and the Infinite

Rahner's analysis raises an important question. Given that an infinite cause is needed to explain change, can the manner of its immanence in substances be further specified? Although Rahner does not directly supply an answer, one can be developed based on his argument. If the dynamism that intrinsically consummates substances can itself be considered an instance of ontological motion, then this dynamism should follow the *a priori* law of motion. It should, in other words, produce a new increment in reality. Consistent with Rahner's analysis, and with his debt to Hegel's notion, this increment should be due to the immanence of the infinite in the motion that produces it. It therefore follows that the infinite should be immanent in the ontological motion by which a substance is constituted. Put another way, the infinite should be immanent in the passing of form into matter and its return through matter to itself. It should further follow that this immanence is the reason why a substance can realize any new determination when it undergoes accidental changes. Let us pursue these thoughts in greater detail.

Rahner affirms that a substance is constituted by the mutual engagement of form and matter. This engagement structures a substance as a *Realsymbol*. We can look more closely into this structure by dividing it

12. Ibid., 90–91. The relation between the infinite cause and the randomness of empirical process requires an independent study in its own right.

into four moments: (1) the original unity of form and matter, which is the source of their difference; (2) their explicit differentiation within their unity; (3) their mediation, which obtains when form is emanated or passes into matter, its own other; and (4) their consummation, which obtains when form passes back into itself, and thus returns through its material mediation. The movement from the first moment of unity to the second moment of explicit differentiation introduces contingency into the core of a substance's structure. When form and matter are actively differentiated within the substance's unity, they necessarily entail negation. To be differentiated means that form and matter are determined in contradistinction to one another. "All determination is negation," Hegel's quotation of Spinoza reminds us (*EL*, 135). Moreover, all negation entails contingency, because what is determined is dependent on its not being something else.[13]

Contingency is thus lodged in the heart of a substance's structure. It is the basis of the differentiation of form and matter. This differentiation, we will recall, entails the mediation of form and matter, and their consummation precisely as a substance. Paradoxically, because contingency becomes a necessity within the motion that structures a substance as a dynamic event, it raises an important question: What carries this event beyond the negation, the contingency, that initiates it? The answer can only be the immanence of the infinite in the event. If it is acknowledged that, in moving beyond negation, the mediation of form in and through matter consummates the substance as a self-transcending event, then the cause of this event should be the same as the cause of self-transcendence in any motion. This cause is the infinite's immanence, which spontaneously generates increments in finite reality whenever new determinations obtain.

It is precisely because of the infinite's immanence in a substance's constitutive event, an event entailing motion, that novelty can appear in the empirical processes of the world. The infinite's immanence

13. Kenneth L. Schmitz, "Postmodernism and the Catholic Tradition," *American Catholic Philosophical Quarterly* 73 (Spring 1999): 233–52, at 250, observes that contingency involves two aspects: lack of necessity and dependence.

endows the substance with what might be called a surplus of reality. Because this surplus is derived from an infinitely creative source, it is able to carry the substance's constitutive dynamism beyond the contingency that initiates it. In doing so, the surplus of reality causes form to return to itself after its emanation in and through matter. This surplus thus explains how real increments can obtain when a substance undergoes accidental change. These are simply the newly determined manifestations of the surplus that is dynamically immanent in the substance's own ontological constitution. If, as Rahner says, a substance transcends itself in motion, this self-transcendence is due to a prior self-transcendence. This is defined by the immanence of the infinite that renders the core of finite substances spontaneously creative. It therefore follows: when substances interact within the empirical processes of the world, the changes they undergo produce new increments in reality. Substance, the basic structure of finite being, is thus the locus and seed bed of the novelty emergent in the cosmos.

A second question raised by Rahner's analysis of change concerns the mode by which the infinite is immanent in the dynamism constituting a substance. Rahner claims that this immanence results from final causality. This is only partially adequate: final causality is a necessary but not a sufficient explanation. Final causality would be a sufficient explanation if the motion of change were defined by the traditional realism that Rahner criticizes. As we recall, traditional realism asserts that motion is merely equivalent to the potential in the substance undergoing the change. In this case, the final cause would sufficiently explain how change draws forth a substance's potency and converts it into an equivalent actuality.

The situation is different, however, when motion is defined as producing an ontological increment. In this case, substances must embody an excess of potency. It is this excess that accounts for spontaneous creativity in the cosmos. Final causality accounts, not for this potency's existence, but for how this potency is drawn forth in motion. We are thus left with a question that Rahner's analysis raises but does not answer:

what cause explains the surplus ontological potency in finite reality?

To answer this question, let us return to the relation between Rahner's definition of substance and Hegel's notion. Rahner adapts the logic of the notion's reciprocal passing-into in order to explain a substance. This means that finite reality is constituted by an immanently dynamic motion. As we have seen, Hegel accounts for this dynamism by the immanence of the infinite in the finite as a formal cause. The essence of the ontological novelty produced by the notion's sublations is sufficiently explained by spirit. This is the infinitely dynamic substance that embraces and drives the notion as its accident. By contrast, Rahner does not posit finite substances as accidents of the infinite being. Nonetheless, if emergent novelty in the cosmos is to be sufficiently explained, it seems necessary to posit the immanence of infinite being in finite substances, not only as a final cause, but also as some mode of formal causality.

We are thus brought to an aporia. On the one hand, the infinite must relate to the finite order as a mode of formal causality. On the other hand, this relation cannot be so construed as to make the finite order the accidents of the infinite substance. It is not possible, therefore, to use Rahner's understanding of the reciprocity between form and matter in finite substances as a model for understanding God's relation with the world. God does not emanate himself forth into the matter of the world and return to himself through the world to constitute himself. Doing so would make God's intrinsic constitution dependent on creation. Therefore, in order to qualify the mode of formal causality that obtains between God and the world's emergent novelty, we need to turn to another theme in Loyola's contemplation: the relation between being and love, first in God, and then between God and the world. If it should be possible to infer from reason that God is love, then it should be credible to claim that freedom is the mode of God's relation with the finite order. If this should be so, then love should explain the dynamism of emergent novelty in the cosmos.

Freedom, God, and Love

Our first question thus concerns whether it is possible, from reason, to infer that God is the subject of love. In his categorical denial, Aristotle has perhaps set the West's philosophical agenda. Early in *Metaphysics,* alluding to Parmenides and Hesiod, he avers that love is the cause of all motion and the reason for the coherence of the cosmos (984b24). But his subsequent discussion of the prime mover makes it clear that, however necessary divinity is, it is not the subject of love. Love would imply that the infinite being desires something that it does not have. This cannot be, since the prime mover is pure actuality, immune to all change, and perfect because it contemplates its own infinite self-knowledge. Were this not the case, the prime mover could not be the necessary and sufficient explanation for finite motion. This is caused precisely by the love of spatio-temporal beings; they yearn for the prime mover as their ultimate object of desire. As infinitely unchangeable, the prime mover draws the motion of their loving desire towards itself. In so doing, it initiates, sustains, and consummates all change. The prime mover's influence on the world does not therefore derive from its inner life. It derives only from the prime mover's infinite finality. Thus spared the passion of love, this infinite finality is also "spared" any freedom (1072b).[14]

Aristotle's position may be slightly nuanced. Thomas, for instance, makes note of an important line in the *Nicomachean Ethics* where Aristotle says: "God rejoices by an operation that is one and simple."[15] Thomas interprets this to mean that God's rejoicing is a function of his intellect and hence is devoid of any passion, sensuous desire being a function of the materiality that God by definition lacks. Thomas concludes that God can love in the same way that Aristotle affirms God can rejoice. Love is the first act of the will because it aims at the universal good. Because God has will, God therefore aims at the universal good, which is himself (*ST* I, q. 20, a. 1).

14. See also W. D. Ross's commentary in *Aristotle's Metaphysics* (Oxford: Clarendon Press, 1924), 1:xiii–clxv, at cxxx–cliv.

15. Aquinas, *ST* I, q. 20, a. 1, citing Aristotle, *Nicomachean Ethics* 1154b26.

Nonetheless, the Angelic Doctor's predication of love in God is merely another way of affirming Aristotle's claim that the prime mover contemplates itself. As a result, Thomas's position does not produce a significant advance. On the one hand, he assumes the existence of God as infinite being endowed with intellect and will and then infers God's love from these assumptions. On the other hand, he does not relate God's love to the finite order. Two pressing issues thus remain. They coalesce around a key question: is it possible to infer from the reality of the finite order that being itself is loving? In other words, is it possible to show that love, and hence the freedom that it entails, are perfections of being, not defects? If so, then the finite order in its contingency could reasonably be shown to stand in relation to a loving and free first cause. As one commentator incisively remarks, Thomas's metaphysics needs restructuring in order to take more explicit account of the personal.[16] Accordingly, let us turn again to Rahner, who develops an argument that, based on the conditions of the human person's ability to know, purports to reach God as a free and loving person.

Rahner begins this argument with the questioning nature of humanity. When inquiring about the world and its causes, we already assume that answers will be delivered, often after lengthy investigation. This seek-and-find dynamic that defines the mind's quest is the principle of intelligibility. It means that what the mind endeavors to know—the reality or being of the world and its causes—is luminous. When answers resolve our questions, reality becomes present not only to us but also to itself, in and through our inquiring minds. The self-presence of being shines nowhere more brightly than in language. By naming and articulating the answers to our questions, language reveals and manifests the implicit intelligibility of being, together with its intrinsic expressiveness and communicability.

That questioning defines humanity constitutes an *a priori*. Rahner warrants this claim by the type of argument that originates in Socrates's

16. Robert O. Johann, *The Meaning of Love: An Essay Towards a Metaphysics of Intersubjectivity* (Westminster, Md.: Newman Press, 1955), 7.

critique of the skeptics and that subsequently finds echoes in Augustine, Descartes, Kant, Newman, and Maréchal. To deny that we are questioners only serves to affirm that we are. In other words, to say that I am not a questioner answers an implicit question. It therefore follows that the mind is capable of affirming at least one axiom that is necessary, absolute, and indubitable. In fact, the mind must make this affirmation if it is to obey the law imposed by its own nature.

That questioning defines humanity entails another *a priori* claim: that we are radically contingent. The mind is not immediately replete with answers to its questions. Often it must grope laboriously before it can even frame a question. To ask questions and secure answers, the mind must turn outward from its own being to that of the external world. Thus dependent on the world, the mind confronts the world as the heteronomous cause of its questions and answers. It follows therefore that humanity is not self-caused, but finite.

Because the human person, in its contingency, can and must affirm eternal *a priori* truths, the nature of the person is revealed as a paradox. Because the objects that the mind knows are finite and mutable, they cannot serve as a sufficient explanation of the mind's capacity to posit these truths. The only other reasonable explanation lies in the mind's own act. It is this act, after all, that affirms the absolute claims. As a result, it follows that the mind's act of affirmation must intend the absolute in its noetic reach, at least implicitly.

As we saw when discussing Rahner's metaphysics of knowledge in chapter 2, this noetic intention does not mean that the mind knows or grasps the infinite as an object of its experience. Such a claim would posit a contradiction. Either the infinite would be made finite, or the contingent mind would be made infinite. Because neither is true, the mind must intend the absolute by yearning for it, just as motion in Aristotle desires the infinite object of love. By way of correcting Aristotle, however, Rahner rightly asserts a reciprocity between the contingent questioner and the absolute. If the activity of the questioner implicitly intends the absolute as a goal, end, or final cause, then the absolute must implicitly be present in the questioner's intention, not as an object of affirmation, but as any cause must be implicit in the effect that it produces.

Because of the reciprocity between infinite being and the contingent mind, a dynamic movement is revealed in the core of human knowing. The mind comes to know contingent objects by contrast with the implicit intentionality of its questioning. Because this intentionality aims at the absolute, the absolute's immanence structures the act of knowledge by which contingent objects are affirmed. As a result, knowing entails a dual motion. On the one hand, the mind's intention moves toward the absolute. On the other hand, the contrast in the mind between the intended absolute and the contingent objects that it draws from the finite world moves the person to know whatever is known.

We now come to the inference important for the argument's claim that being is free. The dynamic core of knowing entails volition or will as a necessary cause. Will after all means yearning, and yearning explains knowing's dual movement. Where there is will, freedom is necessarily entailed. It follows therefore that, when we affirm our own contingency as an *a priori*, we necessarily use will. As a result, freedom lies in the core of existence, and thus in the heart of being's luminous self-presence. Freedom is more than a necessary condition of our own ability to render being self-present in the act of knowing. It constitutes a necessary condition of being as such, of pure being, of being absolutely.

The argument for this claim is twofold. First, the freedom of infinite being is antecedently probable. In other words, before a direct argument is put forth, the infinite's freedom is likely, based on indirect evidence. This indirect evidence emerges from the doubly dynamic nature of knowing. More precisely, it emerges from the analogy of being that this dynamism grounds. Let us pursue this point further.

We have already seen that the human intellect, as questioning, is the locus of being's luminous self-presence. We have also seen that being cannot become luminously self-present without the immanence of the absolute in the dynamic act of affirmation. Being's luminous self-presence thus manifests an analogy between the infinite and the finite.

As we know, analogy means that one reality exists in qualitatively different modes. Accordingly, the one act of knowing that affirms any finite object implicitly affirms the infinite that is implicitly intended in any act of affirmation. Moreover, as we have seen, to be luminously self-present means that being is intelligent, self-expressive, communicative, and free. If the human being is the locus of this self-presence, and if absolute being is implicit in human knowing, then the absolute should be affirmable as intelligent, self-expressive, communicative, and free. We have clear evidence for the first three of these four predicates. The absolute expresses and communicates itself as the qualitatively "other" that is noetically intended in the radical contingency of the human being. If the infinite is known by analogy as intelligent, self-expressive, and communicative, then by analogy it is likely that the infinite should also be the subject of freedom.

Bolstering the antecedent probability of this indirect argument from analogy is a direct argument deduced from the necessity of humanity's nature as radically contingent. As previously shown, this contingency must be claimed by us necessarily and also willed by us. From this claim another one follows. That we will ourselves as contingent is tantamount to ratifying that we are freely posited and do not posit ourselves. In other words, because we are by nature contingent, we are not by nature necessary. We could not have existed; the same applies to the universal cosmos of finite reality. That it, together with ourselves, do in fact exist implies that we are posited by a being who is not contingent but absolute.

Moreover, our being posited by the absolute must be free. If the absolute did not posit us freely but necessarily, then we would be necessary just as our cause is necessary. In that case, we would be posited necessarily by the absolute as beings who could or could not exist. This is a patent contradiction. If we were posited necessarily by the absolute, we would be beings who must exist. However, because we are radically contingent, we could not have existed. It follows, therefore, that it is absurd to claim that a contingent being can be posited necessarily by absolute being.

Several further conclusions ensue from this argument. Because absolute being is free as well as intelligent, the absolute is personal. Where there is free personhood, there is love. As Aristotle observes, love is the root of choice insofar as it intends an end or goal. The finite order, therefore, is lovingly intended by the absolute person. Accordingly, this person and the human person face each other in a reciprocal freedom that is analogous to their mode of being.[17]

It would take us far beyond our purpose to offer a critique of Rahner's argument. Like all arguments, it is not invulnerable.[18] Still, it will serve as a sufficient warrant to proceed with our broader discussion. If it can reasonably be claimed that God is the proper subject of love, then God is the loving end intended by the motion of human knowing. Precisely as this end, God is also lovingly immanent in this motion. Accordingly, we have rendered into a philosophical idiom some key claims of Loyola's contemplation. Absolute love impregnates absolute being. Because this love draws the human being towards itself, it causes humanity's self-transcendence. But this love is also immanent in human intelligence, thus impregnating the motion of questioning and answering. Because human intelligence reveals an analogy between infinite and finite being, it follows that an analogy of love also obtains between them. As a result, God's love explains not only human self-transcendence, but also the transcendence of all finite substances previously discussed. In other words, love is the mode of infinite being's immanence in finite substances. Infinite love renders them dynamically and spontaneously creative. In sum, therefore: the divine love, as a final cause, accounts for the emergent novelty of the cosmos.

Important claims in Loyola's prayer still need to be worked out. These concern the nature of God whose love impregnates being. They

17. Rahner's argument is found in his *Hearer of the Word: Laying the Foundation for a Philosophy of Religion*, trans. Joseph Donceel (New York: Continuum, 1994), chap. 7. My explication involves considerable interpretation.

18. I have discussed criticisms in "Contraries in One: Contingency, Analogy, and God in Transcendental Thomism," in *Metaphysics of Aquinas*, ed. Cullen and Harkins; originally delivered at the 31st Annual Conference of the Center for Medieval Studies, Fordham University, Lincoln Center, New York, March 26–27, 2011, and revised for publication.

also concern specifying the mode of formal causality obtaining between God and the world. We shall begin to explore these issues where Rahner's argument has left us.

God, Love, and Being

Rahner's argument provides a philosophical warrant for the doctrine of creation. Creation means that the radically dependent finite order could not have existed, but was brought into being by the free intention of a being capable of doing so. Rahner argues that the radical contingency of the finite order entails its free positing by the absolute being who is a loving person. If this is the case, then we need to inquire into the nature of the love that initiates the infinite person's free intention to create. On the one hand, the love that Thomas predicates of God is inadequate, because this is the infinitely self-sufficient love that contemplates itself as the universal good. It does not move into the finite order. If it did, it would entail contemplating as a good the contingent other and thus violate the universal good.[19]

On the other hand, if we posit in God a love that freely moves into contingency, then do we still have God? As Thomas (following Aristotle) says, God loves by an operation that is one and simple. Again we confront the problem that we broached in the last chapter. There we were required to show how two principles (being and the beauty) could be introduced into God while still preserving his uncompounded essence. Here we need to clarify two relations in God: that between being and love and that between simplicity and the motion that love entails. For help, let us continue chapter 5's efforts to mine the thought of Pseudo-Dionysius and Basil.

Our previous study of Pseudo-Dionysius revealed that the source of the divine being that mediates the finite cosmos lies in another perfection of the Godhead—the divine love that Pseudo-Dionysius names

19. How, for Thomas, God's omniscience embraces the contingent order is a separate question that cannot be taken up here.

eros. The divine act of being proceeds through eros and in eros being subsists.[20] Eros is thus "the cause of initiation" of being.[21] "Being and well-being" flow through it "to all that is."[22] In specifying God's absolute love as eros, Pseudo-Dionysius eschews two other readily available Greek words, *agape* and *philia*. *Agape*, for instance, is preferred for the divine love throughout the fourth Gospel. Neither *agape* nor *philia*, however, denotes passion, yearning, desire. *Agape* evokes the universally disinterested love that Thomas predicates of God. In using eros, Pseudo-Dionysius thus changes what divine perfection means. A high innovator, he supplants the divine love as beneficent impartiality with extroverted engagement. He lodges motion in divinity's core.

As a perfection, eros, claims Pseudo-Dionysius, is equally convertible with beauty and goodness, and with light.[23] Of special concern to us is the convertibility of eros, beauty, and goodness. In the first place, beauty and goodness are convertible by definition. "The good is celebrated ... as beauty," the Areopagite posits, because goodness "causes the consonance and splendor of all."[24] It "brings all together into unity," thus giving everything the order and symmetry appropriate to it.[25] The divine goodness is eros because the divine does not "abide in itself but has moved" to "the generative thrusting forth of all beings."[26] Accordingly, the "divine eros is ecstatic."[27] "By the beautiful and good eros of all," the divine "comes to be outside of itself and into all things through its providences."[28] As a result, being emerges as anything but a static act. On the contrary, it is generated by the motion of love, even as being generates the motion of God's self-communication in the finite order. Of vital importance, Pseudo-Dionysius asserts that the "preeminent

20. Pseudo-Dionysius, *DN*, chap. 5; in Balthasar, *GL* 2:144–210, at 189.

21. Pseudo-Dionysius, *CH* III.1 (164D); in Balthasar, *GL* 2:196.

22. Pseudo-Dionysius, *EH* I.3 (373CD); in Balthasar, *GL* 2:200.

23. *DN* IV.7 (701C); in Pseudo-Dionysius the Areopagite, *The Divine Names and Mystical Theology*, trans. John D. Jones (Milwaukee, Wis.: Marquette University Press, 1980), 138.

24. Ibid.

25. Ibid., 139; *DN* IV.7 (704A), in Jones, 139.

26. *DN* IV.10 (708B), in Jones, 142–43.

27. *DN* IV.13 (712A), in Jones, 145.

28. *DN* IV.13 (712B), in Jones, 145.

ecstasis of the divinity" is the incarnation.[29] Because the incarnation is free, God's eros must be free. The divine freedom thus grounds both creation and redemption, nature and grace. If the divine eros is free, then so is being that eros mediates, as well as the divine beauty and goodness convertible with eros. Accordingly, Pseudo-Dionysius poses a counterfoil both to Aristotle, who argues for the eternality of the cosmos, and to Neoplatonism, which posits its necessity.

From these rich insights, we can harvest several items important for our current discussion. First, because absolute love generates absolute being, being would seem eternally subordinate to love. Second, because being emerges out of the love that mediates it, being must be infused with love. Third, because God's self-communication is generated in love, the entire order of finite being, human and otherwise, must be impregnated with love. Fourth, if the finite order is impregnated with love, then it must be immanently dynamic. It must yearn to achieve a purpose, to reach an end or a goal. Consistent with Aristotle's teaching, this end or goal must be absolute being. Consistent with Rahner's argument, this absolute being must be the loving person who freely communicates the yearning.

Nonetheless, Pseudo-Dionysius's doctrine of God, however seminal and original, continues to threaten God's simplicity. Aristotle is correct in perceiving a certain necessity in love. Because love is motion, it aims at an end, however spontaneously chosen this end may be. But for the divine eros to be truly free, it must be satisfied within itself as its own end. Otherwise, if the free motion of love immanent in God does not terminate in God as its own immanent goal, then it must terminate in a goal other than God. It must terminate therefore in finite being. In order to avoid this conclusion, God must be seen to communicate his loving being to the finite order precisely because he is perfectly satisfied. In this case, God's loving self-communication would be utterly free and gratuitous, and God's ontological simplicity would remain integral.

29. Jones, "Introduction," *Divine Names*, 15–103, at 59.

For his part, Basil does not explicitly consider the relation between love and being in God, but his insights previously explored can help us to resolve the aporia between motion and the divine simplicity. Let us again exploit his understanding of virtual distinctions in God. In the first place, what was said in chapter 5 about the relation between beauty and being applies equally well to that between love and being. As virtually distinct, love and being do not vitiate God's essential simplicity. Being emerges eternally from the divine eros, which impregnates being, and thus renders being a constitutive moment within itself. As a result, the distinction between eros and being implies no interval or void but constitutes a continuous and uninterrupted unity. Consistent with God's paradoxical nature, this unity might be called a mediated immediacy. In other words, the divine eros is mediated to itself through being that it generates. Because being is the intrinsic product of eros, it follows that eros is mediated to itself through being.

Moreover, if being mediates eros to itself, it also follows that eros mediates being, because eros generates being. Being is therefore mediated immediately by eros. Accordingly, the relation of mediated immediacy obtaining between being and eros is reciprocal. As reciprocal, being and eros subsist in God as a community (*koinonia*) bound together by the immanent motion of virtual distinctions. If love and being subsist in a reciprocal relation of mediated immediacy, then, *pace* Pseudo-Dionysius, neither love nor being is subordinate to the other. Each is necessary for the consummation of the other, even as their mutual consummation subsists as a function of God's essential simplicity. In short, God is supremely free, because God is the end, purpose, and goal of his own loving motion. The love that generates being terminates in God, because eros is reflected to itself through being.

Our synthesis of Pseudo-Dionysius and Basil in light of Rahner's argument for the intrinsic freedom of being has accomplished four purposes. First, Rahner shows us that freedom intrinsically structures the analogy between the infinite and the finite. Second, Pseudo-Dionysius posits that this freedom inheres in God, whose beauty and goodness, convertible with his ecstatic eros, mediate being. Third, Basil demonstrates that these transcendentals, as virtual distinctions, do not vitiate God's absolutely simple *koinonia*. Fourth, our synthesis effectively brings us to an understanding of the divine simplicity consistent with the *Realsymbol*, Rahner's definition of reality that adapts Hegel's notion. This last claim can be laconically explained.

As we know, the *Realsymbol* means that reality expresses itself in order to become itself. Reality is thus mediated immediately. It generates its own other and returns through this other to itself. Reality thus constitutes its own symbol that represents itself to itself. In finite substances, form passes into matter, making matter its own other. As form returns through matter to itself, it constitutes a substance as a unified ontological entity. Accordingly, as *Realsymbolic*, God may be said to express himself in order to constitute his essential simplicity. The divine love generates being as its own other and returns through being to itself. Being is thus love's intrinsic symbol that, impregnated by love, reflects love to itself. The reciprocity between love and being in God entails no gap or void, because they are virtually distinct within his essential simplicity. Moreover, it entails no subordination of one virtual distinction to the other, because each is necessary for the other's consummation, as well as for the consummation of the divine simplicity. As the essentially simple community of reciprocal motion without real distinctions, God is therefore properly called a *Realsymbol* by analogy with finite substances. In fact, as the infinitely self-subsisting being, God is the prime analogate of *Realsymbolism*.[30]

God and Novelty

Our final question concerns using the *Realsymbolism* of God to explain more fully emergent novelty in the world. We have already seen how the divine love as a final cause partially explains this novelty in sub-

30. Rahner, "Theology of the Symbol," in *TI* 4:231–32, uses the *Realsymbol* to explain the relation between Father and Son in the revealed doctrine of the Trinity. I am not aware of his using it anywhere to explain the philosophical doctrine of God.

stances. What remains to be explained is the existence of ontological potency that accounts for the emergence of new being when substances change. As we saw earlier, this excess can be explained by the infinite's immanence in substances as a mode of formal causality. This mode cannot be so construed, however, as to render the finite order the accident of the infinite substance. The explanation that follows, grounded in exemplary causality, sketches a solution.

As the proper subject of eros, God's love can move beyond itself. Nonetheless, because God's eros terminates in himself as its own end, God is supremely free. As *Realsymbolic,* God does not sublate his eros in and through the finite order. God's free intention to create is not driven by the need of his eros to terminate in a heteronomous object. As a result, creation is posited by the divine eros in supreme freedom. As freely given, creation is contingent and therefore radically other than its absolute source. Contingency implies determination, and determination implies, as we have seen, negation. Thus an infinite void separates the infinite from the finite. This void spares the finite from being absorbed as an accident within the absolute substance of its divine creator. Furthermore, because of this void, God and the world can constitute, as Pseudo-Dionysius says, a "like unlikeness."

As Pseudo-Dionysius also observes, God communicates being to the finite order by means of his own being. As *Realsymbolic,* God's being and love are mediated immediately in a reciprocal motion. Because God's being is impregnated with love, the finite order that ensues from it is impregnated with love. Moreover, as Christian Platonism and Thomas both affirm, in creating the contingent order, God is the exemplary cause of all that is and can be. An exemplary cause is often called an extrinsic formal cause because of its transcendent independence to that to which it gives meaning and intelligibility. As creation's exemplary cause, God is the absolute archetype of all contingent beings. These thus become images of the divine. As a principle of being, even pure potency, according to Thomas, owes its origin to the infinite archetype.[31] In exemplary causality, the immanence of the cause in its

31. Aquinas, *Summa contra Gentiles* II, chaps. 45–46; *De potentia* q. 3, a. 1, ad 12.

effects obtains by the will or intention of the cause (*ST* I, q. 14, a. 8; q. 15, a. 1).

Accordingly, the existence of all exemplary images, including potency, must be suffused with the divine eros that inspires God's free intention to create them. Because the divine eros is a dynamic motion impregnating potency, the divine eros explains the existence of the excess of potency in finite substances. The divine eros is a motion that, immanent in being, drives substances in change to realize the spontaneous creativity of ontological newness. Driven by love in the potency of being, emergent novelty in the cosmos is also drawn to its loving end by God as the final cause of all emergent processes. God, the absolute *Realsymbol*, thus initiates and consummates the many *Realsymbols* of the world that, as divine creator, God freely intends.

Up to this point in chapter 6, we have used our sacramental model of nature and grace to evince deeper insights into reality from a datum of faith. Based on the premise that grace constitutes nature as its intrinsic medium, we rendered the contemplation of Loyola into a philosophical idiom. This explains how the absolute person and the extra-subjective cosmos can obtain as an analogy of love. Moreover, in demonstrating how this analogy accounts for the emergent novelty of the cosmos, we continued our dialogue with modernity. Dupré, we will recall, argues that modernity results when subjective mind becomes estranged from the transcendence grounding both it and the physical world. The current chapter shows how analogy can realign God and objective reality into a sympathetic relation. It thus complements chapter 4, which evinces a similar realignment for God and human ingenuity. To complete our dialogue with modernity, we still need to show how the analogy between nature and grace can sympathetically realign mind and world in and through God, who is the source of both. We will do this by drawing out implications in claims already established. Afterward, our conclusion will further develop the reflections on postmodernism begun in the previous chapter.

Modernity

Consistent with the realism of Aristotle and Thomas, Dupré observes that, however creative mind may be, it remains dependent on the cosmos. In other words, mind's apprehension of objective form serves as a precondition for the products of individual genius. For its part, Seckler's study of the instinct of faith in Aquinas shows us that the questing of mind's wonder, which generates all invention, originates in mind's implicit religious vocation. For their part, recent commentators of the Angelic Doctor remind us that, in assimilating the forms of the extra-subjective world, mind cannot be reduced to a passive recipient. Precisely because of its innate creativity, mind, as an endowment of the human spirit, reaches out, as it were, to physical reality in order to grasp its inherent meaning.[32] It seizes on this meaning in a way that defies adequate specification. Having done so, however, mind dynamically acts upon this meaning to build complex systems of culture, such as language, science, and art. Some systems, like the mathematical theorems of physics, can predict future events; others, like the humanities, study the creative products of imagination, develop hypotheses accounting for the spontaneity of people's choices in history, and seek answers for our pressing exigency to ask what Paul Tillich calls questions "of ultimate concern."[33]

We are thus led to conclude that the instinct of faith bears responsibility for the human drive to assimilate the physical world's inherent meaning and to explicate it, not merely mimetically, but creatively. As Goethe would opine, human genius integrates the realm of things into a new harmony that consists, not of pallid copies of the world, but of symbols that interpret humanity's appropriation of the world.[34] The

32. See, for instance, Joseph Maréchal, *A Maréchal Reader*, ed. and trans. Joseph Donceel (New York: Herder and Herder, 1970), 202–3, 128–30, citing *ST* I, q. 77, a. 4; see also Rahner, "Theology of the Symbol," 233.

33. Paul Tillich, *Systematic Theology*, 3 vols. (Chicago: University of Chicago Press, 1951), 1:12.

34. Elizabeth M. Wilkinson, "The Poet as Thinker," in *Goethe: Poet and Thinker*, ed. Wilkinson and Willoughby, 133–52, at 141.

instinct of faith, as Seckler shows us, is oriented to a single supernatural end, the absolute. Because Rahner shows us that this end is the loving God, we can further conclude that the instinct of faith is driven by, and directed to, infinite love. Because we have also seen that infinite love accounts for the dynamism of the physical cosmos, we can also conclude that one and the same infinite love links the emergent intelligibility of extra-subjective reality to the instinct of faith. It is the instinct that causes the world's reality to be penetrated and its meaning developed and expressed.

We might speculate further. Is it possible to say, for instance, that the extra-subjective cosmos is free and that this freedom is owing to grace? We have suggested that change in the physical cosmos effects a spontaneously emerging novelty that, while not compromising the structured forms of reality, nonetheless adds a premium to the intelligibility of the universe. This premium, we further argued, is due to an excess of potency in substances that, in turn, is owing to the creative immanence in them of the infinitely loving person. Accordingly, it seems reasonable to claim that, if substances manifest spontaneity when they change, they might fittingly be called free, although in a sense analogous to human beings. Although they do not determine themselves, their emergent novelty cannot be reduced to a merely mechanistic transition from potency to act.

Furthermore, we have previously offered reasons for equating the instinct of faith with prevenient grace. Because one and the same infinite love endows mind with the instinct of faith on the one hand and the physical cosmos with emergent novelty on the other, it seems reasonable to conclude that the objective world is the bearer of grace, although again in a way analogous to human beings. Rahner observes, for instance, that "the 'relative autonomy' of the natural physical and cultural spheres never extends, in Catholic theology, to the implication that they can achieve even the significance which is their own and immanent to them, except through the grace of God in Jesus Christ."[35] If grace is the

35. Rahner, *The Christian Commitment*, 50.

life of God lovingly sanctifying that to which it is given, then it seems appropriate to affirm that the physical world, recapitulated by Christ, is sanctified for the purpose of rendering it conducive to human beings, who must work out their salvation in and by means of it.

We might therefore claim that at least one manifestation of the extra-subjective world's sanctification consists of its emergent novelty. We might suggest that God would sanctify the world in this way precisely to stimulate the instinct of faith, which renders human creativity an implicit religious vocation. We have said, for instance, that it is impossible for the human mind merely to reproduce the forms of physical reality. On the one hand, reality itself, manifesting a certain spontaneity in the dynamism of its formal structure, defies mere mimesis. On the other hand, when the human mind reaches out to grasp the meaning of the cosmos, it cannot help but assimilate the novel intelligibility that the cosmos evinces. If so, then this assimilation would nourish the mind with an intelligibility exceeding the mere appropriation of the forms of the physical cosmos. In turn, this intelligibility would render mind more creative in relation, as Dupré says, "to that physical reality on which it in other respects depends."[36] Accordingly, the complex systems of human thought, as symbols of subjective genius, would add meaning to reality, even as they would require revision and emendation as reality spontaneously develops and evolves.

If the extra-subjective world can be considered graced, then the upshot is that grace would emerge in nature in order to stimulate the ingenuity of persons and thus feed the instinct of faith. Grace would thus close into a circle the three elements that constitute modernity. The instinct of faith would constitute the meeting point of objective reality and grace active in the human person. God, the infinitely loving person who constitutes the instinct's source and goal, would sanctify the extra-subjective cosmos with an intelligibility that stimulates the instinct. As a result, human beings, working out their salvation by means of the world, would be enabled to attain their one end in God. Emer-

36. Dupré, *Passage to Modernity*, 252.

gent novelty in the cosmos would thus subsist as an efficacious sign. Causing what it signifies, it would return humanity to the one who both creates and redeems it.

Our reflections on emergent intelligibility in the cosmos can aid us further to address the inadequacy of postmodernism that we discussed in chapter 5. There we argued that its "riot of diversity" appears instinctively to be groping for a rich concept of the singular that Balthasar's aesthetics helps to supply. We will recall that the singular does not mean merely the particular, but rather the individual existent, which joins together the universal's commonality and the particular's determinacy. Balthasar's analogous analogy, the crux of nature's relation to grace, reveals in the crucifixion that the singular's contingency constitutes the creative heart of novelty in history. For its part, Rahner's understanding of the singular complements Balthasar's. By innovatively interpreting substances as *Realsymbols*, it shows how the singular accounts for novelty in nonhuman events. In these events, as we have seen, postmodernism suggests that novelty emerges as a "totally other," eluding human knowing. Because knowing thereby reaches an unbreachable impasse, postmodernism infers that novelty is undecidable and that the empirical processes of the world lack any existing center. From this lack, postmodernism infers the irreducibility of radical contingency in empirical process.

By contrast, Rahner demonstrates that it is more reasonable to infer from undecidability deeper levels of intelligibility. As *Realsymbols*, substances are dynamic events that generate these levels precisely through contingency and absence. It is the absolutely loving person, we argued, who carries the dialectic constituting substances beyond negation to their consummation. As a result, deeper levels of meaning, heretofore undetermined, refuse to submit to a full reduction by human knowing. They are derived from an infinitely creative source acting in tandem with the randomness of empirical process. Rahner's account of the singular thus develops Kenneth Schmitz's claim, quoted in chapter 5, that undecidability results, not from any gap in reality, but from "a mysterious active principle" percolating forth novelty from within it.[37] In short, like Balthasar, Rahner deconstructs the relativism in postmodernism's account of the singular. By recovering universality within the singular's contingency, he lends further support to Dupré's view that postmodernism subsists as a moment within what is rightly deemed the modern.

Conclusions

Let us now make clear how our analyses in chapters 5 and 6 are complementary. While addressing our current experience of modernity, they lay out a coherent scheme for the relation between nature and grace. The method used in these chapters represents a development of the model that we put forth in chapter 4. For its part, this model emerged from the probings of our first three chapters into the history of nature and grace's relation. In chapter 4, we asserted that the sacramentality of nature and grace means that nature is grace's "own other." In order for grace to accomplish its saving purpose, nature incarnates grace, even as grace constitutes nature's core. As a result, because nature is never "pure," those data that belong to grace are able to broaden our understanding of those data considered to belong to nature. In other words, revealed doctrines can constitute starting points for philosophy without philosophy's losing its autonomy or faith's forfeiting its gratuity. Accordingly, chapter 5 showed that the image of the crucifixion, central to Christianity, constitutes the paradigm of beauty. Chapter 6 shows that the concluding contemplation of the *Spiritual Exercises* manifests the divine love that drives the novelty of the cosmos.

The coherence of our method is grounded in the claim that absolute reality is analogously analogous. This means that theology can fully affirm philosophy's analogy between infinite and finite modes even as, grounded in faith, it can supplement it. Accordingly, chapter 5, assuming the truth of Christian revelation, demonstrated the convertibility in God of beauty, goodness, and love, which mediate the divine

37. Kenneth Schmitz, "An Addendum to Further Discussion," *American Catholic Philosophical Quarterly* 73 (Spring 1999): 277–90, at 278.

being. It showed that God's beauty is revealed in the self-sacrificing love of the crucified Christ, even as God's being grounds an intramundane aesthetics. Based on these claims, it asserted the consistency of divine and worldly aesthetics. Chapter 5 concluded with the suggestion that revelation causes philosophy to question the ultimacy of its traditional standards of beauty. In other words, theology pushes philosophy to see that the love emblemized in the cross, even by philosophy's own analogical criteria, can be understood as the highest mode of aesthetics. From the explicit perspective of Christianity, therefore, chapter 5 established a coherent correlation between the revealed doctrine of God and philosophy's analogy of being.

Nonetheless, chapter 5 did not demonstrate, from philosophy's perspective, that the analogy of being is also an analogy of love. As a complement to chapter 5, therefore, chapter 6 uses unaided reason to demonstrate that the infinite absolute is a freely loving person. Based on this crucial claim, chapter 6 accounts for the spontaneous creativity of substances. It also shows that philosophy, of itself, can affirm the convertibility in God of beauty, goodness, and love, which mediate being. Accordingly, chapter 6 coherently correlates the philosophical doctrine of God with chapter 5's Christian doctrine of God. The upshot is that philosophy can assert an analogy of beauty, goodness, and love between finite and infinite being. This analogy obtains even as theology, from its perspective, can claim that the same beauty, goodness, and love are themselves analogous when they are predicated of the infinite being who is the absolute person. In other words, the philosophical analogy of beauty, goodness, love, and being is itself analogous from theology's viewpoint, because the freedom of divine revelation cannot be deduced. It follows, therefore, that one and the same God is known analogically by each discipline in a manner appropriate to each. Analogous analogy thus holds the sacramental model of nature and grace together. While protecting the gratuity of revelation, it safeguards the appropriate autonomy of reason.

Let us now turn to our final chapter, which will apply our insights into analogy to another theological problem—the relation between Christianity and other religions.

Chapter 7

RELIGIONS, ANALOGY, AND CHRISTIANITY

Among recent thinkers who affirm Christianity as absolute, discussion of its relation to other religions revolves—and often not too amicably—around the polarity between an "optimistic and broad" inclusivism and a "negative and strict" exclusivism.[1] These approaches are not altogether new. They retrieve and develop three models that have emerged in the tradition of Christian reflection. Inclusivism draws on two models. The first, notable in Thomas, sees non-Christian religions as useful preparations for the Gospel (*praeparatio evangelii*). Its scriptural roots lie in Romans 1:18, where Paul defends knowledge of God and virtue from the natural law. The next model, prominent in the second century apologist Justin Martyr, sees other religions as implicitly embodying the divine Wisdom (*logos spermatikos*). Its scriptural roots extend into Acts 17:22, where Paul's speech on the Areopagus equates the Athenians' "unknown god" with the divinity revealed in Christ. For its part, exclusivism hearkens to the model prominent in the Reformation, although Tertullian already adumbrated it in his third century question: "What indeed has Athens to do with Jerusalem?"[2] Castigat-

1. Yves Congar, *Missionaire pour demain* (Paris: Centurion, 1966), 30, 35, 37; in Thomas F. O'Meara, "Yves Congar: Theologian of Grace in a Wide World," in *Yves Congar: Theologian of the Church*, ed. Flynn, 371–99, at 386–87.

2. Tertullian, *Prescription Against Heretics*, chap. 7, in *Early Latin Theology: Selections from*

ing any analogy to the definitive revelation of God in Christ, it places other religions outside the economy of salvation (*cultus degeneres*).[3]

Following inclusivism, this chapter will work to develop an understanding of Christianity and other religions consistent with the view of nature and grace that we have previously posited. It will then use the results to interpret important questions raised by *Dominus Jesus*. Issued in 2000 by the Congregation for the Doctrine of the Faith, this declaration reconsiders the formula of Cyprian dating to 265: "Outside the Church, there is no salvation."[4] Let us begin by studying the two models underlying our approach in order to discern the contours of the problem before us.

Praeparatio Evangelii

Aquinas's treatment of this model remains ambiguous. On the one hand, in *ST* II-II, q. 10, a. 11, he argues that although "unbelievers sin in their rites, they may be tolerated" in order that some good may result or some evil avoided. Yet he immediately adds that the Jewish rites foreshadow "the truth" of the Catholic "faith" and thus "bear witness" to it. It is, of course, hard to see how a sinful act can, in itself, bear witness to the truth, which is necessarily convertible with the good. On the other hand, we might draw a more positive inference from *ST* I-II, q. 109. As we will recall from our discussion of this text in chapter 1, postlapsarian nature, without grace, can neither know what the law of God demands nor fulfill it with the required charity. Yet as first mover God inspires us toward any good whatsoever. Accordingly, works can be done that lead to a good connatural with fallen nature. These so-called goods of utility cannot effect justification, however much they are grounded in virtuous habits. The position of *ST* I-II, q. 109, leads to the view that

Tertullian, Cyprian, Ambrose, and Jerome, ed. and trans. S. L. Greenslade (Philadelphia: Westminster Press, 1956), 19–64, at 36.

3. For a helpful discussion, both historical and systematic, of all three models, see the neo-orthodox work of Hendrik Kraemer, *Religion and the Christian Faith* (Philadelphia: Westminster, 1957).

4. Cyprian, "Letter 73," in *Letters*, 282.

non-Christian religions can be subsumed under these goods. Although they subsist outside of grace, and hence do not regenerate anyone, they nonetheless ensue from God. His providential ordering of all secondary causes guides everything to himself as its common good. Because other religions can direct humanity to the good proportionate to fallen nature, they can rightly be called preparations for the Gospel. But because only the sacramental culture of the church mediates grace, not the fallen culture of natural virtue, salvation requires the person to be linked to the church, either explicitly or implicitly.

Based on this position, a follower of Aquinas could claim that a non-Christian can be saved when the first mover guides his conscience to a state of acquired virtue sufficient, in the judgment of the redeeming God, to attain baptism of desire. If this claim is accepted, then a more positive interpretation of Aquinas's position in *ST* II-II, q. 10, a. 11, becomes possible. If the non-Christian rites themselves can be seen as unfolding under God's providential guidance, then their ability to foreshadow Christ can be understood as devolving not from sin but from God's goodness. If this claim is accepted, then non-Christian culture, not only the individual human conscience, can be affirmed as mediating God. Accordingly, one could conclude that other rites should not merely be tolerated, but even nurtured and sustained, precisely because they are preambles of Christian faith.

Developments in Thomas like these, which lay a firm theological ground for *praeparatio evangelii*, are eminently reflected in the labors of the early Jesuit missionaries in the Far East. It is clear that their prodigious efforts to inculturate the Christian message contributed to the flourishing of indigenous cultures. Several examples center on the Jesuits' importing of a Gutenburg-style printing press to Goa sometime between 1556 and 1563. On the one hand, this invention allowed for textbooks to be printed for the Society's newly founded schools, as well as for the dissemination of a vernacular Christian literature.[5] On

5. Antoni Üçerler, "The Jesuit Mission Press and João Rodrigues's *Arte da Lingoa Japoa* (1604–08)," paper delivered at the "Coming to Terms: The Quadricentennial of João Rodrigues's *Arte da Língoa de Iapam*" conference at Georgetown University, December 12–13, 2008, 3–4.

the other hand, it allowed Western secular learning, such as astronomy and philosophy, to come through translation into a fecund dialogue with indigenous thought. Furthermore, through the careful preparation of dictionaries, oriental culture was opened to the Occident. The first Western-style dictionary of Japanese, produced in 1604 at the Jesuit college in Nagasaki, distinguished regional dialects. It also clarified both Buddhist terms and the subtle nuances of polite speech.[6]

What demands special note is the distinctive contribution that translated Christian sources provided for native language. The *Imitation of Christ* and the *Acts of the Saints*, for instance, stand as elegant masterpieces of Japanese style and usage. Similarly, the Jesuits' perfecting of the calligraphic cursive style supplemented linguistic beauty with visual beauty, further augmenting Japanese aesthetics.[7] These achievements gave to Japan what the Jesuit lay brother Guiseppe Castiglione, known as Lang Shih-ning, offered in picture to China—an indigenous monument inspired by devout Christian humanism. Adept at oil as well as water-ink, Lang not only mastered traditional Chinese brushwork, but creatively combined it with Western three-dimensional perspective to effect an innovative advance in native virtuosity.[8]

In chapter 3, we cited John Paul II's observation in *Fides et Ratio* that "without the stimulus of the Word of God, a good part of modern [culture] would not exist."[9] By practicing an inculturation of the Gospel that augmented native cultures, the Jesuits evince the Pontiff's claim. Their exploits implicitly affirm the truth, goodness, and beauty already inherent in the civilizations that they encountered. Nowhere is this affirmation more evident than in their approach to translating Christian terms of Greco-Roman provenance into Chinese and Japanese terms of a Buddhist-Confucian-Taoist provenance. João Rodrigues, for instance, well recognized for his sensitivity to lexical connotations, feared that

6. Ibid., 12.

7. Ibid., 10.

8. Cécile Beurdeley and Michel Beurdeley, *Giuseppe Castiglione: A Jesuit Painter at the Court of the Chinese Emperors*, trans. Michael Bullock (Rutland, Vt.: Charles E. Tuttle, 1971), 45, 142, 147.

9. John Paul II, *Fides et Ratio*, par. 76.

imprecise Asian terms were being used to render Christian doctrines.[10] He thus exercised more caution in Japanese than he felt that Matteo Ricci displayed in Chinese.[11] Communicating an errant rendering of a word, albeit subtly, could be prejudicial, not only to the meaning of Christianity, but also to indigenous religions. Nonetheless, Rodrigues did not solve this problem by favoring a wholesale transliteration of Latinate Christian terms into the vernacular. He was more flexible, frequently allowing familiar Buddhist terms to be used in translating Christian literature.[12] His theological prudence sought to balance religious orthodoxy over-against the missionary's ever-pressing zeal to render his message accessible to the local audience.

Although Rodrigues entertained reservations about Ricci's zest for using native words to render Christianity, he nonetheless shared an important theological kinship with him. Despite their tactical differences, a common strategy underlay their approaches to translation. Following the Thomist foundation of *praeparatio evangelii*, both believed that no sharp equivocation obtained between oriental rites and Christianity.[13] For his part, Rodrigues did declare them to be "atheistic," because they denied divine providence and affirmed the eternality of the material cosmos.[14] But his belief in the goodness of God's creating and redeeming activity allowed him consistently to criticize errors while affirming that Asian religions vestigially, dimly, and inchoately reflect the one absolute. By contrast, had he and Ricci believed otherwise, then no theological warrant would have supported their strategy. Had they subsumed indigenous rites under *cultus degeneres*, then it would follow that no language drawn from non-Christian religions would even remotely be serviceable to express Christ's unique revelation to humanity. On

10. William J. Farge, "João Rodrigues vs. Matteo Ricci: Christian Terminology in Japan and China," paper delivered at "Coming to Terms," 8, 11.

11. Ibid., 6.

12. Ibid., 16; see also Isabel Pina, "João Rodrigues Tçuzu and the Controversy over Christian Terminology in China," *Bulletin of Portugese-Japanese Studies* (2003): 47–71, at 57; in Farge, "João Rodrigues," 15.

13. Farge, "João Rodrigues," 2.

14. Michael Cooper, *Rodrigues the Interpreter: An Early Jesuit in Japan and China* (New York: Weatherhill, 1974), 281–82; in Farge, "João Rodrigues," 5.

the contrary, only the explicit language of Christianity would suffice. It would further follow that Christianity could not be translated, if by this is meant finding vernacular terms from other religions to express Christian doctrine. Only transliteration would therefore constitute the missionary's ideal of inculturated evangelization.

In sum, because the Jesuits claimed an affinity between nature and grace, they could claim a lexical affinity between Christian terms and those of other religions. Because they claimed a lexical affinity, Buddhist, Confucian, and Taoist words could serve as a preparation for the Gospel, even as pre-existing human flesh could serve as a preparation for the incarnation. Nonetheless, *praeparatio evangelii* is reluctant to claim, strictly speaking, an analogy between Christianity and other religions. This hesitation is owing to the separation found in Thomas between the good of utility, as proportionate to fallen nature, and the good of grace, as ensuing from the regenerating life of God. By contrast, the next model that we shall treat, *logos spermatikos*, enthusiastically grounds religion in an analogy of truth.

Logos Spermatikos

Deriving from Justin the Apologist, this model's legacy continues in Irenaeus and Athanasius. According to Justin, the divine Logos is preeminently "the seed of God" in Christ, who is also "the seed of Jacob."[15] By Logos, Justin means not only Word but also God's speech, design, reason, thought, and plan (233). As "the First-begotten of God," Christ "is the Reason of which every race of man partakes," the end to whom "every nation" looks "forward to His coming" (272; 262–63). Consequently, "those who lived in accordance with Reason are Christians, even though they were called godless" (272). Plato, for instance, "borrowed from our [Judeo-Christian] teachers, I mean from the Word [speaking] through the prophets, when he said that God made the universe by changing formless matter" (280). For Justin, therefore, the

15. Justin, *Apology* I, ed. and trans. Edward Rochie Hardy, in *Early Christian Fathers*, ed. Cyril C. Richardson et al. (New York: Macmillan, 1970), 225–89, at 262–63. Cited in the text.

divine reason incarnate in Christ diffuses itself as the seminal logos or word that speaks in a divinely vicarious way in the reason of every person (233). Wherever authentic rationality obtains, there also obtains "the divine force" impregnating "the universe" (233). "Hence everything good and true really is [Christian] by right" (233). If so, then everything good and true belongs not only to nature but, participating in the Logos, implicitly to grace.

Irenaeus develops Justin by using the notion of "recapitulation" mentioned in chapter 4. Christ "became what we are," he says in *Against the Heresies,* so that we might become "even what He is."[16] What he is, as Word, means "Creator of the world," who "in an invisible manner contains all things created and is inherent in the entire creation" (546). As Word, he "governs and arranges all things" (546–47). What he has become, as "very man," is the communicator of "invisible things" in virtue of his intelligence (547). As God-man, therefore, he "'sum[s] up in Himself all things which are in heaven, and which are on earth,'" thereby "uniting man to the Spirit" (548, citing Eph 1:10). Thus nature, created by, presided over, and incarnated in the Logos, constitutes, together with the freely offered divine life, a unity-in-diversity. Creation and redemption cohere into a symmetry by their one divine agent, the Word-Wisdom-Son, who refashions from within what he has fashioned and guides. Primordially, therefore, nature participates in the Logos and thus implicitly in grace.

Athanasius in *On the Incarnation* advances a similar position. Like Justin and Irenaeus, he understands that humanity, as made in the divine image, was given "a portion even of the power of [God's] own Word" in virtue of "having been made rational."[17] Significantly, God "has not only made us out of nothing; but he gave us freely by the *grace* of the Word, a life of correspondence with God," the fullness of such grace being lost by sin (59; emphasis added). Nature thus exists primordially within the grace of the Word, a measure of which perdures

16. Irenaeus, *Against the Heresies,* 1:315–567, at 526. Cited in the text.

17. Athanasius, *On the Incarnation,* trans. Archibald Robertson, in *Christology of the Later Fathers,* ed. Hardy, 43–110, at 58. Cited in the text by page number.

through the Fall. Nonetheless, despite this measure, sin turns humans "back to their natural state, so that just as they have had their being out of nothing, so also ... they might look for corruption into nothing in the course of time" (59). Within the cosmic ambit of divine grace, integral and fallen nature are thus distinguished by the tendency of fallen nature to revert to radical contingency. This defines nature over against the radical freedom of God that brings it into being.

Athanasius further draws out his analogy. The Word "alone" possesses the "*natural* fullness" to refashion fallen nature, because as "the image of the Father, he [could] create afresh the man after the image" (62, 67; emphasis added). "It was *naturally* consequent," Athanasius continues, "that the physician and Savior should appear in what had come to be, in order to cure the things that were" (98; emphasis added). Creation and redemption, integral nature and redeemed nature, are thus understood as a continuum. They obtain under the grace of the Logos, which exists "in the whole universe ... illuminated and moved by Him" (96). In sum, this doctor of the church, developing Justin and Irenaeus, affirms that nature, never discontinuous with grace, expresses the same truth embodied in Christ. Created by the Logos and recapitulated by its incarnation, human reason reflects its divine origins. It therefore follows, as Balthasar much later avers, that "supernatural grace ... even of God's revelation of his Word ... has undergirded and enwrapped all natural knowledge of, and relation to, God."[18]

Whereas Justin and his followers ground their analogy of truth in Christology, other versions of *logos spermatikos* subsequently arise on different bases. One continuum runs from Ramon Lull (ca. 1232 to ca. 1315) to Nicholas of Cusa and the Florentine Academy of the fifteenth century. Socratic in provenance, it sees metaphysics primarily as the science of God, not as the Aristotelian science of being evinced from sensuous experience.[19] For instance, Marsilio Ficino, recognized

18. Balthasar, *Theology of Karl Barth*, 319–20.

19. Charles Lohr, "Metaphysics," in *The Cambridge History of Renaissance Philosophy*, ed.

founder of the Academy, seizes on a humanist-inspired Neoplatonism as the hermeneutic of Christian doctrine. Harnessing a theory called the "dynamic unity of truth," he posits a harmony between faith and reason that, he claims, stems from Platonism's divine origins.[20] Although he does not go so far as to assert that, like revelation, Platonism is divinely inspired, still he does not separate it from religion as its mere handmaid.[21] Ficino refuses radically to differentiate this earthly life from the future life. In fact, the Platonic philosopher, in his highest contemplation, can attain "an authentic anticipation" of glory.[22] Consequently, philosophy is able to describe this foretaste of beatitude in an analogy drawn from reason's mundane-conditioned reflection.[23]

To be sure, Ficino never denies the superiority of Christianity or the efficacy of grace. Nonetheless, this very superiority, according to him, rests on the premise that faith and reason possess the highest good as their common goal. Because all human beings dynamically pursue this goal "as the only way to salvation," Christianity can be understood as perfectly effecting its realization.[24] It therefore follows, as Ficino strives to explain in *De Christiana Religione* (1474), that all religions, insofar as they aim at humanity's single end, can lay some claim to the glory that Christianity reveals absolutely. For his part, Pico della Mirandola, initially inspired by Ficino, deals with the correspondence among Christanity, the Hebrew scriptures, Kabbalist mysticism, and classical mythology.[25] Ironically, however, his *On Being and Unity* (1491) ends the Florentine

C. B. Schmitt et al. (Cambridge: Cambridge University Press, 1988), 537–638, traces the development of this continuum.

20. Paul Oskar Kristeller, *Renaissance Thought and Its Sources*, ed. Michael Mooney (New York: Columbia University Press, 1979), 196; Josephine L. Burroughs, "Introduction to Marsilio Ficino," *The Renaissance Philosophy of Man*, trans. and ed. Ernst Cassirer et al. (Chicago: University of Chicago Press, 1948), 185–92, at 187.

21. Burroughs, "Introduction," 186–87.

22. Paul Oskar Kristeller, "Thomism and the Italian Thought of the Renaissance," in *Medieval Aspects of Renaissance Learning: Three Essays by Paul Oskar Kristeller*, ed. and. trans. Edward P. Mahoney (Durham, N.C.: Duke University Press, 1974), 29–91, at 88.

23. Ibid.

24. Burroughs, "Introduction," 187–88.

25. See Paul Oskar Kristeller, *Eight Philosophers of the Italian Renaissance* (Stanford, Calif.: Stanford University Press, 1964), 61–62.

tradition. It leaves Platonism behind by harnessing Aquinas's equivocal-tending theory of nature and grace.[26]

A third version of *logos spermatikos* emerges with the Enlightenment. Unlike its predecessors, it is expressly philosophical. Grounding its analogy in reason's critique of religion's historical forms, its origins lie in Lessing's appropriation of Leibniz. The eighteenth-century Deists facilely dismissed Christianity's doctrines because these were perceived to rest on the authenticity of the Bible's historical evidence. Lessing, agreeing with the proponents of natural religion that such evidence is insupportable, sought to preserve Christianity by abandoning John Locke's criteria of its truth.[27] In *The Reasonableness of Christianity* (1695), the Englishman formulates these as Christ's miracles and his fulfillment of prophecies. Lessing's efforts led him to confront the famous "broad, ugly ditch" between religion's truth and its historical foundation.[28] "Accidental truths of history," he didactically asserts, "can never become the proof of the necessary truths of reason."[29] Initially fearing that "he cannot get across" the ditch, Lessing finds a solution that subsequently changes the course of the study of religion.[30] In "Leibniz on Eternal Punishment" (1773), he opines that the great rationalist endeavors to maintain the truth of the Christian doctrine of hell, not by holding to its actual existence, but by making it agree with his own metaphysics of universal harmony. Accordingly, hell, as a religious doctrine, could be viewed as containing an inner truth wrapped in the outer form of a metaphoric image. When submitted to rational critique, the doctrine means that "nothing in the world is isolated ... nothing is without eternal consequences."[31]

26. Lohr, "Metaphysics," 583.

27. Henry E. Allison, *Lessing and the Enlightenment: His Philosophy of Religion and Its Relation to Eighteenth-Century Thought* (Ann Arbor, Mich.: University of Michigan Press, 1966), 82–83.

28. Gotthold Ephraim Lessing, *On the Proof of the Spirit and of Power*, in *Lessing's Theological Writings*, ed. Henry Chadwick (Stanford, Calif.: Stanford University Press, 1956), 55.

29. Ibid, 53.

30. Ibid.

31. Gotthold Ephraim Lessing, *Gesammelte Werke*, ed. Paul Rilla (Berlin: Aufbau, 1954–58), 7:476; in Allison, *Lessing*, 88.

The upshot is that after Lessing the Enlightenment could envisage religious doctrines as symbols of pure reason. Posited in historically conditioned sensuousness, they require no divine intervention as such to warrant their validity. If this claim can be made of Christianity, then in principle it can be extended to all specific religious forms. Whatever superiority Christianity might possess can be acknowledged based on its conformity to rational criteria over-against other religions. As a result, Kant argues that Christianity constitutes "that portion of the human race in which the predisposition to the unity of the universal church is already approaching its complete development."[32]

For him, the universal church is a symbol. It is the state that will obtain when specific religions, liberated from their historical conditioning, are understood explicitly to correspond to pure practical reason. This correspondence will obtain when the will of God is viewed as coterminous with the categorical imperative: so act that the maxim of the will can simultaneously become a general law of duty. The universal church lies as implicitly in all religious forms as it does in reason itself. Hence, Kant can affirm that Christianity "enriched philosophy with ... purer conceptions of morality than [morality] had been able to furnish before, but which, once they are there, are *freely* assented to by reason and are assumed as concepts to which it could well have come of itself."[33] Consequently, Christianity assumes a hegemony over other religions, many of which nonetheless manifest discrete elements of the universal church. Christianity's superiority, however, does not obviate its need for rational purification, as Kant's ingenious interpretation of original sin in the first book of *Religion Within the Limits of Reason Alone* (1793) demonstrates.

Although Kant establishes an analogy among religions based on the degree to which they embody the pure religion of reason, he does not systematically rank them according to this criterion. For this project,

32. Kant, *Religion Within the Limits of Reason*, 115.

33. Immanuel Kant, *Critique of Judgment*, trans. J. H. Bernard (London: Collier Macmillan, 1951), 325n33.

we must look to Hegel, who culminates the trend of this version of *logos spermatikos* to synthesize reason and religion's pluriform history. Let us linger on his efforts, because they probably constitute the most ambitious of their kind ever undertaken. We observed in chapter 2 that Hegel's entire system may be considered symbolic. All finite forms manifest, in appropriate degrees, the unique spirit that struggles, in and through history, to express itself. Spirit, we will recall, is the infinite act that embraces, transforms, and surpasses all oppositions in the order of experience. Although this entire manifold discloses spirit, it is only through the mediation of the human mind that spirit is able to posit itself finally and fully. It does so in art, religion, and philosophical science.

Both religion and philosophy, for Hegel, share the same source, object, and content, which are nothing less than the self-consciousness of God. Because in religion the human mind first recognizes "the absolute as absolute," it attains a knowledge of "spirit in its completeness."[34] Nonetheless, this knowledge is posited in a form that Hegel calls "representation." Essentially, this means that religion still refers to the absolute under a finitely conditioned form. It perceives the infinite as existing externally to human consciousness.[35] The overcoming of this perception is precisely the task of philosophy. It demonstrates that "when the individual subject knows God, it is God who is doing the knowing."[36] This demonstration constitutes the movement from faith, which knows God as representation, to thought that, in the words of the fourteenth-century mystic Meister Eckhart, is the "eye by which God sees me."[37]

Because representation embodies spirit in its absolute completeness, the origins of religion, according to Hegel, lie in what he calls the "religious consciousness." This constitutes the seed, as it were, that gives structure to all determined religious forms that emerge from it. It

34. Quentin Lauer, "Hegel on the Identity of Content in Religion and Philosophy," in *Hegel and the Philosophy of Religion: The Wofford Symposium*, ed. Darrel E. Cristensen (The Hague: Martinus Nijhoff, 1970), 261–78, at 262.

35. Fackenheim, *Religious Dimension*, 154–55.

36. Lauer, "Identity of Content," 268.

37. Meister Eckhart, "Distinctions are Lost in God," in *Meister Eckhart: A Modern Translation*, ed. and trans. Raymond Bernard Blakney (New York: Harper and Row, 1941), 203–6, at 206.

contains implicitly all of religion's characteristics, which it envelopes in a spiritual manner. In and through the human mind, spirit explicates these characteristics gradually in history.[38] Religious consciousness constitutes the condition for the possibility of what Hegel calls the "consciousness of religion." This embraces the exercise of faith in specific religions. Still, it is only through the existing forms of religion that the elements entailed in the religious consciousness can be inferred. Similarly, for instance, it is only through the mature human being that we can grasp how the full genetic content implicit in the fertilized ovum will unfold.

If the religious consciousness contains religion's elements in an "indeterminate universality," only with "distinction in general" can "religion as such begin."[39] Religious consciousness constitutes for religion what in chapter 5 we identified as the notion. This is the generating source of spirit's immanent dialectic. By logical necessity, the elements implicit in the notion become determined in time and space, where their progressive explication brings the notion to perfection in what Hegel calls the idea. Non-Christian religions, therefore, represent for Hegel partial realizations of the notion; in and through them, spirit works its way to the idea, Christianity, which Hegel calls the consummate religion. Other religions are ranked in a hierarchy based on the degree to which the consummate religion is reflected in them. This ranking varies in the four extant series of lectures that Hegel delivered on the subject. In 1827, his schema from lowest to highest begins with the religions of magic, including Confucianism and Taoism. It moves to Buddhism, then to Hinduism, on to Persian and Egyptian religion, then to Greek religion, to Judaism, finally ending in Roman religion.

As an example of Hegel's analogy of religious truth, let us review how Roman religion serves as a transition from Greek and Jewish religion to Christianity. In manifesting itself in determined religions, the religious consciousness is seeking ever richer expressions of the free-

38. Peter C. Hodgson, "Introduction: The Lectures of 1827," in Hegel, *Lectures on the Philosophy of Religion (1827)*, 75–110, at 101.

39. Hegel, *Lectures on the Philosophy of Religion (1827)*, 128–29.

dom intrinsic to spirit. These expressions give witness to the progressive disengagement of the consciousness of religion from its dependence on finite media. For its part, Greece gives birth to the religion of beauty, which expresses the divine in the freedom of human subjectivity. The natural symbols of the divine in Egyptian religion, like the sun, the floods of the Nile, and the part-animal, part-human sphinx are overcome. The gods of Olympus, now incarnated in mythology and sculpture, achieve for Hegel a balance between spirit and matter that lies in the heart of aesthetics. Yet this very balance causes spirit to leave beauty behind as its adequate medium. Contingent on human freedom, religion becomes capable of irony when the comedies of the amphitheaters begin to show the gods as ridiculous.[40]

Spirit thus requires a higher expression, which it finds in Judaism, the religion of sublimity. In transcendent monotheism, spirit becomes its own medium. Yet the God of the patriarchs and prophets, externally posited to anything finite, acts with arbitrary freedom toward the world. He performs miracles, for instance, and chooses only one ethnic people for his unique covenant. Although intrinsically spirit, the divine freedom now seems to threaten the "alien objectivity" of the material cosmos rather than harmoniously to integrate it.[41] Following Judaism, the Roman cult, although degenerate in its understanding of freedom, serves ironically for Hegel as Christianity's harbinger. It creates a purifying vacuum, so to speak, that allows the spiritual sublimity that Christianity shares with Judaism to embrace the finite within itself. Spirit is, after all, "the freeing of itself from what is null and the elevating of itself to itself."[42] Tantamount to magic, Roman religion sets up in its divine caesars the pretext for the worship of sheer power. Moreover, the rituals of its pantheons are performed empty of mythic narrative, whereas its concept of the person, as the merely legal *suppositum* of assigned rights, stands evacuated of freedom.[43]

40. For Greek religion, see ibid., esp. 331; for Judaism, esp. 358; for Egyptian religion, 313.
41. Collins, *Emergence of Philosophy of Religion*, 273.
42. Hegel, *Lectures on the Philosophy of Religion (1827)*, 132–33.
43. Ibid., esp. 376.

By contrast, the Christian doctrine of the Trinity reveals spirit's absolute freedom. In the Son as the Father's image and Word, we are shown that God has consciousness of himself within himself. Furthermore, in the Holy Spirit who guides us into all truth (Jn 16:13), we see that religious consciousness knows the finite world as itself. Accordingly, Christianity renders "the absolute judgment that God is *as* spirit *for* spirit."[44] This judgment is further evinced in the paschal mystery of the God-man. The death and resurrection of Christ manifest that God, who in the incarnation first embraces the material cosmos, also triumphantly transcends it.[45] Absolute spirit thereby reconciles history in a consummate sublation that displays the self-subsisting unity-in-diversity of time and eternity. What religion "enacts in image and symbol," philosophy "enacts in reflective activity."[46] This last enactment, which accepts "no authority outside human thought as arbiter of that thought's validity," constitutes, according to Hegel, the essence of freedom.[47]

Anonymous Christians

Let us now trace the legacy of *praeparatio evangelii* and *logos spermatikos* in the contemporary debate. We shall focus on Karl Rahner's anonymous Christian, which has enjoyed something of a pride of place within the inclusivist approach. Blending our two models into a synthesis, it represents a development of the supernatural existential treated in chapter 2. As we will recall, Rahner delineates two types of revelation that show how knowledge of God can be correlated to the faculties of the human person. On the one hand, a philosophical analysis independent of Christianity can show that humanity is constituted by a general revelation of the absolute. By means of finite realities, this pre-apprehends the unconditioned being, in a dim and unobjectified way, as the intellect's necessary and sufficient explanation. On the other hand, faith affirms the categorical revelation given in history. This

44. Ibid., 131.

45. Ibid., esp. 432, 464.

46. Collins, *Emergence*, 273.

47. Lauer, "Identity of Content," 261.

manifests Christ as the absolute's definitive Word, who proclaims the Trinity and the other data mediated by scripture and the tradition of the church.

Because only one concrete order obtains, faith makes it clear that general revelation, even as discerned by unaided reason, actually subsists within grace. Although it constitutes a natural desire for God, general revelation is materially united with prevenient grace. From this union, it follows that the pre-apprehension of the absolute constitutes an implicit offer of the sanctifying grace to which prevenient grace is oriented. This offer, the supernatural existential, means that through the incarnation Christ embodies the general revelation of the absolute in time and space. Christ becomes a mirror in which humanity can see the historical fulfillment of reason's orientation to the unconditioned cause of all reality. As a result, general revelation's yearning for the absolute can be seen as a call to justification. This call can terminate explicitly in the regeneration given by the water of baptism's normal mode, or it can become baptism of desire. In this case, God's universal salvific will can justify those outside formal incorporation in the church. Because all grace is necessarily mediated by Christ, it follows that all persons participating in it can be called anonymous Christians. An assent to the absolute who in the pre-apprehension constitutes the goal and term of the human person represents an implicit assent to the absolute's historical utterance. Rahner affirms that sin can always consciously reject grace. This possibility applies as much to the Christian, who can lapse from baptism's state of grace, as to the practitioner of another religion who, deviating from a sincere conscience, fails to realize baptism of desire. Nonetheless, given that the availability of grace ubiquitously conditions history, the confrontation with it, and hence with Christ, either explicitly or implicitly, is inescapable.[48]

Rahner's debt to the two models prominent in the tradition centers on his using the supernatural existential to develop a complex analogy between general and categorical revelation. First, hearkening

48. See Rahner, "Anonymous Christians," in *TI* 6:390–98.

to Hegel, the supernatural existential can establish degrees of membership in the church. On the one hand, an ascending membership would embrace those who, explicitly professing Christianity, are joined by the extent to which they share the fullness of the faith preached by "the one true [Roman Catholic] Church." On the other hand, a descending membership would join the anonymous Christians baptized by desire to explicit Christians baptized by water.[49] An analogy between anonymous and explicit Christians obtains because the pre-apprehended absolute of general revelation and the grace of categorical revelation are yoked. "The express revelation of the word in Christ," Rahner states, "is not something which comes to us from without as entirely strange, but only [as] the explicitation of what we already are by grace and what we experience at least inchoately in the limitlessness of our transcendence."[50] In other words, because general revelation and prevenient grace are materially united, the incarnation, together with its offer of sanctifying grace, comes to humanity as a perfection and fulfillment of its natural desire for God. Consequently, an individual's conscientious fulfillment of the natural desire can confer justification.

Second, Rahner's analogy between faith and reason evokes the Florentine Academy's dynamic unity of truth. Consonant with Ficino, faith for Rahner can be said to integrate reason's end within its own. Together both ends can attain the same object that, without grace, reason could only vaguely, but really, grasp. Furthermore, because the Logos "becomes the explicit statement" of the grace that we always experience "implicitly in the depths of [our] being," Rahner can ratify the claim of the Greek Fathers that Christ is revealed wherever truth obtains.[51] Although Hegel could also ratify this claim, Rahner would reject his model of reason as infinite and would thus align himself with the views of Möhler and Ricoeur on religious symbolism discussed in chapters 2 and 5.

Third, because general revelation does not presuppose grace for its cogency, Rahner can also echo Lessing and Kant, who ground human

49. Ibid., 391.

50. Ibid., 394.

51. Ibid.

religiosity in unaided reason. In fact, the anonymous Christian could be said to agree with Kant that Christianity represents the completion of humanity's predisposition to the universal church. For Kant, humanity's transcendental aspirations, implicit in moral reason, are adequately reflected in the Christianity that aids in their fruition. For Rahner, "Anyone who does not say in his *heart*, 'there is no God,'" but who "lives the duty of each day in" virtue "is a believer."[52] The difference, of course, turns on their understandings of grace. By contrast with the supernatural existential, Kant assigns grace to the *parerga*: those "high-flown ideas" that, although logically possible, cannot be incorporated into reason's "maxims of thought and action."[53]

Fourth, by grounding the anonymous Christian in natural virtue, Rahner renders it a preamble of Christian faith. In Thomas, such virtue, subsumed under the good of utility, cannot claim an analogy, strictly speaking, with the grace that leads to glory. It can only claim an affinity with it, or at least no sharp equivocation to it, based on God as the common origin of the goods of nature and grace. By materially uniting general revelation and prevenient grace, Rahner makes possible just such an analogy, which can implicitly incorporate the anonymous Christian into the church. Although goods inspired by prevenient grace alone do not cause justification, still they are drawn within the ambit of grace. Thus they join the orders of creation and redemption into the harmony that, as previous chapters have argued, rightly belongs to them. It bears repeating, however, that ultimately how and when the virtuous non-Christian guided by prevenient grace becomes the anonymous Christian sanctified by baptism of desire remains a mercy hidden in the divine economy of salvation.

The ingenuity of the anonymous Christian as a synthesis of diverse strains of theology and philosophy explains why it rightly enjoys a high regard in relating other religions to Christianity as absolute. Despite the significance of its contribution, however, it embodies at least three

52. Ibid., 394–95.
53. Kant, *Religion*, 47–48.

problems. The first concerns the supernatural existential on which it depends. If prevenient grace and nature are materially joined, then it could appear that this union is sufficient to cause justification. This does not represent Rahner's doctrine as we have explained it. He sees the union only as the call to justification, whose consummation requires baptism, either by water or desire. Nonetheless, as we have previously observed, the supernatural existential does not adequately explain the unity-in-difference between nature and grace. It leads to the appearance that nature and grace are univocal. If nature's integrity as grace's sacrament is thus compromised, then the distinction between prevenient and sanctifying grace could precariously be lost. No qualitative difference could seem to obtain between reason's assent to general revelation and faith's assent to categorical revelation. In that case, the anonymous Christian, as Balthasar argues, would attenuate, even eliminate, Christianity's distinctive claim as uniquely salvific.[54] At root, therefore, the anonymous Christian suffers from a limping analogy.

The second problem is related to the previous one. Consistent with its vague notion of nature, the anonymous Christian gives insufficient attention to the destructive, false, and idolatrous elements in other religions. According to Balthasar, Hinduism, for instance, contrasts sharply with Judaism, whose appreciation of the material cosmos provides the seed bed for the incarnation. This cult of the subcontinent dispenses with the dignity of form and structure. Similarly, Buddhism climbs toward the divine without waiting for God's gratuitous action from above.[55] When non-Christian religions overstress spirit at the expense of matter, they become prone to the delusions of the Gnosticism that Christianity has long countered. Such deceptions include pantheism, which stands at odds with the incarnation; syncretism and claims to esoteric knowledge, which undermine the ecclesial structure of revelation; and emphases on extraordinary psychological phenomena, which

54. Hans Urs von Balthasar, *The Moment of Christian Witness*, trans. Richard Beckley (Glen Rock, N.J.: Newman Press, 1969), 60–68.

55. Balthasar, *GL* 1:217, 314, 336–37, 496; in Louis Dupré, "Balthasar's Theology of Aesthetic Form," *Theological Studies* 49 (1988): 299–318, at 315–16.

can obviate the redemptive value of suffering epitomized in the cross.

The third problem concerns the inattentiveness of the anonymous Christian to a key insight in the work of the early Jesuits in Asia: that indigenous cultures play a decisive role in shaping humanity's religious conscience. By making original contributions to the nurturing of local societies, these zealous pioneers believed that local realizations of truth, goodness, and beauty could lead individual consciences to recognize Christ as the perfection of the transcendentals. Unlike Rahner, Yves Congar, the titan ecclesiologist of the twentieth century, hearkened more intently to their belief as his thought matured. His earliest considerations conceived salvation as a function principally of the "person, existence in history, grace outside of baptism and dogma."[56] Implying a "somewhat negative" view of non-Christian and non-Biblical religions, his approach later did "not exclude that the religions of humanity might be habitually an occasion or a canal" of justifying grace.[57] Moreover, his reflections concluded with a frank admission that the cultures in which people live, and the religions embedded in them, are humanity's usual and "ordinary ways to salvation."[58] These are "inclusive" within Jesus Christ, who as the God-man represents "the absolute religion, the fullness and the perfect example of the religious relationship."[59]

Congar's later thought moves the issue of salvation outside formal incorporation in the church from a single focus on the individual conscience invincibly ignorant of Christ. It suggests that, despite their errors, other religious forms, as the media of baptism by desire, can themselves lay some claim to association with the body of Christ. It may be no accident that so schooled a Thomist as Congar would refer to non-Christian religions as "habitually" a canal of grace.[60] Could this

56. O'Meara, "Theologian of Grace," 373, referring to Yves Congar, *The Wide World, My Parish: Salvation and Its Problems*, trans. Donald Attwater (Baltimore: Helicon Press, 1961).

57. O'Meara, "Theologian of Grace," 385; Congar, *Missionaires*, 37; in O'Meara, "Theologian of Grace," 387.

58. Yves Congar, *Fifty Years of Catholic Theology: Conversations with Yves Congar*, ed. Bernard Lauret (Philadelphia: Fortress Press, 1988), 15; in O'Meara, "Theologian of Grace," 388.

59. Congar, *Fifty Years*, 18; in O'Meara, "Theologian of Grace," 388.

60. Congar, *Missionaires*, 37; in O'Meara, "Theologian of Grace," 387.

be an adroit pun? As we know, habitual grace in Aquinas is sanctifying grace, the very life of God that, through Christ, reforms the sinner. By contrast with the French cardinal, the anonymous Christian, despite its optimistic inclusivism, says nothing about the implicit truth, goodness, and beauty of Christianity in other religions as cultural forms. Consequently, it accounts neither for their value nor their delusion.

Inclusivism Revisited

In light of our critique of the anonymous Christian, our next task concerns integrating into our previously posited model of nature and grace the central elements that structure the problem of Christianity's relation to other religions. As this chapter thus far shows, these elements include personal conscience, religions as cultural forms, sinfulness and error, the necessity of Christian faith, and the inclusion of all humanity in the incarnation. Let us begin by turning to Vatican II in order authoritatively to develop the prescient shift just mentioned in Congar's thought.

Gaudium et Spes, the council's *Pastoral Constitution on the Church in the World of Today*, shows sensitivity to the reciprocal mediation between personal acts of thinking, judging, and willing and the sociocultural context of the persons exercising them. It frankly acknowledges that "real and full humanity" can "only" be achieved "through culture," which aims at developing the physical world and refining family and civic life.[61] Culture fosters institutions that express humanity's "spiritual experiences and aspirations" so that, in turn, these can inspire others and contribute to their progress (1106). Culture "flows immediately from the rational and social nature of human beings" as transcendent spirits embodied in time and space (1109). Intelligent and creative activity produces symbols such as "literature and the arts," "human sciences," "history," and "the laws of society," together with "the mathematical, natural and social sciences" and "technology" (1070–71, 1073).

61. Vatican Council II, *Gaudium et Spes*, par. 53, in *Decrees*, ed. Tanner, 2:1069–1135, at 1106.

In addition, culture embraces those phenomena that affect how these symbols change, develop, and are proliferated, such as industrialization, urbanization, mass media, and emigration (1072).

According to the Council, if the symbols of culture emanate from humanity's rational and social nature, they nonetheless form the basis for the exercise of that nature. Conditioning the yearnings of the transcendent spirit in time and space, they constitute the milieu from which "people of every race and age" draw the values needed "to cultivate their human and social life" (1106). But cultural symbols not only elevate us above the chaos of brute sensuousness; they also "redound" on us, on our "judgments and wishes," and on our "ways of thinking and acting" (1071). Changes in symbols, brought about by phenomena like materialism and atheism, unsettle traditional modes of thought (1072–73). Such disturbances make it increasingly difficult for individual consciences to balance the norms of morality over-against the demands of the society where these norms must be applied (1073).

Although the symbols of culture affect the individual conscience, they are not the sufficient cause of moral tension. This results from the fundamental paradox of human nature. Though "unlimited in [our] desires ... [for] a higher life," we are beset by the shortcomings of finitude and sin (1074). These impair our ability to create symbols adequate to our potential. When impoverished symbols arise, they disturb culture with "so many disharmonies," from the false immanence of scientism to the false transcendence of utopianism (1074). Nonetheless, these discords can shock our conscience and serve as a fresh impetus for questions about the destiny of humanity and the meaning of suffering, evil, and death (1074).

This select overview of *Gaudium et Spes* brings into relief several important teachings relevant to our project. First, if culture springs from humanity's rational and social creativity, still culture conditions that creativity. Second, like humanity, culture is ambivalent. Its capacity to manifest the transcendent order is flawed by limitation, error, and sin. Yet even these can spur human aspiration and so expand culture. Third, grace "continually renews" not only the individual person but also the culture "of fallen humanity" (1109). In combating sin and error, the Gospel purifies morality, stimulating and advancing "human and social culture." It thus contributes to the freedom of conscience (1109).

Significantly, grace accomplishes its renovation not by standing outside of culture in stern judgment but "from the inside" of it (1109). Divine revelation takes "the spiritual endowments and talents of every people and age," and with its own abundance "strengthens, completes and restores [them] in Christ" (1109, citing Eph 1:10). Most importantly, renovating "from the inside" means that wherever culture's symbols lead humanity to a deeper awareness of truth, goodness, and beauty, conscience is further enlightened by "the wonderful wisdom which was with God at the beginning" (1108, citing Prv 8:30–31). In this last teaching, *Gaudium et Spes* undoubtedly alludes to the Fathers' version of *logos spermatikos,* although it does not explicitly cite it.

We can therefore draw the following conclusion. If, according to Vatican II, culture mediates transcendence because of the divine's implicit immanence, then it follows that the religions embedded in culture can implicitly embody, manifest, and communicate the Wisdom of the Trinity. It further follows that where the Logos abides, there the grace of Christ must likewise be active.

The constitution's teaching dovetails with the model of nature and grace that our previous chapters have framed. We have argued that prevenient grace and nature obtain as an analogous unity-in-difference. We might therefore claim, in virtue of their unity, that culture vestigially embodies prevenient grace. This embodiment explains how religious symbols can be renovated "from within." Prevenient grace, in and through non-Christian forms of human worship, is able not only to enlighten personal conscience but also, in so doing, to mediate sanctifying grace, God's very life, to the moral judgment of the sincere practitioner. Because prevenient grace is oriented toward sanctifying grace, culture can be viewed as serving the one single end of the human person, the beatific vision. These claims do not mean that a non-Christian religion, in and of itself, causes justification. They mean only that baptism of desire can be mediated through its culturally conditioned symbols that are vestigially graced. How could it be otherwise, we might ask, if God is implicit in these religions; if they are people's usual means to salvation; and if, as the Holy See affirms, salvation is accessible to the invincibly ignorant outside of formal ecclesial incorporation?[62] Nonetheless, these claims must be qualified by the analogical difference between nature and prevenient grace. As we have argued, nature, within its synthesis with grace, continues to exercise its own exigency. This includes the struggle with its propensity to sin and delusion. While Christ consummates the truth, goodness, and beauty of other religions, he also purifies their error.

Thus far we have integrated into our model of nature and grace the following elements structuring Christianity's relation to other religions: personal conscience, religions as cultural forms, sinfulness, and error. Let us now address the crucial issue of the necessity of Christian faith and the inclusion of all humanity in the incarnation. We will tackle this issue by developing an analogy of religious experience. As we will recall from chapter 5, in the analogy of intrinsic attribution, a quality is predicated authentically of a principal subject and only secondarily of other subjects insofar as they bear a relation to it. Accordingly, if we can establish Christian faith as the prime analogate of religious experience, then no religious experience at all would be possible without Christ. He would constitute its principal subject from which the religious experience of other subjects would be derived.

Let us begin by examining the common origins of humanity's religious experience in the instinct of faith. Studied by Seckler in Aquinas, the instinct, as chapter 2 explained, represents the divine impulse prompting all persons to respond to objective value. As the ground of transcendence located in the cradle of nature, the instinct yearns for supernatural satisfaction. In light of Congar's view that indigenous religions are humanity's usual and normal means to salvation, we might

62. See "Letter of the Holy Office to the Archbishop of Boston (1949)," in *The Christian Faith in the Doctrinal Documents of the Catholic Church*, ed. Josef Neuner and Jacques Dupuis (New York: Alba House, 1996), 305–7.

claim that the instinct's yearning finds satisfaction in the ordinary religious symbols of the culture in which it is exercised. When it does, it accomplishes what is characteristic of religion. It brings all the person's powers into a synthesis: the sensory intuitions of the material world, the products of the imagination, the concepts and judgments of the intellect, and the desires and choices of the will. Moreover, in light of the reciprocity posited by Vatican II between culture and the human powers, we can claim that indigenous religious symbols, for their part, form and stimulate the instinct of faith.

As Seckler further maintains, humanity's response to objective value is consummated and fulfilled specifically in Christian faith. Unless all the human faculties are immersed in the new covenant as the formal object of faith, they remain open to the spuriousness of a subjectivity held hostage by the Fall. Balthasar reminds us, for instance, that the truth of faith's content, *fides quae creditur,* is to be stressed over faith's existential activity, *fides qua creditur* (1:131).[63] *Fides quae creditur* reveals the Trinity as evidence concretely in and through the incarnation of the Logos (1:151). Through this faith, the intellect is rendered capable of perceiving the forms of grace manifested explicitly in Christ and implicitly in creation. Insofar as the intellect is transformed, so are the other faculties, because they are animated by it and subordinated to it. Without the reception of Christian *fides quae creditur,* the vestiges of grace in fallen nature are insufficient to overcome sin, error, and delusion, and hence to elevate and justify nature. When faith is received in a noetic act that confers on all the human potencies a share in its formal object, religious experience is spared from errors like Gnosticism. On the one hand, faith integrates matter into spirit, because it permeates the bodily senses and the imagination. On the other hand, faith does not confine spirit to the myths of mere fancy, because it is divinely revealed knowledge (1:131–33, 139–40). In a word, Christian faith becomes the prime analogate of religious experience because it draws the faculties into sanctifying grace.

63. For Congar's treatment of this distinction, see *Tradition and Traditions,* 315.

We are now in a position to evince our analogy that derives non-Christian religious experience from Christianity as its principal subject. In so doing, we need to recall an important claim of Seckler's: the instinct of faith is joined with the natural desire for God. This union means that the natural desire, embraced by prevenient grace, cıonstitutes the material cause of justification, whose formal cause is sanctifying grace. The union of nature and prevenient grace, we have argued, subsists as an analogous unity-in-difference. In virtue of the unity of nature and prevenient grace, the natural desire for God is oriented toward the human person's one supernatural end. Consequently, non-Christian religious experience shares with Christianity a common source in preveniently graced nature and a common goal in the beatific vision. In virtue of the analogous difference between nature and prevenient grace, the attainment of this goal is not necessary, but only remotely possible. Anyone may seek to satisfy the instinct of faith in a host of base, selfish, and sinful objects at odds with the best symbols of transcendence culturally available. The instinct represents only a call to justification. It can be answered in the freely chosen disvalues of this world, which would prevent its proper response in baptism, whether explicitly in water or implicitly in desire. As a call to justification, the instinct is oriented to sanctifying grace, but it is not as such formally endowed with this grace, which alone makes the beatific vision existentially attainable. Even after justification, anyone can sin grievously and forfeit the loss of the final end.

Furthermore, if the union of the natural desire for God and prevenient grace constitutes humanity's disposition to sanctifying grace, then sanctifying grace "calls forth" the disposition oriented to it. We saw in chapter 4 how Rahner makes this argument. He contends that sanctifying grace gives the natural desire for God, as the preveniently graced instinct of faith, its reason for existing. The final cause, end, purpose, and goal of the instinct can be nothing less than the person's justification. Consequently, without its final cause, religious experience would lack any ground, basis, or warrant. It therefore follows that Christian faith, as the prime analogate of religious experience, is necessary and essential. Other religions can mediate a call to justification, as well as sanctification itself through baptism of desire, but only because they derive their efficacy from Christ.

These considerations emphatically underscore Balthasar's astute observation that the notion of transcendence posited by Christianity and other religions is analogous. On the one hand, from the perspective of Christian theology, it is legitimate to affirm that the instinct of faith, even in other religions, aims at the beatific vision because such religions mediate baptism of desire. On the other hand, we need to recall Seckler's claim that, although the natural desire for God and the instinct of faith are materially joined, they are formally distinct. In the case of Christian faith, the instinct of faith and the natural desire share the same formal object, sanctifying grace. In this case, in other words, the natural desire is in fact explicitly an instinct for Christian faith. In the case of non-Christian religious experience, the instinct of faith has not been purified by explicit contact with Christian *fides quae creditur*. As a result, it is open to the errors and delusions that spring from nature's own exigencies. Nonetheless, in non-Christian religious experience, the natural desire is preveniently graced. Whatever truth, goodness, and beauty that its symbols contain are oriented, therefore, to the beatific vision, however remotely. For this reason, Balthasar can go so far as to claim that, "because of our *natural* relation to" God, "even in unbelief and worship of idols man is continually dealing with the" one and only God of grace.[64] Philosophy, too, deals with this same God. As we saw in chapter 5, the absolute posited by its analogy of being subsists in an analogous relation to the freely revealing divine person.

In sum, because of the unity-in-difference of prevenient grace and the natural desire for God, the fundamental drive of human transcendence aims at, and is drawn by, the same God revealed by Jesus Christ, despite the different names that this transcendence knows. As a consequence, although baptism of desire is available to every sincere conscience, Hegel's insight remains trenchant. Because they are analogous, the various objects of human transcendence could, at least theo-

64. Balthasar, *Theology of Karl Barth*, 319 (emphasis added).

retically, be ranked according to the degree of their participation in the truth proclaimed by the Roman Catholic church. Carrying out such a project, however, would face large, if not insurmountable, obstacles because of the vast erudition it would require.

Dominus Jesus

Let us draw this chapter to a close by showing how the analogous model of inclusivism that we have worked out can be used to interpret the Holy See's declaration "on the unicity and salvific necessity of Jesus Christ and the Church."[65] The document raises questions that call for "free theological debate" and "further development" (par. 3). These arise from its reassertion of Catholicism's paradoxical teaching. On the one hand, "'the Church rejects nothing of what is true and holy'" in other religions (par. 2).[66] On the other hand, it does reject "relativistic theories" that undermine the church's claim to embody "the full and complete revelation" (pars. 2, 6) Expanding on this paradox, *Dominus Jesus* draws an important distinction at the heart of its argument. On the one hand, "*theological faith* ... is the acceptance in grace of revealed truth"; whereas on the other hand, "*belief* in other religions ... is that sum of experience and thought that constitutes the human treasury of wisdom and religious aspiration, which man in his search for truth has conceived and acted upon in his relation to God and the Absolute" (par. 7).[67] Theological faith is "'*a gift*'" of "'*a supernatural virtue infused*" by God involving an adherence "to the truth which he reveals" (par. 7).[68] "'In order to have [this] faith, the grace of God must come first and give assistance'" (par. 7).[69] By contrast, belief "is religious experience still in search of the absolute truth and still lacking assent to the God who reveals himself" (par. 7).

The declaration sustains the tension between theological faith and

65. Congregation for the Doctrine of the Faith, *Dominus Jesus* [hereafter "*DJ*"], June 16, 2000; all English translations are drawn from www.vatican.va. Cited in the text by paragraph.

66. See *DJ*, n. 4, citing Vatican Council II, *Declaration "Nostra aetate,"* par. 2.

67. See *DJ*, nn. 21–22, citing John Paul II, *Fides et Ratio,* pars. 13, 31–32.

68. See *DJ*, nn. 17–20, citing *Catechism of the Catholic Church,* § 144, 150, 153, 178.

69. See *DJ*, nn. 16, citing Vatican Council II, *Dei Verbum,* par. 5.

belief throughout its teaching. It claims, for instance, that only the Old and New Testaments are properly "*inspired*" (par. 8). Nonetheless, the texts of other religions "receive from the mystery of Christ the elements of good and grace which they contain" (par. 8). These elements explain how "countless people throughout the centuries" can "maintain their life-relationship with God" (s. 8). Other religions cannot claim "a divine origin" or the sacraments' *ex opere operato* efficacy, which places the salvific economy within "the visible boundaries of the Church" (pars. 12, 21). Yet "'grace is active invisibly'" in the hearts of "'all men of good will,'" who receive Christ's "salvific action … through his Spirit" (par. 12).[70] Without using the phrase "baptism by desire," the document affirms that invisible grace makes accessible non-Christians' "'salvation in Christ'" (par. 20).[71] While this grace confers on them "'a mysterious relationship to the Church,'" it does not mitigate "that *objectively speaking* they are in a gravely deficient situation in comparison with" the church's offer of salvation's fullness (pars. 20, 22).[72]

The declaration brings its tensions to a head and hints at a resolution by several times referring to "'one and the same [divine] destiny'" to which "'all men are in fact called'" (par. 12, echoed in par. 22).[73] This "single goal" is the "one salvific economy of the One and Triune God" (par. 12). Importantly, this one end can embrace "the historical figures and positive elements" of other religions in "the divine plan" (par. 14). Christ's unique revelation enables in them "'a manifold cooperation which is but a participation in this one source'" (par. 14).[74] As such, other religions become a "preparation for the Gospel" (par. 21). Because of the "elements of good and truth present among" them, they can prompt the human heart "to be open to the action of God" (pars. 8, 21).[75]

70. See *DJ*, n. 37, citing Vatican Council II, *Gaudium et Spes*, par. 22.

71. See *DJ*, n. 81, citing John Paul II, *Redemptoris Missio*, par. 10.

72. See *DJ*, n. 92, referring to Pope Pius XII, *Mystici Corporis*.

73. See *DJ*, n. 37, citing Vatican Council II, *Gaudium et Spes*, par. 22.

74. See *DJ*, n. 43, citing Vatican Council II, *Lumen Gentium*, par. 62.

75. See *DJ*, n. 23, citing Vatican Council II, *Lumen Gentium*, par. 16; and *DJ*, pars. 86–87, citing John Paul II, *Redemptoris Missio*, par. 29; and *Catechism*, § 843.

The view of religious experience that we have developed in this chapter supports and develops *Dominus Jesus*. In the first place, the declaration can be understood as positing a unity-in-diversity of theological faith and belief that effectively establishes them as an analogy. For instance, although "theological faith" and "belief" stand opposed as "God's infused virtue" to "humanity's religious aspiration," still both are oriented toward a single goal, the triune God's universal salvific will. As a result of their sharing a unique divine destiny, the grace of God grounds a participation in Christ of those elements in other religions that are true and beautiful. Belief can thus mediate grace's "invisible activity" to all people of good will, whether Christian or not. Perhaps influenced by de Lubac, this teaching of *Dominus Jesus* consistently applies the rule discussed in chapter 3: that the end, goal, and destiny of any process must be contained implicitly within the process itself. On this point, it is noteworthy that the declaration never mentions a merely natural end for humanity. Consequently, it seems to eclipse the theory of Cajetan.

In the second place, the document's understanding of participation affirms that grace can be mediated not only through the consciences of individual non-Christians, but also through their sacred texts, historical figures, and other elements of their cults. When the declaration says that these cooperate with Christ, it supports our argument that non-Christian religions themselves, as cultural forms, can be embraced within the order of grace. Although *Dominus Jesus* never refers to Justin's doctrine of *logos spermatikos,* still the declaration seems effectively to subsume *praeparatio evangelii* under this ancient model. If invisible grace is immanent in other religions, and if the belief that they engender can lead to theological faith, then *Dominus Jesus* seems to support the analogy of religious experience that we have argued is characteristic of *logos spermatikos* but not of *praeparatio evangelii.* The unmentioned Martyr-Apologist therefore emerges as the chief inspiration of the document's model of inclusivism.

Third, the declaration's compatibility with our model's analogy of religious experience is further evinced when we probe into its understanding of invisible grace. *Dominus Jesus* does not explicitly associate invisible grace with prevenient grace, but the association is implied when it affirms that an assisting grace must precede theological faith. It does not explicitly refer to sanctifying grace. Nor does it posit an understanding of the relation of justifying grace to prevenient or assisting grace. We can reasonably conclude that these questions are left open for theological inquiry. We suggest, therefore, that invisible grace, understood as prevenient grace, accounts for whatever authentic religious experience subsists outside of Christianity. It also accounts for the ability of belief to constitute a call to justification and to culminate in the baptism of desire that vindicates the single salvific end of humanity. It also accounts for the assisting grace that precedes theological faith. If, as we have argued, grace is analogous, then *Dominus Jesus* can be said to affirm an analogy of religious experience, even as sanctifying grace establishes Christian *fides quae creditur* as the prime analogate of this experience. In sum, our model resolves tensions ensuing from the paradox rightly maintained by *Dominus Jesus*: that despite their errors, non-Christian cults possess a saving potential.

AFTERWORD

If this modest work has achieved its purpose, it has indicated the need, within the human person's single graced end, for a robust concept of nature. Although weakened, it can be rebuilt, we have argued, by developing a better understanding of the complex analogies that constitute its relation with its partner. We have also argued that the sacramental model constituted by these analogies can address modernity. Moreover, in the essay's last part, we have shown how this model can deepen insights into several of Christianity's perennial problems: the doctrine of God, God's relation with the world, and the relation of the unique savior to other religions. It is not sufficient, however, for theology solely to ponder recondite questions important to the academy. Any model of nature and grace must also possess capital enough to support the church's ever-pressing kerygmatic mission. It must contribute to the practical life of Christians seeking to grow in faith, hope, and love, as well as to the Lord's great commission to "go into the whole world and make disciples of every creature" (Mk 16:15–16). Let us therefore conclude with some reflections on these twin issues in light of our model.

In some ways, we may look with a longing nostalgia on the theory of pure nature. As we seek to cope with current quandaries, we might feel that it undergirded the church's kerygmatic task better than the model which we have favored. Despite our claim in chapter 1 that pure nature contributed to secularism, it did provide a clarity that gave internal coherence to the Catholic clan. In Evelyn Waugh's 1945 novel

Brideshead Revisited, Sebastian Flyte offers lapidary insight into how Catholics understood nature and grace before Vatican II. "Everything they think important," he says, "is different from other people." When his benighted chum Charles Ryder opines, "They seem just like other people," the young nobleman brusquely retorts, "That's exactly what they're not."[1] Sebastian is suggesting that nature, aiming at its own proportionately distinctive end which grace supernaturally alters, offers strong motivation for the economy of salvation. It leaves no doubt, for instance, why, without juridical membership in the one body of Christ that comes with the water of baptism, hell or limbo results. This certainty set charity for the non-Christian world ablaze in the hearts of Francis Xavier and other heroically self-sacrificing missionaries like him. Similarly, understanding nature as sinfully devoid of grace gives persuasive necessity for the frequent reception of the sacraments as grace's unique channels. Because of their eagerness to escape and transcend a profane nature, zealous persons teemed into the priesthood and religious life in order to pursue vocations that they deemed better because more surely and fully graced. In a word, few reared under pure nature would have questioned Cardinal Newman's 1864 thesis that in religion the human mind only has two logically consistent options: Catholicism or atheism. Every position between them is but a halfway house.[2]

Two reasons stand out for the eclipse of a robust theology of nature since Vatican II. The first concerns this essay's argument that the vital distinction between prevenient and sanctifying grace has become blurred. Although those fine minds that rejected pure nature did in fact preserve the difference, still it does seem confined to the small print of their writings. This confusion merged with popular views of *aggiornamento* as enthusiastically embracing a world far less profane than pure nature avers. An impression was thereby fashioned that justification was not only potentially available to all, but actually achieved by all.

1. Evelyn Waugh, *Brideshead Revisited: The Sacred and Profane Memories of Captain Charles Ryder* (Boston: Little, Brown, 1945), 89.

2. Newman, *Apologia*, 291.

In turn, this impression quickly rendered as censoriously Jansenistic Newman's view of postlapsarian nature as an "aboriginal calamity," whose "length and breadth" manifests "no reflection of its Creator."[3] The demise of pure nature seems to have taken all of nature into the grave along with it.

Another reason for the crippling of nature concerns confusion over how Catholics should receive and implement the developments of Vatican II. It goes without saying that, when a council introduces developments, it often effects a shift that questions accepted paradigms and disrupts habitual sensibilities.[4] Accordingly, we need to probe into the root cause of Vatican II's developments. On the one hand, no one can deny that deep and consistent continuity of doctrine obtains between it and the tradition. Avery Dulles, when surveying some of its key documents on its fortieth anniversary, found core doctrines reasserted. Salvation is found only in Jesus; baptism, as the gateway to the church, is required for salvation; the church of Christ subsists in the Catholic church; and only the church authoritatively interprets the scriptures, which nonetheless normatively guide it.[5] On the other hand, Vatican II does interpret and apply these doctrines according to a subtle and sophisticated hermeneutics. We can identity it by taking some clues from Newman's *Essay on the Development of Christian Doctrine*. In this 1845 work, he outlines seven "notes" that allow us to distinguish a doctrinal development from a corruption. Two of these notes are especially relevant to our discussion.

The first is "continuity of principles." According to Newman's theory, developments ensue from a doctrine even as a doctrine embodies a

3. Ibid., 319–21.

4. For Vatican II as a paradigm shift, see John W. O'Malley, "Developments, Reforms, and Two Great Reformations: Towards a Historical Assessment of Vatican II," *Theological Studies* 44, no. 3 (September 1983): 373–406.

5. Avery Cardinal Dulles, "Vatican II: The Myth and the Reality," *America* (February 24, 2003). The term "subsists in" has been authoritatively defined as: "has always existed and will always exist, and in which alone are found all the elements that Christ himself instituted" in Congregation for the Doctrine of the Faith, "Responses to Some Questions Regarding Certain Aspects of the Doctrine of the Church," June 29, 2007, Second Question, Response; www.vatican.va.

principle. A development, therefore, must be faithful to both doctrine and principle. For their part, principles tend to be "abstract and general."[6] Hence, opines Newman, the doctrines of Protestantism develop as it ramifies into different sects and denominations. But these doctrines themselves bear the general principle of private judgment as necessary and sufficient to interpret the scriptures.[7] This principle, he states, is opposed *a priori* to the Catholic principle of private judgment's interpretive insufficiency. Newman cites another instance of a general principle: the transitoriness of the world's goods. It can be embodied either in the religious doctrine of ascetical mortification (in view of eternal life) or in the secular doctrine of epicurean licentiousness.[8] The religious doctrine, in turn, can develop, as it did, into the efficacious application of the merits received from our earthly ascetical works to those in purgatory. This development preserves both the doctrine and the principle embodied in it.

Now concerning the principle governing Vatican's II's hermeneutics of development, our essay has, in fact, already identified it. It is analogy. This is the "abstract and general" rule according to which the council interprets key doctrines whose reassertion establishes its continuity with the tradition. The argument for this claim has been put forth, at least implicitly, in our first chapter's treatment of *Dei Verbum* and in the important references to *Lumen Gentium* in *Dominus Jesus,* treated in our final chapter. These two products are arguably the council's most important, because they are its only dogmatic constitutions. In them, therefore, we should expect to find whatever doctrinal development, properly speaking, the council should have intended.

We have seen, for instance, how the council uses analogy to reassert the Catholic understanding of divine revelation. It is defined as an interlocking system of intrinsic symbols, in which each level of

6. John Henry Cardinal Newman, *An Essay on the Development of Christian Doctrine,* in *Conscience, Consensus, and the Development of Doctrine,* ed. James Gaffney (New York: Doubleday, 1992), 38–428, at 180.

7. Ibid., 182.

8. Ibid., 181.

symbol proceeds analogously from Christ, whose incarnation of the Father's image in history constitutes the prime symbol. Christ's acts and speech become symbols that manifest the Father to the apostles in time and space. Their preaching, in turn, establishes the next symbol, sacred tradition, in which the apostolic witness is embodied. From tradition emerges the New Testament, a written symbol of tradition. Vatican II therefore views human acts and speech, both written and spoken, when they become media of revelation, as analogous. As *Dei Verbum* states, "God's words … have taken on the likeness of human speech, just as the Word … took on the likeness of human beings."[9]

The council uses the same principle to reassert the doctrine of the church. Divine revelation, uniquely subsisting in the Catholic church, nonetheless enables in other religions "a manifold cooperation which is but a participation in this one source."[10] Where participation obtains, there analogy also obtains. Because of it, "elements of good and truth [are] present among" other religions so that they can prompt the heart "to be open to the action of God."[11] These elements of good and truth, derived only from Christ, are reflective of him in a decidedly different and less adequate manner than in Catholicism. We have also seen how Rahner implicitly uses analogy to express this doctrine of the council. An ascending membership in the church embraces all those who, even while professing Christianity apart from Rome, are joined in unity to the extent that they share the fullness of Catholic faith. A descending membership joins those baptized by desire to professing Christians baptized by water.[12]

Our final chapter also showed how *Gaudium et Spes,* although a "pastoral" and not a dogmatic constitution, makes a broad use of analogy to develop a theology of culture. This it defines as those institutions, like government and the university, and those symbols, like the

9. Vatican Council II, *Dei Verbum,* par. 13, in *Decrees,* ed. Tanner, 2:971–81.

10. Vatican Council II, *Lumen Gentium,* par. 62, in *Decrees,* ed. Tanner, 2:849–900, quoted in *DJ.*

11. *DJ,* par. 21, referring to *Lumen Gentium,* par. 16.

12. Karl Rahner, "Anonymous Christian," in *TI* 6:390–98, at 391.

arts and sciences, that express humanity's "spiritual experiences and aspirations."[13] Grace continually renews "from the inside" culture's intrinsic truth and beauty.[14] Wherever authentic value inheres in institutions and symbols, there likewise inheres "the wonderful wisdom which was with God from the beginning."[15] Because this wisdom is the incarnate Logos, Christ is implicit wherever truth and goodness are found. The pastoral constitution thus extends the principle of analogy used in the dogmatic statements. Together they promulgate a coherent teaching that embraces Catholicism, non-Catholic Christianity, and other religions, as well as the truth, goodness, and beauty of human endeavor in general.

Regarding the second of Newman's notes that concern us, his theory claims that a doctrinal development exercises a "conservative action upon its past." By this he means that a new development illustrates and corroborates the principle, doctrine, and previous developments from which it springs.[16] To be sure, a development can represent a "real and perceptible" change, but it nonetheless protects "what was before" in such a way that, without the development, the church's patrimony would not be so effectively supported, articulated, and understood.[17] It may be that developments "appear at first sight to contradict that out of which they grew," yet sober reflection shows them otherwise.[18]

As an example of this note, we might recall the standard defense of Nicaea in its recourse to the term *homoousios* (consubstantiality) to define the Trinitarian relations. Given the fragmented references to these relations in the scriptures, the council harnessed an expression not found in them in order precisely to articulate their inner coherence and underlying meaning. Although the term introduced a marked change, and to the Arians even a heterodox one, it was warranted under the

13. Vatican Council II, *Gaudium et Spes*, par. 53, in *Decrees*, ed. Tanner, 2:1069–1135, at 1106.
14. Ibid., par. 58 (1109).
15. Ibid., par. 57 (1108).
16. Newman, *Development*, esp. 195–98, at 196.
17. Ibid., 198; see also esp. 363–77, at 363.
18. Ibid., 365.

council's apostolic authority to conserve the tradition. Developments can thus be paradoxical; their conservatism sometimes results from boldly liberal initiatives. Without Nicaea's innovation, Arianism would have held sway, and the Christian doctrine of God would have been corrupted, not conserved.[19] Even as it was, many Eastern bishops retained forms of Arianism for at least sixty years after the council.[20]

In recovering analogy as its hermeneutical principle, Vatican II, although precipitating "real and perceptible change," nonetheless exercises a conservative action upon the past. We have indicated in chapter 7 that the principle can be traced to Justin's *logos spermatikos* and Ireneaus's "recapitulation."[21] But these ancient understandings are only dressing in different garb what Chalcedon in 451 declared as the orthodox faith. Because humanity and divinity unite in the one person of Christ, a congenial blending of infinite and finite obtains in God's plan for salvation, even though each remains integral and distinct. Complementary in their disparity, nature and grace, creation and redemption, exist to serve each other.

In a word, Vatican II, in grasping hold of an insight lodged deep in Christianity, puts contemporary Catholicism squarely in an analogous world. It offers little support for the equivocal world of pure nature's sharp distinction between nature and grace. Nonetheless, its great *aggiornamento* does not render anachronistic Newman's claim that all religious positions between Catholicism and atheism are halfway houses. But it does differ with pure nature in its own tendency to see those halfway houses as perhaps inclining more toward Catholicism than atheism. Similarly, the council vindicates Sebastian Flyte's conviction that Catholics are not "just like other people." Yet its analogous vision would suggest that they have more in common with other people than Sebastian may have thought.

19. For a critical study of this development, see Bernard Lonergan, *The Way to Nicea: The Dialectical Development of Trinitarian Theology* (Philadelphia: Westminster, 1976).

20. John Henry Cardinal Newman, *On Consulting the Faithful in Matters of Doctrine*, in *Conscience*, 392–428, at 409.

21. Justin, *Apology*, 262–63; Irenaeus, *Against the Heresies*, 548.

Undoubtedly, living in Vatican II's analogous world is more difficult than living in pure nature's equivocal one. The council, even as it exercised a conservative action on its past, called into question past certainties, just as Nicaea did. The weakening of nature bears much of the blame. But as we argued in chapter 4, an analogous understanding of nature's relation to grace presents no obstacle to a robust conception of it as grace's "own other." Revitalizing nature requires a fresh appreciation of the distance obtaining between it and grace, even in their union. In chapter 6, we cited Hegel's quotation of Spinoza that all distinction implies negation.[22] All analogy, insofar as it embraces two integral partners, entails an apophatic moment between them. The last fifty years of the council's reception have established the partners' similarity; the future must attend to the "unlikeness" that, as Pseudo-Dionysius the Areopagite reminded us in chapter 5, constitutes analogical "likeness."[23]

We can only glimpse from anecdotal experience how creative pastoral practice is currently recovering an existential sense of nature's otherness to the grace in which it abides. Frequently, instances concern young people, the *spes gregis* religiously cultivated under the last two pontiffs, whose harvest is now teeming forth. Their zeal appreciates Christianity as a prophetic alternative to the dominant secularism. We might speculate that, as the offspring of drugs and alcohol, divorce, a wide range of sexual liberation, and purposeless affluence, they are spiritually and emotionally burned out from a culture deficient in truth and goodness. They are not, however, flocking, as previous generations did, to the priesthood and religious life. They seem to want to renew culture "from within" by devout lay vocations. For support, they turn to the model that Benedict XVI foresees as the future of Christianity: small groups who, sharing a strong commitment, come together to be shaped by the eucharist in order to disperse into the world as leaven.[24]

22. Hegel, *EL*, 135.

23. Pseudo-Dionysius, *CH* XV.8 (337B), in Balthasar, *GL* 2:179.

24. Ratzinger, *Principles of Catholic Theology*, 54.

New forms of celebrating the eucharist that differ from general practice seem attractive to them. One pastor in New Orleans encourages his more mature congregants to attend the parish "youth mass." This turns out to be the extraordinary form, often called by the misnomer "Tridentine" mass. We might speculate that its allure results from its contemplative silence, welcomed as a salutary contrast to the banality of ubiquitous cell-phone chat. Entering this silence for the sake of participating in a transcendent action symbolized by the common position before the high altar makes it clear that the profane world of nature is left well behind. Similarly, in Quebec, where the "quiet revolution" of the 1960s remains aggressively indifferent to the once culturally dominant Catholicism, a cathedral-sized abbey church along a rural stretch of Lake Memphrémagog is filled each Sunday for the principal mass. At St. Benoit, affiliated with the Solesmes Benedictines, the "ordinary form" is concelebrated with the priests facing the people. We might speculate that its allure, like the traditional mass, also results from forms which challenge the hegemony of the profane world: the creatively adapted Gothic of the contemporary church, the Gregorian chant, the elevated altar clearly signifying transcendence, and the conspicuous reverence of the ritual that eschews the impromptu and improvised.

An instance of a different sort is provided by a middle-aged pastor in suburban Baltimore, who recounts his experience of challenging secularism.[25] For some years, his ministry was sustained by the assumption that a parish's mission was to provide services of ever-higher quality to its members, who in turn would respond by contributing generously to support them. This assumption collapsed when he realized that it was emerging from and sustained by a consumerist model. The *quid pro quo* of expected benefits for dollars paid reduced growing in faith, hope, and love to a mercantile transaction. In addition, it locked the congregation in a self-enclosed cycle that precluded an evangelizing concern for others outside of it. Introducing new forms

25. Michael White and Tom Corcoran, *Rebuilt: Awakening the Faithful, Reaching the Lost, and Making Church Matter* (Notre Dame, Ind.: Ave Maria Press, 2013).

into parish life confronted the previous profane assumption. These forms, some adapted from Protestant worship, noticeably enhanced faith, attendance, and zeal to spread the Gospel.

Above all, the single end theory of nature contends that nature yearns for a final purpose that it cannot know without God's free revelation. When examples like those just described define the gap between nature and grace, they effectively bring this "good news" home. However much nature subsists within the prevenient grace that renders the desire for God an implicit Christian vocation, nature cannot explain itself. Pascal reminds us, for instance, that nature confronts us as a cipher of two meanings—one clear, one hidden. Although partially intelligible by its own discernible rules, it conceals its ultimate meaning. Without the code, the cipher will ever appear fraught with the deepest of contradictions.[26] Even when working to achieve our noblest aspirations, we discover how embedded they still remain in the recalcitrant "aboriginal calamity" within.[27] Christians know the code, but the code is useless without the cipher. No better description of the cipher can be found than the epigraph from Newman that appears before the introduction to this book. Fresh even now fifty years after Vatican II, it continues to deliver the Christian kerygma its mission. With it this essay began, and now closes by evoking it.

26. Blaise Pascal, *Pensées*, trans. H. F. Stewart (London: Routledge and Kegan Paul, 1950), § 520 (299).

27. For a cinematic depiction of this theme, see *The Wind That Shakes the Barley*, a 2006 Irish film directed by Ken Loach.

Appendix

The *Realsymbol* and Selected Modern Symbols

In framing the argument of this book, we referred throughout to a number of prominent theories of the symbol in Western thought. We mentioned, for instance, that the medieval theory flowered because it was used to interpret the scriptures and to develop a theology of the sacraments (chapter 1). Extending into Augustine and the great Scholastics, this theology, we said, influenced John Paul II's retrieval of efficacious causality (chapter 3). We treated Möhler's theory, together with its impact on *Dei Verbum*, subsequently tracing Vatican II's doctrine of the symbolism of divine revelation to the patristic *logos spermatikos* (chapters 1, 2, 7). In studying recent theorists, we underscored Hegel, singling out his aesthetics, dialectic of the notion, and mythic structure of religion (chapters 2, 6, 7). This last theme assumed prominence in our treatment of Ricoeur (chapter 5). Our purpose in dealing with these theories was overarching: to shed light on the sacramental relation of nature and grace, which finds congenial formulation, we argued, in Rahner's *Realsymbol* (chapter 4). Its mediated immediacy entails a unity-in-difference between the symbol and what it symbolizes; it thus grounds the analogy between Christian transcendence and the empirical order (chapters 2, 6, 7).

It may be helpful now if we fill in some gaps by locating our central concept within several other important modern and contemporary theories so that its distinctiveness can be more amply appreciated.

We will organize these under four types. The first will place Kant and Ernst Cassirer under the "phenomenal" symbol, whose referent communicates no ontological value.[1] The second will place Paul Tillich and Roger Haight under the "ontological" symbol that is nonetheless culturally relative. The third will place Jean-Luc Marion, Louis-Marie Chauvet, Ghislain Lafont, David Power, and George Steiner under the "apophatic" symbol dismissive of, or hesitant about, the analogy of being. The fourth is David Tracy's "analogical" symbol compatible with the argument of our book.

Kant lays out the symbol's process of formation in the *Critique of Judgment*. He had already shown in the *Critique of Pure Reason* that the mind's ideas of God, soul, and world are purely regulative and not constitutive of reason; no empirical datum intuited as experience could ever correspond to them. They therefore possess no epistemic value as such, although they do serve as architectonic ideals toward which reason strives and under which reason necessarily operates. Yet because the mind ineluctably seeks to give utterance to these ideals, it generates symbolism as a creative dynamism. God comes to be exhibited, for instance, in the doctrinal propositions of the Nicene Creed. Although these do not import the ontological value that they purportedly intend, still they do possess rational content. This content is due not to speculative but to practical reason, which, for Kant, can frame a sound argument for God as morality's necessary ground. They can be purified of their symbolic husk to reveal their inner kernel. This manifests some aspect of the "moral governor," who is the guarantor of the categorical imperative, which gives practical reason its weight and force. Historically revealed religion thus stands to the moral religion of reason as the symbol stands to what it symbolizes (see above, chapter 7).

In addition to pure reason's ideals, the mind entertains other ideas embedded in historical religion, such as love, envy, death, hell, eternity, creation, and the kingdom of the blessed. Kant calls these aesthetic.

1. We might affirm Kant, together with Goethe, as the co-origins of the modern symbol. For Goethe's theory, which is ontological, see Fields, *Being as Symbol*, 61–65.

They surpass sensible experience and so can never rely on specific data of intuition for their adequate exhibition. Such symbols expand intuition and so enrich experience, whereas those symbols expressive of God are impoverished when compared to their referent. Nonetheless, both types of symbol, by producing "arbitrary forms of possible intuition," stretch reason beyond the limits of its properly determining powers.[2] In short, in seeking to approximate their universal referents, symbols animate reason and so depend on, even while revealing, a genius in human thinking that nature "is hardly likely ever to allow us to discover."[3] Whatever religious value that they signify beyond the moral can be claimed only by a fideism, to which Catholic thought has traditionally been opposed (see above, chapters 1, 2, 3).[4]

Ernst Cassirer's four-volume *Philosophy of Symbolic Forms* extends Kant's suppositions into the twentieth century, but not without significantly qualifying them. Although indebted to the *Critique of Judgment* that lays out a unifying bridge between speculative and practical reason, Cassirer nonetheless reads this work through the lens of Fichte, Schelling, and Hegel. On the one hand, his project, like Kant's, seeks to frame the unity of experience. On the other hand, like the Romantics, it finds this unity far less in the conditions for the possibility of any object than in the conditions for the unity of mind itself. The source of this unity lies in the dynamism of life, which Cassirer counterpoises to spirit. Life means "flux without pause."[5] Nonetheless, in its very midst, life becomes individualized by spirit, creative subjectivity, which Cassirer defines as the workings of the intellect as finalized in its judgments.

2. Immanuel Kant, *Critique of Judgment*, trans. J. H. Bernard (New York: Hafner Press, 1951), 77.

3. Immanuel Kant, *Critique of Pure Reason*, trans. Norman Kemp Smith (New York: St. Martin's Press, 1929), 183 (A141/B181).

4. "I have therefore found it necessary to deny *knowledge*, in order to make room for *faith*" (*Critique of Pure Reason*, 29 [Bxxx]). See also Avery Dulles, "The Cognitive Basis of Faith," in *Philosophy and Theology* 10, no. 1 (1998): 19–31.

5. Ernst Cassirer, *The Metaphysics of Symbolic Forms*, vol. 4 of *The Philosophy of Symbolic Forms*, ed. John Michael Krois and Daniel Philip Verene, trans. John Michael Krois (New Haven, Conn.: Yale University Press, 1996), 9, quoting Georg Simmel, "The Transcendent Character of Life," in his *Individuality and Social Forms*, trans. and ed. Donald N. Levine (Chicago: University of Chicago Press, 1971), 363.

When spirit's judgments halt life, "the objective products of culture unfold" from subjectivity, thus constituting the symbolic forms of science, art, religion, and language.[6] These, when and as founded by spirit, subsequently become unbounded by life, the active principle of both their origin and elimination. Thus, whereas the symbolic productivity of spirit "stands opposed to life," it never turns against life or rages antagonistically toward it.[7] Similarly, even as life indirectly accepts spirit's judgments, it rejects them. Yet without them, all the symbolic forms that unify the mind would be devoid of meaning and "amount to nothing but empty phantasmagoria."[8] Meaning originates in the realm of spirit, which establishes the measuring norms of life.

Despite his debt to Romanticism, Cassirer's symbolic idealism remains Kantian in its rejection of any claim of the mind to knowledge of the thing-in-itself. Although Cassirer would agree with Hegel's critique of Kant's erroneously static conception of mind, he would reject Hegel's ontology of the absolute. Similarly, he also adamantly rejects any reproductive or mimetic metaphysics according to which "some positively given being" is separate from the intelligent formulations of spirit.[9] Reality is given only in and through intelligent action, not in any chimeral notion of substances. Hence, Cassirer equates reality with the sequence of the plurality of symbolic forms. In them, percept and concept, particular and general, the one and the many find reconciliation. In this reconciliation, *Geist* achieves an awareness precisely of its unity within the multiplicity of its activities.[10] The upshot, as Paul Tillich puts it, is that while culture is irreducibly symbolic for Cassirer, culture does not reflect reality, but its symbols create reality.[11]

6. Ibid, 7.

7. Ibid., 31.

8. Ibid.

9. Ibid., 223.

10. Habermas criticizes Cassirer for so eliminating the mimesis of language that he in fact risks losing the transcendental self altogether; see Stephen Fields, review of Jürgen Habermas, *The Liberating Power of Symbols: Philosophical Essays*, in *The Review of Metaphysics* 56 (2003): 650–51.

11. Paul Tillich, "The Religious Symbol," trans. James Adams and Ernst Fraenkel, in *Symbolism in Religion and Literature*, ed. Rollo May (New York: George Braziller, 1960), 75–98, at 84; originally in *The Journal of Liberal Religion* 2 (1940): 13–33.

It is on this very point that Tillich takes strong issue with Cassirer. The Lutheran divine asserts the uniqueness of religious symbols, which cannot "be merely constructed" but only "created."[12] Religious symbols exert a distinctive power over the human person owing precisely to the fact that the cosmos is not free-standing but embraced by the objectivity of the unconditioned transcendent. Accordingly, religious symbols, unlike all others, express "an object which never can become an object," however much we must assign the transcendent a name such as God.[13] If therefore the transcendent is the all-encompassing source of meaning, then it follows that all cultural symbols, such as language, art, and science, bear the potential to become religious symbols. But it is these and these alone that can integrate human experience and orient the mind to its ultimate destiny and purpose. Nonetheless, precisely because the religious symbol participates in the transcendent that it signifies, the mind cannot constitute religious symbols unless, ironically, it also denies them. In this dialectic, claims Tillich, "the profoundest aspect of the religious act is manifested."[14]

Despite his criticism of Cassirer, Tillich does share his symbolic relativism. It is grounded in his view that, in religion, "it is not God that is given, but the symbol of the encounter between God and man."[15] Clearly at odds with Rahner's understanding Christ as the divine *Realsymbol,* Tillich attenuates the ontological distance between the revealing God and the medium of the revelation.[16] Based on an apophatic view of God as the "abyss" beyond symbols, he strongly asserts that "in all cases, the confusion of the holy itself with the bearer of the holy is the beginning of the distortion of religion."[17] His intent to avoid this confusion leads him to underscore the cultural and historical conditioning of all religious symbols. Although these do indeed

12. Ibid., 76; also Paul Tillich, "Theology and Symbolism," in *Religious Symbolism,* ed. F. Ernest Johnson (New York: Institute for Religious and Social Studies, 1955), 107–16, at 109.

13. Tillich, "Religious Symbol," 77.

14. Ibid., 90.

15. Tillich, "Theology and Symbolism," 111.

16. See Rahner, "Theology of the Symbol," 236–40, and the commentary in Joseph Wong, *Logos-Symbol in the Christology of Karl Rahner* (Rome: Libreria Ateneo Salesiano, 1984).

17. Tillich, "Theology and Symbolism," 114–15.

import transcendence, still, he observes, "the truth of a symbol depends on its inner necessity for the symbol-creating consciousness."[18] In other words, the process of becoming a symbol and its acceptance as a symbol are one and the same. As a result, because symbols commence signifying and cease doing so, they are held hostages to the evolving transitions among paradigms and world views.

It is true that, for Tillich, Christ belongs to a distinctive set of religious symbols called "objective." This term appears to mean that the prophet of Nazareth will always remain an authoritative bearer of the holy. But the claims that we make about Christ are culturally relative interpretations of the objective symbol. Even so, we might wonder whether, given the apophatic reach of Tillich's thought, the distinctiveness of the objective religious symbol can ever survive what Cassirer calls the unbounding of all symbols by relentless flux.

Tillich's use of the symbol's dialectic to relativize Christianity's doctrines finds a recent duplication in the work of Roger Haight. A symbol, he reminds us, both is and is not what it symbolizes. Accordingly, Chalcedon teaches us that "Jesus is truly human, that is, not divine but consubstantial with us; [and also that] Jesus is truly divine."[19] The tension between Jesus's divine and human natures cannot be "resolved," he claims, because a dialectic by definition cannot be resolved.[20] Nonetheless, when Chalcedon-based Christology has successively tried to achieve a resolution, it consistently compromises Jesus's human nature in favor of the divine nature. The upshot is that Chalcedon's point of departure, "the Logos and its incarnation," seems flawed from the beginning. It must therefore be abandoned for a fresh starting point capable of more credibly accounting for Jesus precisely as a human bearer of the holy.[21] Buttressing this challenge to orthodoxy, Haight contends that "the shift in western culture" to historically self-conscious modes of thought means that the classical ontology undergirding Chalcedon

18. Tillich, "Religious Symbol," 91.

19. Roger Haight, *Dynamics of Theology* (New York: Paulist Press, 1990), 220.

20. Ibid., 139n10.

21. Roger Haight, *Jesus, Symbol of God* (Maryknoll, N.Y.: Orbis Books, 1999), 290–91.

has, in any case, become moribund.[22] Echoing Tillich, he declares: "Symbols live and die in culture."[23] The symbol putatively relevant to the contemporary world that *Jesus, Symbol of God* presents can broadly be termed Adoptionist; it has been further specified as second-century Ebionism.

As a brief commentary on Haight's theory, we might observe that it seems anachronistic to impose Tillich's "purely dialectical" theory of the symbol on Chalcedon, when in fact the council establishes its own rules for interpreting its Christological symbolism. That the dialectic between the human and divine natures of Christ cannot achieve a resolution reductively satisfactory to human reason should in no measure surprise us. Chalcedon is seeking to do no more than exclude erroneous understandings of a paradox divinely revealed in the scriptures. Yet the dialectic does admit of resolution, chiefly because it is the one person who is the dialectic's unified subject. According to the nuances of Christological predication, whatever belongs to this person according to one nature may simply be affirmed of him. Thus, we may say that "Jesus died." But what does not belong to the person according to one nature may not simply be denied.[24] Thus we may not say that Jesus is "not divine," as Haight says, even though, precisely as human, he is not. The reason we cannot is owing to the integrity of the two natures that subsist "without confusion," but also "without [hypostatic] separation."[25]

By contrast, Jean-Luc Marion's analysis of the icon in *The Crossing of the Visible* offers us a theory whose use of dialectic resembles, at first view, the *Realsymbol*'s mediated immediacy. On the one hand, the icon manifests a "trace of the brilliance of the holiness of the Holy," yet on the other hand, it does not devolve into a blasphemous idol claiming to replicate it.[26] Holding with John Damascene that icons are models

22. Ibid., 291.

23. Haight, *Dynamics*, 162–63.

24. J. F. Rigney, "Communication of Idioms," *NCE* 4:36.

25. "The Chalcedonian Decree," in *Christology of the Later Fathers*, ed. Hardy, 372–74, at 373.

26. Jean-Luc Marion, "The Prototype and the Image," trans. James K. A. Smith, in Marion,

or "types of that which has no type," Marion also follows the teaching of Nicaea II that they should conform themselves to the cross, the paradigm of all sacred types.[27] The cross becomes sanctified because it serves as the means by which Christ's death transfers in perfect obedience "all holiness to One other than himself, the Father."[28] Accordingly, common icons become sanctified because, by eliciting the obedient faith of those who venerate them, they enable the pious transferring of holiness from the visible medium to its invisible prototype.

Marion is adamant, however, that this transfer shuns any logic of mimesis. If it did not, he claims, the icon would devolve into sacrilege. Hence, strictly speaking, the icon does not "represent" the invisible. It constitutes "a sign and not (a) nature of the invisible [*sic*]," with which it therefore makes no claim to an "intrinsic correspondence."[29] Nonetheless, the icon "reaches the invisible by never ceasing to transgress itself, according to the paradox of anatyposis."[30] In other words, icon veneration is fed by an act of dialectical negation made in the intention of the faithful. Marion thus echoes Tillich's caution not to confuse the holy with its bearer.

Once mimesis as a link between visible and invisible is obviated, the key question concerns the ground of the visible's merit to elicit an act of veneration on the believer's part. Reminiscent of Balthasar's theological aesthetics, Marion avers that the invisible itself takes the initiative in sanctifying the icon, which can thus "approximately" make present "the holiness of the Holy One" (see above, chapter 5).[31] This initiative is accomplished by the Spirit, who can cross "definitive and unsurpassable" distances.[32] The Spirit produces for the icon an effect not unlike the incarnation. In it, Christ's "human nature becomes, en-

The Essential Writings, ed. Kevin Hart (New York: Fordham University Press, 2013), 273–87, at 275; reprinted from *The Crossing of the Visible* (Stanford, Calif.: Stanford University Press, 2004), 66–87; originally *La croisée du visible* (Paris: Presses universitaires de France, 2007).

27. Ibid., quoting John of Damascus, *The Orthodox Faith*, IV.16, in *PG* 94:172b.

28. Ibid., 280.

29. Ibid., 280–81.

30. Ibid., 281; *anatyposis* is spelled in Greek.

31. Ibid., 280.

32. Ibid., 285.

tirely, the type whose prototype consists of nothing less than the divine nature."[33] Just as the hypostatic union does not dispel "the ambiguous commerce" between the natures, so in the icon's veneration, the Spirit bridges the inimitable divide by enabling "a transition that does not cease to exchange" the medium and what it presents.[34] In short, even as Marion fixes the symbol's efficacy in apophatic anatyposis, his appeal to the action of the Spirit allows the symbol to mediate the holy to the faithful immediately.

Our critique would note that, in developing his symbol theory, Marion makes a one-sided use of Basil. On the one hand, he cites the great Cappadocian's claim that "the honor given to the icon passes to its prototype."[35] On the other hand, however, he ignores Basil's assertion that guided our analysis in chapter 5: that "from the beauty of created things, the nature of the creator is correspondingly inferred."[36] Unlike Basil, Marion denies any natural analogy between the symbol and its prototype, allowing only the action of the Spirit to overcome the mimetic vacuity between them. Accordingly, although the icon mediates the invisible immediately, still its power to do so finds its basis only on a fideism inimical to one of Marion's patristic sources. After all, when the symbol forfeits any claim to represent or correspond to its apophatically mute prototype, fideism is all that remains to ground its efficacy.

Ironically, Marion's fideism may be as far-reaching as Kant's regulative metaphysics. It seems consistent with his treatment of the relation between God and being in Thomas. There, Marion tells us, because God's essence transcends all finite beings and concepts and hence remains unknown, it follows that God's act of being is not being at all. As a result, when we speak of it, we must do so in a strictly apophatic, "nonontological way."[37] Marion thus collapses the all-important distinction in Thomas between the mind's knowing that God exists and

33. Ibid.

34. Ibid., 285–86.

35. Ibid., 275, citing *DS* 392, referring to Basil the Great, *De Spiritu Sancto*, XVIII.45.

36. Basil the Great, "Letter 8," in *Letters*, 1:93.

37. Jean-Luc Marion, "Thomas Aquinas and Onto-theo-logy," trans. B. Gendreau et al., in Marion, *Essential Writings*, 288–311, at 310; reprinted from *Mystics: Presence and Aporia*,

knowing what God is, thus leaving us with a dialectic without any effective synthesis. Destroying the very notion of a natural analogy between visible and invisible, finite and infinite, Marion cannot seem to allow the divine any kataphatic manifestation in the world other than what faith professes. Christian theology therefore seems to sacrifice any hermeneutics according to which it could do its work: to render the truths of revelation credibly intelligible to both believer and nonbeliever alike. Truth itself seems to have become an equivocal term.

Louis-Marie Chauvet's work on the sacraments rings its own changes on Marion's theme. We find, for instance, the same resistance to symbolic mimesis, especially as expressed in the instrumental causality that, for both, purportedly debases grace as divine gift.[38] Accordingly, Chauvet underscores "the nonadequation" of any visible symbol to the transcendent mystery, while at the same time accounting for the sacraments' "constant creativity."[39] To accomplish the first aim, he devises the notion of "anti-ritual," thus ingeniously adapting the apophatic dialectic with which we are by now familiar. Echoing Marion, this term means that all symbolic rituals must be measured against the cross. Even as graced, they should be experienced as breaking "the pattern of the theophanic."[40] To realize the second aim, Chauvet delves into anthropology, mining for theological profit an understanding of traditional societies. Both aims congenially coalesce in his view of language's overarching efficacy.

In order to cross the inimitable divide between symbol and divine mystery, Chauvet harnesses an insight from Stanislas Breton that also accords with Marion. While decidedly avoiding any analogy, Chavet affirms that, when God acts in time, he does not effect a representa-

ed. Michael Kessler and Christian Sheppard (Chicago: University of Chicago Press, 2007), 38–74; originally "Saint Thomas d'Aquin et onto-théo-logie," *Revue thomiste* 95 (1995): 31–66.

38. See Bernhard Blankenhorn, OP, "The Instrumental Causality of the Sacraments: Thomas Aquinas and Louis-Marie Chauvet," *Nova et Vetera (English Edition)* 4 (2006): 255–94, at 258.

39. David N. Power, OMI, "Louis-Marie Chauvet," in Regis A. Duffy, OFM, Kevin W. Irwin, and David N. Power, OMI, "Current Theology – Sacramental Theology: A Review of Literature," in *Theological Studies* 55 (1994): 657–705, at 685–86.

40. Ibid., 687.

tion, but rather leaves "the trace" of his action.[41] Such a trace does not entail causality, but it does keep the reference to the divine "gratuity alive."[42] Present in the sacraments, God's trace is expressed and specified in human speech. As the law of prayer, language interprets the immanent trace and thus assumes priority over the visible aspects of the ritual, even overshadowing them. In so doing, the human word acts as a dialectic guarantying the sacraments' apophatic anti-ritual.

Language also explains the sacraments' enduring efficacy for those who receive them. Studies have made clear, Chauvet writes, that "symbolic exchange" constitutes the essence of ritual.[43] In it, subjects not only give and receive objects but, by means of them, exchange themselves in generous gratuity. All such exchanges, however, "are [necessarily] encompassed by language," because speech articulates the underlying intentionality that renders them distinctively human.[44] If the sacraments embody God's free offer to enter into exchange with us, then the language that specifies the divine gift must perforce incorporate us into grace's continuous renewal. Precisely because of language's pivotal sacramental importance, Chauvet approvingly quotes de Lubac, who castigates the "'deadly dichotomy'" introduced in the twelfth century between Christ's eucharistic and ecclesial body.[45] Over-elevating the intrinsic symbolism of the visible signs of the "real presence" undermines the eucharist's intrinsic union with the church. After all, this union is specified by the liturgical words of public prayer, and these are the very means by which the church effects itself.

41. Ibid., 688, referring to Chauvet, *Symbole et sacrement: une relecture sacramentelle de l'existence chrétienne* (Paris: Éditions du Cerf, 1987), 74–78, 214–16, discussing Stanislas Breton, *Le Verbe et la croix* (Paris: Éditions Desclée de Brouwer, 1981), 133–37.

42. Ibid., 687.

43. Louis-Marie Chauvet, *The Sacraments: The Word of God at the Mercy of the Body* (Collegeville, Minn.: Liturgical Press, 2001), 119; originally *Les sacrements: parole de Dieu au risque du corps* (Paris: Éditions de l'Atelier, 1993); referring to Marcel Mauss, *The Gift: Forms and Functions of Exchange in Archaic Societies*, trans. Ian Cunnison (New York: Norton, 1967), and Georges Duby, "Les attitudes mentales," in *Guerriers et paysans: VIIe-XIIe siècle, premier essor de l'économie européenne* (Paris: Éditions Gallimard), 1973.

44. Ibid., 122.

45. Ibid., 141, citing Henri de Lubac, "Du symbole à la dialectique," in *Corpus mysticum: l'eucharistie et l'église du moyen âge, étude historique* (Paris: Aubier, 1944), esp. 280–83.

In emphasizing language as the means of synthesizing the symbol's apophatic and kataphatic dimensions, Chauvet posits an advance over Marion. Nonetheless, as in Marion, we finally remain stagnant in one of nominalism's problems, an equivocal view of truth. Without a more sustained metaphysics of the analogous unity of reality, no demonstrable natural link obtains between the divine trace and the human speech that interprets the trace and so specifies the sacrament. Once again, therefore, fideism speaks the final word, because only it can sew trace and speech together.

Although also reluctant to posit a causal ontology, Ghislain Lafont in *God, Time, and Being* does signal a decided turn away from nominalism and fideism. Similar to the argument of our book, he posits a reciprocal continuity between nature and grace, speaking of God's "*creative* word" and "*addressed* word."[46] Reminiscent of Pseudo-Dionysius the Areopagite, he views both as springing from the amplitude of God's own dynamic act of being (see above, chapter 5). On the one hand, creation constitutes all particular beings in their own act of being, which is simultaneously specific and dynamic.[47] Without reluctance, therefore, Lafont supports the analogy of being. On the other hand, redemption proposes a "*symbolic rupture*" in creative being for the human person whose freedom ranges infinitely open.[48] In other words, Christian faith dialectically negates the analogy precisely in order for reality to attain a new synthesis.[49] Although grace causes a hiatus with nature, it nonetheless allows the human person's natural openness "to expand to the point of divine communion." In turn, this graced expansion of intellect and will brings about the transformation of the world.[50]

We might view Lafont as undertaking an apologetic project designed to bring postmodern theology within the ambit of the tradition. While entering into dialogue with those who fear building Christianity into the kind of grand system inimical to Lyotard, he also implicitly hear-

46. Ghislain Lafont, *God, Time, and Being*, trans. Leonard Maluf (Petersham, Mass.: Saint Bede's Publications, 1992), 315; originally *Dieu, le temps, et l'être* (Paris: Éditions du Cerf, 1986).

47. Ibid.

48. Ibid.

49. Ibid., 308.

50. Ibid., 315.

kens to Balthasar. Both thinkers understand the caesura between grace and nature as neither definitive nor reductively apophatic (see above, chapter 5). On the contrary, this caesura achieves a resolution in reality's higher union with God even while revelation remains in its essence not a cause and effect, but an event and a gift. As a result, for Lafont, language can authentically specify the gift-event because it is joined intrinsically to God's hidden being "at the core of the world."[51] Thus, unlike his compatriots whom we have surveyed, Lafont implicitly traces for us the skeletal outline of the *Realsymbol*: the emanation of nature and grace from their divine source, their dialectical mediation in history, and their return in grace to their source (see above, chapters 4 and 5).[52]

The skepticism of postmodern thinkers like Marion, Chauvet, and Lafont about causality is owing to Heidegger's criticism of the sharp dichotomy purportedly drawn by Western thought since Plato between being and particular beings. In the German's view, this division has led to the exclusion of being to the mind's rational concept and thus, ironically, to the forgetfulness of authentic being. Accordingly, Heidegger seeks to recover being's rich communications to humanity, its "mittances," in volitional and affective experience. But in doing so, he is clear that being, and the human beings to whom being is unveiled, are essentially conditioned by history and so finite.[53]

It follows, therefore, as George Steiner argues in *Real Presences*, that only metaphor can yield any "systematic theory of meaning."[54] Meta-

51. Ibid., 274.

52. David N. Power, in *Sacrament: The Language of God's Giving* (New York: Crossroad, 1999), cursorily approves of Lafont's understanding of the analogy of being (281–82), even as he integrates into his symbol theory Marion's analysis of the icon (282–90). Yet because he shows reluctance to "look for some causative force outside language usage itself" (75), we remain unclear about how language and being are related other than "in the grace of the Spirit" (295). Even though "being [is] given to us in sacrament" (295) and "being is possessed only through language" (294), without a fuller elaboration of analogy, we are left with the same equivocal view of truth and the same fideism. See the commentary on Power and Chauvet in Joy Harrell Blaylock, "Ghislain Lafont and Contemporary Sacramental Theology," *Theological Studies* 66 (December 2005): 841–61, at 851.

53. William J. Richardson, *Heidegger: Through Phenomenology to Thought* (The Hague: Martinus Nijhoff, 1967), 42–43.

54. George Steiner, *Real Presences* (London: Faber and Faber, 1989), 164.

phor constitutes the essence of language in its unveiling of intelligibility. Words consist of a nexus of symbols inescapably embedded in the context of the flux of experience from which they emerge. "Context," Steiner avers, "is at all times dialectical." Metaphor, and indeed all symbols, like the plastic arts and music, compel us to modify the spatio-temporal manifold, even as this manifold modifies our symbols. In other words, "nature imitates art" just as art imitates nature.[55] "Summer nights," for example, "notably to the south, have changed since Van Gogh." As a result, symbols introduce us into "the naked presence" of freedom itself.[56] Because no symbol admits of any definitive or stable interpretation, the onus falls on us to decide its value, and to do so in the face of an abyss of meaning, an "illusory absolute," that, paradoxically, does not obviate meaning itself.[57]

As a riposte to the Heidegger-inspired view of the symbol, we would note that Rahner attended the distinguished existentialist's seminars in Freiburg-im-Breisgau between 1932 and 1934. In his critique, he underscores his mentor's emphasis on death as thoroughly pervasive of the human person. On account of it, the Jesuit judges Heidegger's concept of the intelligibility of being to devolve into pure nothingness. Despair and atheism thus speak the ultimate metaphor that confronts us with an absolute far from illusory.[58] It is therefore surprising that Catholic thinkers seem so eager to come under its influence. Given its fundamental presuppositions, it poses a major problem, even an insuperable block, to its use as Christianity's handmaid (*ancilla theologiae*). Its final darkness seems to continue to cast its shadow over Marion and Chauvet in their one-sided apophaticism, unresolved dialectic, and fideism, and over them and Lafont in their distrust of elucidating the causality of the divine effects in the world.

In the view of this book, it would be far more profitable to deal

55. Ibid., 163.

56. Ibid., 164.

57. Ibid., 165.

58. Karl Rahner, "The Concept of Existential Philosophy in Heidegger," trans. Andrew Tallon, in *Philosophy Today* 13 (1969): 127–37, at 135–36; originally "Introduction au concept de Philosophie Existentiale chez Heidegger," in *Recherches de science religieuse (Paris)* 30 (1940): 152–71.

with Heidegger as his distinguished student did. Rahner demonstrates by the "pre-apprehension of the Absolute" that being is not confined to the rational concept. On the contrary, through it, an analogy of *Realsymbols*, which respects the causative order of intelligible finitude, can be vindicated, even as this order subsists under the divine mystery that constitutes its origin and destiny (see above, chapters 2, 4, 6).

A more satisfying account of the interrelation among event, symbol, analogy, and dialectic emerges in David Tracy's *The Analogical Imagination: Christian Theology and the Culture of Pluralism*. Three events, he claims, constitute the core symbols of Christianity: incarnation, cross, and resurrection. As events, they proclaim the divinely gratuitous action in history; as symbols, they contain and manifest God's very being, his self-communication in grace. Echoing Lafont, Tracy thus emphasizes the fundamentally kataphatic origins of Christianity. Echoing Ricoeur, to whom his book is throughout indebted, he affirms that Christianity's core symbols ever give rise to thought (see above, chapter 5). As "symbol-events," they cry out for critical and creative interpretation as human reason seeks to plumb their meaning. The scriptures, offering Gospel narratives and epistolary reflections, represent the events in a privileged language claiming inspiration. Theology, a "second order" language, is subsequently conducted on their basis. Although theology does its work while embedded in a particular situation—and although theology modifies our understanding of the symbol-events, even as they modify our understanding of reality—still the kataphatic symbol-events remain paramount as the primary analogues of all theology.

According to Tracy, therefore, theology's work is inescapably analogical. It seeks to achieve an integration among the world, the human person, and revelation. To do this, it must find, in its second-order interpretive language, a similarity to the language of the symbol-events as primary analogues. Accordingly, it must discover a criterion according to which the coherence among the divine symbol-events can be demonstrated. (Luther, for instance, adverts to *simul justus et peccator* and Rahner to the *Realsymbol*.) It must then relate this criterion to the coherence of mundane experience. Moreover, in so doing, it must scrupulously attend to the oppositions inherent in the objects under comparison, such as God and the world, the human person as spirit and matter, nature and grace, faith and reason. All opposition entails dialectic; dialectic insures that similarities do not overshadow differences and that the *via eminentiae* maintains harmony with the *via negationis*.

Crucially, Tracy does not abandon the dialectic embedded in theology's work in an unresolved apophatic limbo. On the contrary, it is reconciled in the renewed synthesis that it brings about. Theology, generated by reason's enriching encounter with the divine symbols, and aware of the opposition between them and mundane experience, recognizes its inability to reduce the revealed symbols to adequate rational discourse. As a result, thought must continually return "reflectively" to the symbols to find nourishment afresh for deeper insights.[59] Throughout its work, theology is intrinsically tethered to the symbols from which, dialectically, it emanates and to which it returns. Tracy thus achieves an equilibrium between the kataphatic and apophatic dimensions of the symbol-events. Always and necessarily related to these, theology's interpretations remain open "to correction at every crucial moment" in their formulation.[60] We might therefore say that the Chicago academic has rendered into a contemporary idiom the dynamic paradox of the Areopagite. For Pseudo-Dionysius, even as the theologian immerses himself in the aesthetics of divine symbols, he is driven irresistibly to fulfill an impossible task: to dissolve all symbols "in the light of the unimaginable" that shines luminously in them.[61]

In conclusion, it remains simply to say that Tracy's analogical understanding of theology leaves us at the doorstep of the *Realsymbol*. If theology's task entails using a criterion to demonstrate the overarching coherence between the truths of natural experience and the truths

59. David Tracy, *The Analogical Imagination: Christian Theology and the Culture of Pluralism* (New York: Crossroad, 1981), 411.

60. Ibid.

61. Balthasar, *GL* 2:179.

of graced revelation, and to do so by respecting the inherent oppositions among them, then the *Realsymbol* emerges as Christianity's most adequate hermeneutic when viewed against the theories just surveyed. As integrated by Rahner into a realist vision of the human mind's power to affirm the analogy of being and to express it as language, the *Realsymbol* refuses to reduce the "positive intelligibility" of the divine merely to metaphor and arbitrary sign.[62] On the contrary, by embracing event and contingency into an analogous analogy, the *Realsymbol* guarantees that, in Christianity's saving message, the order of nature mediates the order of grace immediately (see above, chapters 4–7). Both orders are intelligible, according to the differentiated harmony of Augustine's adage that has long guided Catholicism: "I believe that I may understand."[63] An equivocal view of truth and the fideism that devolves from it assault the human person; they needlessly suffocate our God-given potential. As quipped by the late John E. Smith, a wise mentor during his long career teaching philosophy at Yale: if a great mind begins to think from a false premise, it simply gets to the wrong answer much faster than the average fellow.[64]

62. Avery Dulles, "Criteria of Catholic Theology," *Communio: International Catholic Review* 22 (Summer 1995): 303–15, at 305–6. See also Stephen Fields, "Rahner and the Symbolism of Language," *Philosophy and Theology* 15, no. 1 (2003): 165–89.

63. Augustine, *Tractates on the Gospel of John* 29.6.

64. John E. Smith (1921–2009), Clark Professor of Philosophy emeritus (from 1991), fellow of Silliman College, editor of the Yale *Works of Jonathan Edwards*, author of articles and at least nine books on American pragmatism, philosophy of religion, and German Idealism.

Selected Bibliography

Albertson, James S. "Instrumental Causality in St. Thomas." *New Scholasticism* 28 (1954): 409–35.

Allison, Henry E. *Lessing and the Enlightenment: His Philosophy of Religion and Its Relation to Eighteenth Century Thought*. Ann Arbor: University of Michigan Press, 1966.

Anselm of Canterbury. *Why God Became Man, and The Virgin Conception and Original Sin*. Translated and edited by Joseph M. Colleran. Albany, N.Y.: Magi Books, 1969.

Aristotle. *Metaphysics: A Revised Text with Introduction and Commentary by W. D. Ross*. 2 vols. Oxford: Clarendon Press, 1924.

———. *Nicomachean Ethics*. Translated by Robert C. Bartlett and Susan D. Collins. Chicago: University of Chicago, 2011.

———. *On the Soul*. Translated by J. A. Smith. Oxford: Clarendon, 1931.

Athanasius. *On the Incarnation*. In *Christology of the Later Fathers*, edited by Edward Rochie Hardy and translated by Archibald Robertson, 55–110. Philadelphia: Westminster Press, 1954.

Augustine. *Confessions*. Translated by R. S. Pine-Coffin. Harmondsworth: Penguin, 1961.

———. *The Grace of Christ and Original Sin*. In *An Augustine Reader*, edited by John J. O'Meara, 2:443–90. Garden City, N.Y.: Image, 1973.

———. *On the Trinity*. In *A Select Library of the Nicene and Post-Nicene Fathers of the Christian Church*, edited by Philip Schaff, translated by Arthur Hadden and W. T. G. Shedd, 3:17–228. 14 vols. Grand Rapids, Mich.: Eerdmans, 1980.

———. *Tractates on the Gospel of John*. *PL* 35.

Balasuriya, Tissa. "A Companion to the Encyclical of Pope Benedict XVI on 'God is Love.'" *Cross Currents* 56, no. 2 (Summer 2006): 229–60.

Balthasar, Hans Urs von. *The Glory of the Lord: A Theological Aesthetics*, vol. 1: *Seeing the Form*. Translated by Erasmo Leiva-Merikakis, edited by Joseph Fessio and John Riches. 7 vols. San Francisco, Calif.: Ignatius Press, 1982–91.

———. *The Glory of the Lord: A Theological Aesthetics*, vol. 2: *Clerical Styles*.

Translated by Andrew Louth et al. 7 vols. San Francisco, Calif.: Ignatius Press, 1982–91.

———. *The Moment of Christian Witness*. Translated by Richard Beckley. Glen Rock, N.J.: Newman Press, 1969.

———. *The Theology of Karl Barth: Exposition and Interpretation*. Translated by Edward T. Oakes. San Francisco, Calif.: Ignatius Press, 1992.

Barrett, C. K. *The Gospel According to St. John: An Introduction with Commentary and Notes on the Greek Text*. Philadelphia: Westminster Press, 1978.

Barth, Karl. *The Humanity of God*. Translated by John Newton Thomas et al. Atlanta: John Knox Press, 1960.

Basil of Caesarea. *The Letters*. Translated by Roy J. Deferrari. 4 vols. London: W. Heinemann, 1926.

Benedict XVI, Pope. *Caritas in Veritate*. Encyclical Letter. June 29, 2009. www.vatican.va. *Acta Apostolicae Sedis* 101 (2009): 641–709.

———. *Deus Caritas Est*. Encyclical Letter. December 25, 2005. www.vatican.va. *Acta Apostolicae Sedis* 98 (2006): 217–52.

——— (as Joseph Ratzinger). "Dogmatic Constitution on Divine Revelation, Origin and Background." In *Commentary on the Documents of Vatican II*, edited by Herbert Vorgrimler, 3:155–66. 5 vols. New York: Herder and Herder, 1967–69.

———. "Faith, Reason, and the University: Memories and Reflections." Lecture, University of Regensburg. September 12, 2006. www.vatican.va.

———. *Jesus of Nazareth: From the Baptism in the Jordan to the Transfiguration*. Translated by Adrian J. Walker. New York: Doubleday, 2007.

——— (as Joseph Ratzinger). *Principles of Catholic Theology: Building Stones for a Fundamental Theology*. Translated by Sister Mary Frances McCarthy, SND. San Francisco, Calif.: Ignatius Press, 1987.

———. *Spe Salvi*. Encyclical Letter. November 30, 2007. www.vatican.va. *Acta Apostolicae Sedis* 99 (2007): 985–1027.

——— (as Joseph Ratzinger). *The Theology of History in St. Bonaventure*. Translated by Zachary Hayes. Chicago: Franciscan Herald Press, 1971.

Blankenhorn, Bernhard. "The Instrumental Causality of the Sacraments: Thomas Aquinas and Louis-Marie Chauvet." *Nova et Vetera (English Edition)* 4 (2006): 255–94.

Blondel, Maurice. *Action* (1893). Translated by Oliva Blanchette. South Bend, Ind.: University of Notre Dame Press, 1984.

———. *The Letter on Apologetics and History and Dogma*. Translated by Alexander Dru and Illtyd Trethowan. New York: Holt, Rinehart, and Winston, 1964.

Bonaventure. *The Mind's Road to God*. Translated by George Boas. New York: Macmillan, 1986.

Bouillard, Henri. *Conversion et grâce chez saint Thomas d'Aquin: étude historique.* Paris: Aubier, 1944.

———. "Philosophy and Christianity in the Thought of Maurice Blondel." In Bouillard, *The Logic of the Faith*, 161–85. New York: Sheed and Ward, 1967.

Boyer, Charles. "Nature pure et surnaturel dans le *Surnaturel* du Père de Lubac." *Gregorianum* 28 (1947): 279–95.

Buckley, Michael J. *At the Origins of Modern Atheism.* New Haven, Conn.: Yale University Press, 1987.

Burgaleta, Claudio. "Benedict XVI: Theology of the Word of God." Paper presented at the Eleventh Jesuit Colloquium on Papal Thought, Georgetown University, June 7–10, 2009.

Caputo, John D. "Commentary on Ken Schmitz, 'Postmodernism and the Catholic Tradition.'" *American Catholic Philosophical Quarterly* 73 (Spring 1999): 253–60.

———. "Philosophy and Prophetic Postmodernism." *American Catholic Philosophical Quarterly* 74 (Autumn 2000): 549–68.

Carlyle, Thomas. *Sartor Resartus: The Life and Opinions of Herr Teufelsdröckh.* Edited by Charles Frederick Harrod. New York: Odyssey Press, 1937.

Cassirer, Ernst. *The Philosophy of Symbolic Forms*, vol. 4: *The Metaphysics of Symbolic Forms.* Edited by John Michael Krois and Daniel Philip Verene, translated by John Michael Krois. 4 vols. New Haven, Conn.: Yale University Press, 1996.

Cassirer, Ernst, et al., trans. and eds. *The Renaissance Philosophy of Man.* Chicago: University of Chicago Press, 1948.

Chauvet, Louis-Marie. *The Sacraments: The Word of God at the Mercy of the Body.* Collegeville, Minn.: Liturgical Press, 2001.

———. *Symbole et sacrement: une relecture sacramentelle de l'existence chrétienne.* Paris: Éditions du Cerf, 1987.

Clarke, W. Norris. "Central Problems in the History of Metaphysics"; "Central Problems in Metaphysics"; "Notes on St Thomas's Philosophy." Photocopy, course notes, Department of Philosophy, Fordham University.

Collins, James. *The Emergence of Philosophy of Religion.* New Haven, Conn.: Yale University Press, 1967.

Congar, Yves. *Fifty Years of Catholic Theology: Conversations with Yves Congar.* Edited by Bernard Lauret. Philadelphia: Fortress Press, 1988.

———. *Missionaire pour demain.* Paris: Centurion, 1966.

———. *Tradition and Traditions: A Historical and a Theological Essay.* Translated by Michael Naseby et al. New York: Macmillan, 1967.

———. *The Wide World, My Parish: Salvation and Its Problems.* Translated by Donald Attwater. Baltimore: Helicon Press, 1961.

Congregation for the Doctrine of the Faith. *Dominus Jesus.* June 16, 2000. In *Sic et Non: Encountering "Dominus Jesus,"* edited by Stephen J. Pope and Charles Hefling, 3–23. Maryknoll, N.Y.: Orbis, 2002. www.vatican.va.

———. "Responses to Some Questions Regarding Certain Aspects of the Doctrine of the Church." June 29, 2007. www.vatican.va.

Conley, John, and Joseph Koterski, eds. *Creed and Culture: Jesuit Studies of Pope John Paul II*. Philadelphia: St. Joseph's University Press, 2004.

Council of Chalcedon. *The Chalcedonian Decree*. In *Christology of the Later Fathers*, edited by Edward Rochie Hardy and translated by Archibald Robertson, 55–110. Philadelphia: Westminster Press, 1954.

Council of Trent. *Decree on Justification*. January 13, 1547. In *Decrees*, edited by Tanner, 2:671–81.

Cyprian of Carthage. *Letters*. Translated by Sister Rose Bernard Donna, CSJ. Fathers of the Church 51. Washington, D.C.: The Catholic University of America Press, 1965.

D'Ambrosio, Marcellino. "*Ressourcement* Theology, *Aggiornamento*, and the Hermeneutics of Tradition." *Communio: International Catholic Review* 18 (1991): 530–55.

de Lubac, Henri. *Catholicisme: les aspects sociaux du dogme*. Paris: Cerf, 1941.

———. *Corpus mysticum: l'eucharistie et l'église du moyen âge, étude historique*. Paris: Aubier, 1944.

———. *Exégèse médiévale: les quatre sens de l'Écriture*. 4 vols. Paris: Aubier, 1959–64.

———. "Le mystère du surnaturel." *Recherches de science religieuse* 36 (1949): 80–121.

———. *The Mystery of the Supernatural*. Translated by Rosemary Sheed. New York: Herder and Herder, 1967.

———. *Scripture in the Tradition*. Translated by Luke O'Neill. New York: Crossroad, 2008.

———. *Surnaturel: études historiques*. Paris: Aubier, 1946.

Duffy, Regis, et al. "Current Theology—Sacramental Theology: A Review of Literature." *Theological Studies* 55 (1994): 657–705.

Duffy, Stephen J. *The Graced Horizon: Nature and Grace in Modern Catholic Thought*. Collegeville, Minn.: Liturgical Press, 1992.

Dulles, Avery (Cardinal). "The Cognitive Basis of Faith." *Philosophy and Theology* 10, no. 1 (1998): 19–31.

———. "Criteria of Catholic Theology." *Communio: International Catholic Review* 22 (Summer 1995): 303–15.

———. "Vatican II: The Myth and the Reality." *America* (February 24, 2003).

Dunbar, Helen Flanders. *Symbolism in Medieval Thought and Its Consummation in the Divine Comedy*. New Haven, Conn.: Yale University Press, 1929.

Dupré, Louis. "The Broken Mirror: The Fragmentation of the Symbolic World." *Stanford Literature Review* 5 (Spring–Fall 1988): 7–24.

———. “Hans Urs von Balthasar’s Theology of Aesthetic Form.” *Theological Studies* 49 (1988): 299–318.

———. “Ignatian Humanism and Its Mystical Origins.” *Communio: International Catholic Review* 18 (Summer 1991): 164–82.

———. *The Other Dimension: A Search for the Meaning of Religious Attitudes*. New York: Seabury Press, 1979.

———. *Passage to Modernity: An Essay in the Hermeneutics of Nature and Culture*. New Haven, Conn.: Yale University Press, 1993.

———. *Transcendent Selfhood: The Loss and Rediscovery of the Inner Self*. New York: Seabury Press, 1976.

Fackenheim, Emil L. *The Religious Dimension in Hegel’s Thought*. Boston: Beacon Press, 1967.

Farge, William J. “João Rodrigues vs. Matteo Ricci: Christian Terminology in Japan and China.” Paper presented at the “Coming to Terms: The Quadricentennial of João Rodrigues’s *Arte da Língoa de Iapam*” conference, Georgetown University, December 12–13, 2008.

Feingold, Lawrence. *The Natural Desire to See God according to St. Thomas and His Interpreters*. 2d ed. Ave Maria, Fla.: Sapientia Press of Ave Maria University, 2010.

Ferré, Frederick. “The Logic of Analogy.” In *The Challenge of Religion: Contemporary Readings in Philosophy of Religion*, edited by Ferré et al., 104–13. New York: Seabury Press, 1982.

Ficino, Marsilio. *Opera Omnia*, vol. 1: *De christiana religione*. Basel, 1576; reprinted in Turin: Bottega de’ Erasmo, 1983.

Fields, Stephen M. “Balthasar and Rahner on the Spiritual Senses.” *Theological Studies* 57 (June 1996): 224–41.

———. “The Beauty of the Ugly: Balthasar, the Crucifixion, Analogy, and God.” *International Journal of Systematic Theology* 9, no. 2 (2007): 172–83.

———. *Being as Symbol: On the Origins and Development of Karl Rahner’s Metaphysics*. Washington, D.C.: Georgetown University Press, 2000.

———. “Contraries in One: Contingency, Analogy, and God in Transcendental Thomism.” In “The Metaphysics of Aquinas and Its Modern Interpreters: Theological and Philosophical Perspectives,” edited by Christopher M. Cullen and Franklin T. Harkins.

———. “Mediating the Non-Christian Religions: Congar, Balthasar, Nature and Grace.” In *Yves Congar: Theologian of the Church*, edited by Gabriel Flynn, 401–26. Louvain: Peeters, 2005.

. “Nature, Grace, and the Public Square.” In *Catholicism in America: Proceedings from the 33rd Annual Convention of the Fellowship of Catholic Scholars, Sep-*

tember 24–26, 2010, Baltimore, Maryland, edited by Elizabeth C. Shaw, 123–38. Notre Dame, Ind.: Fellowship of Catholic Scholars, 2012.

———. "Rahner and the Symbolism of Language." *Philosophy and Theology* 15, no. 1 (2003): 165–89.

———. "The Singular as Event: Postmodernism, Rahner, and Balthasar." *American Catholic Philosophical Quarterly* 77 (2003): 93–111.

Fitzmyer, Joseph A. *The Interpretation of Scripture: In Defense of the Historical-Critical Method*. New York: Paulist Press, 2008.

Flynn, Gabriel, ed. *Yves Congar: Theologian of the Church*. Louvain: Peeters, 2005.

Flynn, Gabriel, and Paul D. Murray, eds. *Ressourcement: A Movement for Renewal in Twentieth Century Catholic Theology*. Oxford: Oxford University Press, 2012.

Flynn, Thomas R. "A Reply to Kenneth L. Schmitz." *American Catholic Philosophical Quarterly* 73 (Spring 1999): 261–66.

Garland, Peter B. *The Definition of Sacrament According to St. Thomas*. Ottawa: University of Ottawa Press, 1959.

Habermas, Jürgen. *The Liberating Power of Symbols: Philosophical Essays*. Translated by Peter Dews. Cambridge, Mass.: MIT Press, 2001.

Haight, Roger. *Dynamics of Theology*. New York: Paulist Press, 1990.

———. *Jesus, Symbol of God*. Maryknoll, N.Y.: Orbis Books, 1999.

Hegel, G. W. F. *Hegel's Logic*. Translated by William Wallace. Oxford: Clarendon Press, 1975.

———. *Lectures on the Philosophy of Religion: One-Volume Edition—The Lectures of 1827*. Edited by Peter C. Hodgson, translated by R. F. Brown et al. Berkeley: University of California Press, 1988.

———. "On Art." In *On Art, Religion, and Philosophy*, translated by Bernard Bosanquet, edited by J. Glenn Gray, 23–127. New York: Harper and Row, 1970.

Heidegger, Martin. "The Origin of the Work of Art." In *Poetry, Language, and Thought*, translated and edited by Albert Hofstadter, 17–87. New York: Harper and Row, 1971.

Henrici, Peter. "The One Who Went Unnamed: Blondel in the Encyclical *Fides et Ratio*." *Communio: International Catholic Review* 26 (Fall 1999): 609–21.

Henry of Ghent. "Can a Human Being Know Anything without Divine Illumination?" *Summa Quaestionum Ordinariarum, q. 2, a. 1*. In *Medieval Philosophy: Essential Readings with Commentary*, edited by Gyula Klima. Malden, Mass.: Blackwell, 2007.

Himes, Michael J. *Ongoing Incarnation: Johann Adam Möhler and the Beginnings of Modern Ecclesiology*. New York: Crossroad, 1997.

Hooper, J. Leon, ed. *Religious Liberty: Catholic Struggles with Pluralism/John Courtney Murray*. Louisville, Ky.: Westminster John Knox Press, 1993.

Hunt, Robert P., and Kenneth L. Grasso, eds. *John Courtney Murray and the American Civil Conversation*. Grand Rapids, Mich.: Eerdmans, 1992.

Ignatius Loyola. *The Spiritual Exercises of St. Ignatius*. Translated and edited by Louis J. Puhl. Chicago: Loyola University Press, 1951.

Irenaeus of Lyons. *Against the Heresies*. In *Ante-Nicene Fathers*, translated and edited by Alexander Roberts and W. H. Rimbaud, 1:315–567. 10 vols. Peabody, Mass.: Hendrickson, 1996.

Janssens, John Baptist. "A Letter of Very Rev. Father General on the Encyclical 'Humani Generis' (11 February 1951)." *Woodstock Letters* 80 (1951): 291–316.

John of Damascus. *The Orthodox Faith. PG* 4.

John XXIII, Pope. *Mater et Magistra*. Encyclical Letter. May 15, 1961. www.vatican.va. *Acta Apostolicae Sedis* 53 (1961): 401–64.

John Paul II, Pope (as Karol Wojtyła). *The Acting Person*. Translated by Andrzej Potocki. Analecta Husserliana 10. Dordrecht: D. Reidel, 1979.

——— (as Karol Wojtyła). *Amore e Responsibilità*. 2nd ed. Translated by A. Milanoli. Torino: Marietti, 1978.

———. *Centesimus Annus*. Encyclical Letter. May 1, 1991. www.vatican.va. *Acta Apostolicae Sedis* 83 (1991): 793–867.

———. *The Church: Mystery, Sacrament, Community*. Boston: Pauline Books and Media, 1998.

———. *Dominicae Cenae*. Encyclical Letter. February 24, 1980. *Acta Apostolicae Sedis* 72 (1980): 113–48. In Edward J. Kilmartin, *Church, Eucharist, and Priesthood: A Theological Commentary on "The Mystery and Worship of the Most Holy Eucharist."* New York: Paulist Press, 1981.

———. *Fides et Ratio*. Encyclical Letter. September 14, 1998. www.vatican.va. *Acta Apostolicae Sedis* 91 (1991): 5–88.

——— (as Karol Wojtyła). "The Person: Subject and Community." *The Review of Metaphysics* 33 (1979): 273–308.

Justin Martyr. *Apology* I. Edited and translated by Edward Rochie Hardy. In *Early Christian Fathers*, edited by Cyril C. Richardson et al., 225–89. New York: Macmillan, 1970.

Kant, Immanuel. *Critique of Judgment*. Translated by J. H. Bernard. New York: Hafner Press, 1951.

———. *Religion Within the Limits of Reason Alone*. Translated by Theodore M. Greene and Hoyt H. Hudson. New York: Harper and Row, 1960.

Klubertanz, George P. *St. Thomas Aquinas on Analogy: A Textual Analysis and Systematic Synthesis*. Chicago: Loyola University Press, 1960.

Kockelmans, Joseph. "On Religious Myths." In *Challenge of Religion*, edited by Ferré, 213–33.

Komonchak, Joseph A. "Fifty Years After *Humani Generis*." Paper presented to annual meeting of Catholic Theological Society of America, Milwaukee, Wis., June 8, 2001. Photocopy, privately circulated.

Kraemer, Hendrik. *Religion and the Christian Faith*. Philadelphia: Westminster, 1957.

Kristeller, Paul Oskar. *Eight Philosophers of the Italian Renaissance*. Stanford, Calif.: Stanford University Press, 1964.

———. *Renaissance Thought and Its Sources*. Edited by Michael Mooney. New York: Columbia University Press, 1979.

———. "Thomism and the Italian Thought of the Renaissance." In *Medieval Aspects of Renaissance Learning: Three Essays by Paul Oskar Kristeller*, edited and translated by Edward P. Mahoney, 29–91. Durham, N.C.: Duke University Press, 1974.

Lafont, Ghislain. *God, Time, and Being*. Translated by Leonard Maluf. Petersham, Mass.: St. Bede's, 1992.

Langan, John P. "What Jerusalem Says to Athens." In *The Faith That Does Justice: Examining the Christian Sources for Social Change*, edited by John C. Haughey, 152–80. Ramsey, N.J.: Paulist Press, 1977.

Lauer, Quentin. "Hegel on the Identity of Content in Religion and Philosophy." In *Hegel and the Philosophy of Religion: The Wofford Symposium*, edited by Darrel E. Cristensen, 261–78. The Hague: Martinus Nijhoff, 1970.

Le Grys, James L. "The Christianization of Modern Philosophy According to Maurice Blondel." *Theological Studies* 54 (1993): 455–84.

Leeming, Bernard. *Principles of Sacramental Theology*. Westminster, Md.: Newman Press, 1960.

Leo XIII, Pope. *Rerum Novarum*. Encyclical Letter. May 15, 1891. www.vatican.va. *Acta Sanctae Sedis* 23 (1890–91): 641–70.

Lessing, Gotthold Ephraim. *On the Proof of the Spirit and of Power*. In *Lessing's Theological Writings*, edited by Henry Chadwick. Stanford, Calif.: Stanford University Press, 1956.

Lewis, C. S. *The Allegory of Love*. Oxford: Oxford University Press, 1936.

Locke, John. *The Reasonableness of Christianity*. Edited by I. T. Ramsey. Stanford, Calif: Stanford University Press, 1958.

Long, Steven A. *Analogia Entis: On the Analogy of Being, Metaphysics, and the Act of Faith*. Notre Dame, Ind.: University of Notre Dame Press, 2011.

———. *Natura Pura: On the Recovery of Nature in the Doctrine of Grace*. New York: Fordham University Press, 2010.

Louth, Andrew. *The Origins of the Christian Mystical Tradition from Plato to Denys*. Oxford: Oxford University Press, 1981.

Maréchal, Joseph. *Le Thomisme devant la philosophie critique*. Vol. 5 of Maréchal, *Le point de départ de la métaphysique*. Brussels: Édition universelle, 1949.

Marion, Jean-Luc. *The Essential Writings*. Translated by James K. A. Smith and edited by Kevin Hart. New York: Fordham University Press, 2013.

———. "The Prototype and the Image." In Marion, *Essential Writings*, 273–87.

———. "Thomas Aquinas and Onto-theo-logy." In Marion, *Essential Writings*, 288–311.

Markus, R. A. *Saeculum: History and Society in the Thought of St Augustine*. Cambridge: Cambridge University Press, 1970.

Marrone, Steven P. *The Light of Thy Countenance: Science and Knowledge of God in the Thirteenth Century*. Boston: Brill, 2001.

McCabe, Herbert. "Analogy." Appendix 4 in Thomas Aquinas, *Summa theologiae*, 3:106–7.

McCool, Gerald A. *Catholic Theology in the Nineteenth Century: The Quest for a Unitary Method*. New York: Seabury Press, 1977.

———. "Twentieth-Century Scholasticism." *Journal of Religion* 58 (1978 Suppl.): S198–221.

McDermott, John M., ed. *The Thought of Pope John Paul II: A Collection of Essays and Studies*. Rome: Editrice Pontificia Gregoriana, 1993.

McDermott, John M., and John Gavin, eds. *John Paul II on the Body: Human-Eucharistic-Ecclesial*. Philadelphia: St. Joseph's University Press, 2007.

Migne, J.-P., ed. *Patrologiae cursus completus. Series graeca*. 161 vols. Paris, 1857–66.

———. *Patrologiae cursus completus. Series latina*. 220 vols. Paris, 1844–64.

Millbank, John. *The Suspended Middle: Henri de Lubac and the Renewed Split in Modern Catholic Theology*. 2d ed. Grand Rapids, Mich.: William B. Eerdmans, 2014.

Möhler, Johann Adam. *Symbolism or Exposition of the Doctrinal Differences Between Catholics and Protestants as Evidenced by Their Symbolical Writings*. Translated by James Burton Robertson. 5th ed. London: Thomas Baker, 1906.

Murray, John Courtney. "The Declaration on Religious Freedom." *Concilium: International Journal of Theology*, 15:3–16. New York: Paulist Press, 1966.

———. "Government Repression of Heresy." *Proceedings of the Catholic Theological Society of America* (1948): 26–98.

———. *We Hold These Truths: Catholic Reflections on the American Proposition*. New York: Sheed and Ward, 1960.

Nemec, Ludvik. *Pope John Paul II: A Festive Profile*. New York: Catholic Publishing, 1979.

Newman, John Henry Cardinal. *Apologia Pro Vita Sua*. New York: Doubleday, 1989.

———. *An Essay on the Development of Christian Doctrine*. In *Conscience, Consensus, and the Development of Doctrine*, edited by James Gaffney, 38–428. New York: Doubleday, 1992.

———. *On Consulting the Faithful in Matters of Doctrine*. In Newman, *Conscience, Consensus, and the Development of Doctrine*, 392–428.

Nichols, Aidan. "Thomism and the Nouvelle Théologie." *The Thomist* 64 (2000): 1–19.

O'Meara, Thomas F. "Yves Congar: Theologian of Grace in a Wide World." In *Yves Congar: Theologian of the Church*, edited by Flynn, 371–99.

Pascal, Blaise. *Pensées*. Translated by H. F. Stewart. London: Routledge and Kegan Paul, 1950.

Paul VI, Pope. *Humanae Vitae*. Encyclical Letter. July 25, 1968. *Acta Apostolicae Sedis* 60 (1968): 481–503. www.vatican.va.

———. *Populorum Progressio*. Encyclical Letter. March 26. 1967. www.vatican.va. *Acta Apostolicae Sedis* 59 (1967): 257–99.

Pegis, Anton C. "Nature and Spirit: Some Reflections on the Problem of the End of Man." *Proceedings of the American Catholic Philosophical Association* 23 (1949): 62–79.

Pico della Mirandola, Giovanni. *On Being and Unity*. Translated by Victor Michael Hamm. Milwaukee, Wis.: Marquette University Press, 1943.

Pieper, Josef. *The Four Cardinal Virtues: Prudence, Justice, Fortitude Temperance*. Translated by Daniel F. Coogan et al. New York: Harcourt, Brace, and World, 1954.

Pius XI, Pope. *Quadragesimo Anno*. Encyclical Letter. May 15, 1931. www.vatican.va. *Acta Apostolicae Sedis* 23 (1931): 177–228.

Pius XII, Pope. *Humani Generis*. Encyclical Letter. August 12, 1950. www.vatican.va. *Acta Apostolicae Sedis* 42 (1950): 561–78.

Power, David. *Sacrament: The Language of God's Giving*. New York: Crossroad, 1999.

Pseudo-Dionysius the Areopagite. *De coelesti hierarchia; De divinis nominibus; De ecclesiastica hierarchia. PG* 3.

———. *The Divine Names and Mystical Theology: Translated from the Greek with an Introductory Study*. Translated and edited by John D. Jones. Milwaukee, Wis.: Marquette University Press, 1980.

Rahner, Hugo. *Ignatius the Theologian*. Translated by Michael Barry. New York: Herder and Herder, 1968.

Rahner, Karl. *The Christian Commitment: Essays in Pastoral Theology*. Translated by Cecily Hastings. New York: Sheed and Ward, 1963.

———. "The Concept of Existential Philosophy in Heidegger." Translated by Andrew Tallon. *Philosophy Today* 13 (1969): 127–37.

———. *Foundations of Christian Faith: An Introduction to the Idea of Christianity*. Translated by William V. Dych. New York: Seabury Press, 1978.

———. *Hearer of the Word: Laying the Foundation for a Philosophy of Religion.* Translated by Joseph Donceel. New York: Continuum, 1994.

———. *Hominization: The Evolutionary Origin of Man as a Theological Problem.* Translated by W. T. O'Hara. Freiburg-im-Breisgau: Herder, 1965.

———. "Salvation." In *Sacramentum Mundi: An Encyclopedia of Theology,* edited by Karl Rahner et al., 5:425b–33a. 6 vols. New York: Herder and Herder, 1969.

———. *Spirit in the World.* Translated by William V. Dych. New York: Herder and Herder, 1968.

———. *TI* 1. Translated by Cornelius Ernst. Baltimore, Md.: Helicon, 1961.

———. *TI* 4. Translated by Kevin Smyth. Baltimore, Md.: Helicon, 1966.

———. *TI* 6. Translated by Karl-H. and Boniface Kruger. Baltimore, Md.: Helicon, 1969.

———. *TI* 19. Edited by Paul Imhof, translated by Edward Quinn. New York: Crossroad, 1983.

Richardson, William J. *Heidegger: Through Phenomenology to Thought.* The Hague: Martinus Nijhoff, 1967.

Ricoeur, Paul. *The Symbolism of Evil.* Translated by Emerson Buchanan. New York: Harper and Row, 1967.

Rigney, J. F. "Communication of Idioms." In *New Catholic Encyclopedia,* edited by staff at the Catholic University of America, 4:36. 19 vols. New York: McGraw Hill, 1967–96.

Sacred Congregation of the Holy Office. "Letter of the Holy Office to the Archbishop of Boston (1949)." In *The Christian Faith in the Doctrinal Documents of the Catholic Church,* edited by Josef Neuner and Jacques Dupuis, 305–7. New York: Alba House, 1996.

Schillebeeckx, Edward. "The Non-Conceptual Intellectual Element in the Act of Faith: A Reaction." In Schillebeeckx, *Revelation and Theology,* translated by N. D. Smith, 2:30–75. 2 vols. New York: Sheed and Ward, 1967–68.

Schindler, David L. "Charity, Justice, and the Church's Activity in the World." *Communio: International Catholic Review* 33 (Fall 2006): 346–76.

———, ed. *Love Alone Is Credible: Hans Urs von Balthasar as Interpreter of the Catholic Tradition.* Grand Rapids, Mich.: Eerdmans, 2008.

———. "Religious Freedom, Truth, and American Liberalism: Another Look at John Courtney Murray." *Communio: International Catholic Review* 21, no. 4 (Winter 1994): 696–741.

Schmitz, Kenneth L. *At the Center of the Human Drama: The Philosophical Anthropology of Karol Wojtyła/Pope John Paul II.* Washington, D.C.: The Catholic University of America Press, 1993.

———. "Postmodernism and the Catholic Tradition"; "An Addendum to Further

Discussion." *American Catholic Philosophical Quarterly* 73 (Spring 1999): 233–52; 277–90.

Seckler, Max. *Instinkt und Glaubenswille nach Thomas von Aquin*. Mainz: Matthias-Grünewald-Verlag, 1961.

Smith, John E. "The Relation of Thought and Being: Some Lessons from Hegel's *Encyclopedia*." *New Scholasticism* 38 (1964): 22–43.

Steiner, George. *Real Presences*. London: Faber and Faber, 1989.

Stolz, Anselm. *The Doctrine of Spiritual Perfection*. Translated by Aidan Williams. New York: Crossroad, 2001.

Tanner, Norman P., ed. *Decrees of the Ecumenical Councils*. 2 vols. London: Sheed and Ward, 1990.

Tertullian. *Prescription against Heretics*. In *Early Latin Theology: Selections from Tertullian, Cyprian, Ambrose, and Jerome*. Edited and translated by S. L. Greenslade. Philadelphia: Westminster Press, 1956: 19–64.

Thomas Aquinas. *On the Truth of the Catholic Faith, Summa Contra Gentiles*. Translated by Anton C. Pegis. 5 vols. Garden City, N.Y.: Hanover House, 1955–57.

———. *The Power of God* (De Potentia). Translated by Richard J. Regan. New York: Oxford University Press, 2012.

———. *Summa theologiae*. Translated and edited by the Fathers of the English-Speaking Dominican Provinces. New York: McGraw-Hill, 1964–66.

Tillich, Paul. "The Religious Symbol." In *Symbolism in Religion and Literature*, edited by Rollo May, translated by James Adams and Ernst Fraenkel, 75–98. New York: George Braziller, 1960.

———. "Theology and Symbolism." In *Religious Symbolism*, edited by F. Ernest Johnson, 107–16. New York: Harper, 1955.

Toomey, D. Vincent. "The Mind of Benedict XVI." *Claremont Review of Books* 4 (Fall 2005): 66–71.

Tracy, David. *The Analogical Imagination: Christian Theology and the Culture of Pluralism*. New York: Crossroad, 1981.

Üçerler, Antoni. "The Jesuit Mission Press and João Rodrigues's *Arte da Língoa Japoa* (1604–08)." Paper presented at the "Coming to Terms: The Quadricentennial of João Rodrigues's *Arte da Lingoa de Iapam*" conference at Georgetown University, December 12–13, 2008.

Urban, Wilbur M. *Language and Reality: The Philosophy of Language and the Principles of Symbolism*. London: Allen and Unwin, 1939.

Vander Kerken, Libert. *Religieus Gevroel en Aesthetisch Ervaren*. Antwerp: Standaard-Boekhandel, 1947.

Vatican Council I. *Dei Filius*. April 24, 1870. In *Decrees*, edited by Tanner, 2:804–11.

Vatican Council II. *Dei Verbum.* November 18, 1965. In *Decrees,* edited by Tanner, 2:971–81.

———. *Dignitatis Humanae.* December 7, 1965. In *Decrees,* edited by Tanner, 2:1001–11.

———. *Gaudium et Spes.* December 7, 1965. In *Decrees,* edited by Tanner, 2:1069–1135.

———. *Lumen Gentium.* November 21, 1964. In *Decrees,* edited by Tanner, 2:849–900.

Vermeil, Edmond. *Jean-Adam Möhler et l'école catholique de Tubingue (1815–1840).* Paris: Librarie Armand Colin, 1913.

Voss, Gustav. "Johann Adam Möhler and the Development of Dogma." *Theological Studies* 4 (1943): 420–44.

Wicks, Robert. "Hegel's Aesthetics: An Overview." In *The Cambridge Companion to Hegel,* edited by Frederick C. Beiser, 348–77. Cambridge: Cambridge University Press, 1993.

Wilkinson, Elizabeth M., and Leonard A. Willoughby, eds. *Goethe: Poet and Thinker.* New York: Barnes and Noble, 1962.

Williams, George Huntston. *The Mind of John Paul II: Origins of His Thought and Action.* New York: Seabury Press, 1981.

Wood, Susan. *Spiritual Exegesis and the Church in the Theology of Henri de Lubac.* Grand Rapids, Mich.: Eerdmans, 1998.

Index

INDEX

INDEX

Analogies of Transcendence: An Essay on Nature, Grace, and Modernity was designed in Arno Pro and composed by Kachergis Book Design of Pittsboro, North Carolina. It was printed on 60-pound Natures Book Natural and bound by Thomson-Shore of Dexter, Michigan.